State
Constitutional
Conventions

Elmer E. Cornwell, Jr.
Jay S. Goodman
Wayne R. Swanson

The Praeger Special Studies program—utilizing the most modern and efficient book production techniques and a selective worldwide distribution network—makes available to the academic, government, and business communities significant, timely research in U.S. and international economic, social, and political development.

State Constitutional Conventions

The Politics of
the Revision Process
in Seven States

Praeger Publishers   New York   Washington   London

PRAEGER SPECIAL STUDIES IN U.S. ECONOMIC, SOCIAL, AND POLITICAL ISSUES

Library of Congress Cataloging in Publication Data

Cornwell, Elmer E
    State constitutional conventions.

    (Praeger special studies in U. S. economic, social,
and political issues)
    Includes bibliographical references and index.
    1. Constitutional conventions—United States—
States.   2. Constitutions, State.   I. Goodman, Jay S.,
joint author.   II. Swanson, Wayne R., joint author.
III. Title.
JK2413.C67   342'.73'02   74-30707
ISBN 0-275-05940-5

PRAEGER PUBLISHERS
111 Fourth Avenue, New York, N.Y. 10003, U.S.A.

Published in the United States of America in 1975
by Praeger Publishers, Inc.

Printed in the United States of America

Most books have long gestation periods and many mid-
wives who assist the principal author or authors in the
labor of creation. For this volume, however, the gestation period has been, of necessity, exceptionally long,
and the roster of those assisting at various stages in
the lengthy process of its development has been especially
long. Such is often the case when, as here, the research
is collaborative, and the data are wide ranging and designed to produce a broadly based comparative study.

The project had its beginnings more than 10 years ago.
One of the questions on the general election ballot in
November 1964 in Rhode Island was a call for a state constitutional convention. The ballot was so arranged that
if the voters approved this call, delegates, for whom they
also voted at the same time, would meet before the end of
the year to constitute the first full-dress, "open" constitutional convention to be held in Rhode Island since
1942. The voters did approve, the convention did begin
meeting, and by early in 1965, two of the authors, Cornwell and Goodman, had been appointed research director and
assistant research director, respectively.

Neither Cornwell nor Goodman had been professionally
interested in constitutional revision as such previously,
though both had done research on state government and politics. It quickly became apparent, however, that the process of rewriting the basic law of Rhode Island was to become a highly political process intimately intertwined
with the larger political processes of the state. It also
became obvious that a golden opportunity was in the making
to examine the workings of a state convention in its total
political context from a firsthand vantage point.

Funding was sought to make such an enterprise possible, and through the advice and assistance of Robert C.
Wood (then a professor at MIT, now president of the University of Massachusetts) and John E. Bebout (then director of the Urban Center at Rutgers University), we got in
touch with William N. Cassella, Jr., of the National Municipal League and, through him, with Frederic A. Mosher
of the Carnegie Corporation of New York. Carnegie was interested in state government and the quality of state legislative operations. They were thus responsive to our

suggestion that processes of state constitutional revision had a direct bearing on these concerns. As concrete evidence of their interest, the corporation funded a modest study proposal dealing with the Rhode Island convention.

As our work on the staff of the Rhode Island convention proceeded (the meetings stretched out for an incredible four years!), we gathered data for our own analysis. Interviews were conducted with the delegates on our behalf by Barbara Karp, then a graduate student in Political Science. In time the results of this Rhode Island study were published by the National Municipal League under the title The Politics of the Rhode Island Constitutional Convention (1969).

On the basis of this initial "pilot" study and our resulting conviction that constitutional revision by convention posed very interesting theoretical and practical questions for investigation we made a successful joint proposal to the Carnegie Corporation with the National Municipal League for support of a very much larger study. By the time this proposal was funded, the states of New York and Maryland had conventions in prospect, and it seemed apparent that in the aftermath of the legislative reapportionment decisions that began in 1962 with Baker vs. Carr, there would be others.

In essence, our proposal was for a study of approximately half a dozen additional conventions both as individual political phenomena and ultimately on a comparative basis. The League, for its part of the task, would commission and publish an essentially descriptive chronological study of each convention, while the research team at Brown University (Cornwell and Goodman, and Swanson, who soon joined the group) would do a more analytical and quantitative analysis in each instance.

In time, the Brown group would also produce two comparative volumes, the first (published by the League in 1974: Constitutional Conventions: The Politics of Revision) would be designed to distill from our findings conclusions and generalizations that would be of aid to those planning, conducting, or participating in future conventions. In other words, this was to be a political manual, which would supplement existing materials available through the League. The other volume would be a comparative study using methods and dealing with questions of interest to political scientists and others professionally interested in constitutional revision, conventions, state government, and politics. The present book is the result of this effort.

The first two chapters that follow set forth in some
detail the characteristics of the states and conventions
studied and the methodological approaches used. We should
note here, however, that the general approach we followed,
which involved an individual interview with each delegate
at the start of each convention, and a second round of interviews at the end, entailed reliance on very substantial
numbers of people in each state to supervise and conduct
this data gathering. In addition, in several states, we
enlisted the aid of local associates to work on the preparation of the draft monographic manuscript pertaining to
that state. Furthermore, there were several convention
officers, delegates, and convention staff personnel who
were especially helpful in a variety of ways. Finally,
the individuals who prepared the studies commissioned by
the League frequently were of great assistance to us in
our parallel efforts.

It would be impossible for us to mention by name
everyone upon whom we have leaned for assistance, and hence
some categories of people, such as the numerous individuals who did the actual interviewing, can only be thanked
collectively, which we hereby do in the case of the inter-
viewers, and most sincerely. Very high on the list of
people due a major portion of deep gratitude are of course
the convention delegates themselves. Few indeed of the
hundreds we sought to have interviewed were anything but
enormously cordial and helpful. Without their experiences
and their willingness to take time out of their busy rounds
to tell us about them, there would have been no book.

Individuals in the various states who should be sin-
gled out by name for special thanks include for New York,
Leon Cohen and Alan K. Campbell; for Maryland, H. Vernon
Eney, Royce Hanson, John P. Wheeler, Jr., Parris Glenden-
ning, and Ben Laime; for Hawaii, David Tabb; for New Mexico, Kenneth M. Johnson and Dorothy Cline; for Arkansas,
Calvin R. Ledbetter, Jr., George E. Dyer, Walter H. Nunn,
and Robert E. Johnston; and for Illinois, Samuel K. Gove,
Thomas Kitsos, Charles Pastors, and Joseph P. Pisciotti.
In Rhode Island, it would be virtually impossible to single out individuals, since most of the delegates became
personal friends who made countless contributions to our
research and education. Mention should be made, however,
of the convention's executive secretary, Edward Conaty,
with whom collaboration in both our staff and research
capacities was invariably a pleasure.

Though the Commonwealth of Kentucky did not have an
elected convention comparable to the others studied, an

appointed commission did produce a major constitutional
revision proposal. This body seemed useful to study, and
we did so with the aid of John E. Reeves, Frederic J.
Fleron, who supervised our data collection, and David A.
Booth who drafted the resulting monograph manuscript.

At Brown we enjoyed a happy collaborative relationship with a succession of secretarial assistants: Virginia Emmert, Claire Duffy, and the late Kay Johnson.
Similarly, a series of Political Science graduate students
played important supportive roles in our efforts; several
were coauthors of articles published from the accumulating
data and analysis: Alan Arcuri, Arthur English, Robert
Arseneau, and Sean Kelleher. Richard J. Croteau helped
us untangle knotty computer program difficulties and generally made valuable contributions as programmer.

We could never adequately express our gratitude to
Bill Cassella, of the League, for the breadth of knowledge
about constitution revision he placed at our disposal,
for his invaluable assistance in threading our way through
the intricacies of securing and managing research grants,
and for his congenial and supportive colleagueship throughout nearly a decade of association.

If one had to pick the ideal foundation with which to
work, it might well be the Carnegie Corporation of New
York. Their sympathetic appreciation of our goals and
problems, their flexibility in allowing us to manage our
research and funds in our own way, and their willingness
to follow a project through to final fruition, all were
unsurpassed. In particular, our contact with Carnegie
throughout was Frederic A. Mosher. The qualities of insight
and sympathy just listed were in fact qualities we found in
him. It is really to Fritz that we address our thanks and
deep sense of appreciation. Also of enormous help to us
in the final stages of placing this volume for publication
was Avery Russell. Thus to her also we owe a very large
debt.

No cumulation of contributions made by others can of
course absolve the authors of full responsibility for what
is found between these covers. We shared equally in the
long and complex process of preparation of this study, and
we willingly take blame equally for errors of fact or interpretation that may be found in it.

We must and willingly do acknowledge permissions received to include in the book quotations from the work of
others and from our own previously published studies.

We are indebted to Professor Albert Sturm and the
Bureau of Government Research at West Virginia University

for permission to quote from Professor Sturm's <u>Major Constitutional Issues in West Virginia</u> published by the Bureau in 1961.

Selected materials from the following articles appear with the permission of Wayne State University Press:

Cornwell, Elmer E. Jr., Jay S. Goodman, and Wayne R. Swanson, "State Constitutional Conventions: Delegates, Roll Calls, and Issues," <u>Midwest Journal of Political Science</u> 14, 1 (February 1970): 105-30.

Swanson, Wayne R., Jay S. Goodman, and Elmer E. Cornwell, "Interaction Patterns in an Unstructured Legislative Setting," <u>Midwest Journal of Political Science</u> 15, 3 (August 1971): 563-70.

Goodman, Jay S., Robert Arseneau, Elmer E. Cornwell, Jr., and Wayne R. Swanson, "Public Responses to State Constitutional Revision," <u>American Journal of Political Science</u> 17, 3 (August 1973): 571-96.

Portions of the following two articles were reprinted by permission of the University of Utah, copyright holder:

Goodman, Jay S., Wayne R. Swanson, and Elmer E. Cornwell, Jr., "Political Recruitment in Four Selection Systems," <u>Western Political Quarterly</u>, March 1970, pp. 92-103.

Swanson, Wayne R., Jay S. Goodman, and Elmer E. Cornwell, Jr., "Voting Behavior in a Nonpartisan Legislative Setting," <u>Western Political Quarterly</u>, March 1972, pp. 39-50.

Selections from the following two articles are also reprinted with the permission of the journals:

Swanson, Wayne R., Jay S. Goodman, and Elmer E. Cornwell, "Leadership Perception and Voting Behavior in the Nonpartisan Legislature," <u>Polity</u>, Fall 1972, pp. 129-35.

Swanson, Wayne R., Sean A. Kelleher, and Arthur English, "Socialization of Constitution-makers: Political Experience, Role Conflict, and Atti-

tude Change," <u>Journal of Politics</u>, February 1972,
pp. 183-98.

Finally, we appreciate the efforts of Nancy Shepard-
son of Wheaton College, who typed this manuscript patiently
through three drafts.
This has been a long and complicated project. We
hope that those reading this volume will judge the fruits
of the effort worthwhile.

CONTENTS

LIST OF TABLES AND FIGURES

xv

State
Constitutional
Conventions

1

AN INTRODUCTION TO
THE STUDY OF STATE
CONSTITUTION-MAKING

The 1960s will likely go down as one of the most significant periods in U.S. history. Presidential assassina-
tion, the Vietnam war, and the urban crisis were among the
most dramatic events of an era in which the hopes of the
New Frontier and Great Society were somewhat tragically
transformed into a spirit of frustration. The federal
government, which had been looked upon as a cure-all for
society's ills at the beginning of the decade, had by the
late 1960s become incapable of meeting the challenges posed
by an increasingly complex society. The spirit of confi-
dence that prevailed in America had quickly eroded. The
key question to confront the nation by the end of the 1960s
was not "How will government solve the problems facing
America?" but "Can the government solve the problems facing
the country?" In other words, Americans were beginning to
ask themselves if they had deluded themselves into believing that all it would take is the proper response by the
federal government to rid society of its political, social,
and economic problems.

One of the unfortunate by-products of recent developments in U.S. politics has been a rather glaring neglect
for the politics of state governments at a time when these
instrumentalities have been facing an identity crisis of
their own. We sometimes forget that although since the
New Deal the burden for solving most of the major problems
facing society has fallen on the national government, state
governments have also expanded their functions and respon-
sibilities, as demands for education, welfare, and any number of other services have been thrust upon them. Indeed,
with the passage of general revenue sharing in 1972 and
the proposal of special revenue sharing, the Nixon adminis-

1

tration and the national government itself turned to the
states as a device to offset what was perceived as the
sluggish federal bureaucracy. The results of those efforts
are still uncertain, but it is clear that the problems con-
fronting the nation in the 1970s will demand a vigorous
response from both the national and the state governments.

In some ways the state governments are unlikely instru-
ments to be chosen to lead a new wave of governmental responsiveness to citizen needs. It is true that historically they have innovated in some program areas and that
their individual rate of adopting new ideas has actually
increased in recent years.[1] At the same time, they have
been strongly criticized as impotent subsystems within the
federal structure, lacking both the means and the will to
respond to pressing contemporary needs.[2] Certain of their
problems the state governments are unlikely ever to be
able to do much about. They can never recapture the
kinds of citizen loyalties they apparently had in the 18th
and 19th centuries. Whatever adjustments it may make,
the federal government will not go back to its trim shape
and the limited operations of the era prior to the New
Deal. Similarly, foreign policy questions, on which the
federal government is preeminent, are likely to retain
their saliency for the United States indefinitely, so that
any thought that the states might become first again in
the "nationalistic" loyalties of residents or be the major
governmental units for most important issues is purely
wishful thinking.

At the same time, the position of the states is not
without some potential. We know that there is a substantial public that follows state politics.[3] Some aspects
of state performance are within the decision-making scope
of the states themselves, especially their basic institutional systems as set forth in state constitutions. Most
state constitutions in effect today were written to ex-
pound a political philosophy for a society far less complicated than the one in which we live. An underlying
assumption of most state constitutions was that politics
was somewhat evil. The government that governed least
governed best. Well before the present crisis in U.S.
politics appeared, the Commission on Intergovernmental Relations observed that "many state constitutions restrict
the scope, effectiveness, and adaptability of state and
local action. These self-imposed constitutional limitations make it difficult for many states to perform all of
the services their citizens require."[4] The myriad of con-
straints in most state charters caused former North Caro-

lina Governor Terry Sanford to characterize state constitutions as "the drag anchors of state progress, and the permanent cloaks for the protection of special interests."[5]

The events of the 1960s produced a new sense of concern about the inadequacy of state constitutions. One of the most immediate stimuli was the reaction to the Supreme Court's one-man, one-vote decisions in <u>Baker vs. Carr</u> (1962), <u>Reynolds vs. Sims</u> (1964), and <u>Lucas vs. Colorado</u> (1964). Malapportionment of the state legislature had perpetuated an advantage for the more conservative rural areas in the country and within each state. However, having been made aware that their apportionment schemes violated the Equal Protection Clause of the federal Constitution, most states, in some instances under considerable prodding from the courts, made a concerted attempt to correct the imbalance.

In some states the housecleaning that took place as a consequence of reapportionment also called attention to other aspects of state governmental organization and structure that tended to stifle innovation. The new legislatures elected after reapportionment were more receptive to the idea that wholesale constitutional reform was needed if state governments were to survive. The previously unheard cries for constitutional reform made by good-government groups such as the League of Women Voters and the National Municipal League drew more support as public officials, state and local opinion leaders, and influential private organizations threw their weight behind the need for constitutional reform.

Thus a combination of factors led many states to call constitutional conventions to revise their basic documents. This volume is a study of conventions in the seven states that held open, unlimited conventions between 1964 and 1970. We are mindful of the warning that it is possible to overstress the hobbling effects of constitutions on state government.[6] Our perspective, however, is not ameliorative. We believe that a comprehensive inquiry into one method of constitutional revision can raise and answer many questions about the nature of constitution-making, many of them often discussed but rarely examined in an empirical context. Is constitution-making, the setting of basic structural arrangements for a political system in a written document, something special in the eyes of the citizenry? What are the attitudes of those entrusted with the responsibility of writing the document, the convention delegates? Is what comes out the product of rationalistic deliberations searching for the "good law?"

Or can we discover, using empirical methods, the ways in which constitution-making is comprehensible in terms of our regular political processes?

Unlike many other studies of this kind, in ours we will try to cope, almost simultaneously, with the concerns of two quite different audiences. One audience consists of those who are interested in the substance and politics of constitutional revision—the activists, delegates, reformers, lawyers, public officials, and citizens in the states. Another audience is more specialized and is concerned with how the data of this study can be connected to social science knowledge about activists' behavior, about actors in quasi-legislative bodies, about the substantive roots of voting blocs, about the role of party in different settings, and many other similar matters. The latter audience is comprised mainly of academic political scientists, primarily students of state politics, but, we hope, also those who analyze many different aspects of political behavior upon which our data may shed new light. At one point, however, we suspect that the concerns of these two audiences do come together. Both are concerned with whatever can be uncovered about the dynamics of structural change and how different segments of the public react to proposals for change in different settings. We hope that, by the end of the book, we will have satisfied the curiosity and concerns of both audiences.

Before we describe the specific contexts in which the seven states in our study attempted to revise their constitutions, in the section that follows we will briefly outline some of the specific characteristics of U.S. constitutions today and also discuss the various methods, in addition to conventions, that have been used to adapt constitutions to the changing requirements of state government.

STATE CONSTITUTIONS TODAY

The most frequently stated normative prescriptions for written constitutions are that (1) they be relatively brief documents that set forth the structure of government and (2) they state clearly the major limitations placed upon government. Governments are said to function more effectively under constitutions that contain a simple digest of fundamental principles rather than a series of long and detailed statutory provisions. The U.S. Constitution is frequently cited as a model that incorporates the qualities

4

of simplicity and brevity but that also has proven to be an extremely effective and enduring charter of government.

Most of the original state constitutions drawn up in the 18th and 19th centuries were noted for their brevity, rarely containing more than 5,000 words and conforming to the principle that constitutions should be restricted to matters of fundamental importance. However, the course of U.S. history has produced basic changes in the political, social, and economic make-up of the country, which manifested themselves rather dramatically in the substance and style of state constitutions. Whereas the federal Constitution has been adapted to a changing society by a liberal interpretation of the delegated powers contained in that document, states have more often than not resorted to the formal amending procedure and wholesale revision as methods to keep pace with an increasingly complex society. The consequence of this trend has been to generate lengthy documents cluttered with detail.

Constitutional scholars often note that American states have been the world's principal laboratories for experimentation in the formation of written constitutions.[7] In the course of U.S. history, 140 different constitutions have governed the American states. Twenty states have managed to survive with only one constitution, but others have engaged in periodic rewriting of their charters. Louisiana leads in the number of constitutions; 12 different constitutions have governed the state since it became a state in 1812. The average age of state constitutions today is 87 years: Massachusetts has the oldest constitution at 192 years; the Montana constitution of 1972 is the newest state constitution. The average length of state constitutions is now approximately 30,000 words. They range in length from Louisiana's, with 254,000, to Vermont's, with approximately 5,000. As of June 1, 1969 the existing 50 state constitutions had been amended 4,883 times. The number of amendments ranged from the 654 in the Georgia constitution to zero in Connecticut's.[8]

Duane Lockard has pointed out that the length and complexity of state constitutions are not negative qualities per se.[9] The significance of length and complexity lies in the fact that they usually contain rules that are to the advantage of some contestants in the political process and to the disadvantage of others. By and large the statutory-code-like restrictions that clutter most state constitutions come, at the time reform becomes a possibility, to protect the interests of those in society who benefit from the preservation of the status quo. In this way constitution-making and the attempts at constitutional reform become part of the struggle for power in the U.S. political system.

We cannot outline the specific problems constitutions cause in the operations of state governments, in part because documents vary considerably and in part because different observers would disagree about what constitutes a constitutional "problem." Those who view state constitutions from one perspective, however, have been quite explicit about the "deficiencies" of state documents. That perspective is the progressive, good-government, reform movement, epitomized institutionally by the National Municipal League.[10] One outstanding scholar of state constitutions who seems to share this perspective, Albert L. Sturm, has catalogued what he considers the typical deficiencies, and we have reproduced Professor Sturm's listing below.[11]

Deficiencies of American State Constitutions

1. A cumbersome, unrepresentative legislature, inadequately staffed to perform the lawmaking function intelligently, with excessively restricted powers, often unresponsive to public needs, especially in urban areas, and subject to manipulation by selfish interests.

2. A disintegrated and enfeebled executive with power widely dispersed and responsibility divided among a large number of elective officials on all levels, and an administrative structure of great complexity featured by duplication, overlapping, inefficiency and waste.

3. A diffused, complicated and largely uncoordinated judiciary, often lacking independence, with judges selected on a political basis and frequently without professional qualifications on the lower levels.

4. Rigid restrictions on local government that seriously impede home rule.

5. A long ballot listing a bewildering array of candidates and issues and rendering the task of even the most intelligent voter exceedingly difficult.

6. Provisions for amendment and revision so rigid, in some constitutions, as practically to

deprive the people of the opportunity to alter
their basic law, and, in others, so lax as to encourage too frequent changes.

7. Inclusion of a mass of detail in the constitution, blurring the distinction between constitutional and statutory law, and necessitating
frequent amendments.

METHODS OF CONSTITUTIONAL CHANGE

State constitutions may not change as quickly as many
persons would like, and the specific changes may not always produce wholly desirable effects, but they do change.
The methods of constitutional change in the states are extremely varied. For our purposes we can separate them into
three types: (1) change by interpretation, (2) change by
amendment (by which we mean a specific and limited altera-
tion), and (3) change by wholesale constitutional reform
(which implies an extensive rewriting of a major part of
the document).

INTERPRETATION

Students of constitutional law are aware that constitutions have never been written with a degree of specifi-
city that would anticipate in advance every constitutional
question to confront the political system. Indeed the
constitutional law of a nation or state is ultimately
comprised of the cumulative effects of how a given political
system has used its charter to govern its constituency.
Whether by legislative elaboration, executive interpretation, judicial decree, or simply custom and usage, states
have resorted to "interpretation" as a means to clarify,
expand, and modernize broadly and vaguely constructed
tenets of their charters. Ernest Bartley notes that the
evasive action of many states to overcome strict prohibition on state borrowing is probably the most significant
illustration of constitutional change by interpretation
at the state level.[12] When constitutional restrictions
have prevented the state from securing funds to carry out
needed capital improvement projects, they have resorted to
the issuance of specific revenue certificates or bonds for
financing the program. Thus in a strict legal sense, it
is the program and not the state that has incurred the
debt. The credit of the state has not been pledged and
the constitution has been legally circumvented.

We should not overemphasize the importance of constitutional change by interpretation at the state level, however. Because of the detailed language of most state constitutions, conservative legislatures and judges have been inclined to follow a rather strict construction. There has been far less interpretative constitutional development at the state than at the national level. As a method of constitutional change, it is probably true that interpretation has been less important than the more formal processes of amendment and revision.

AMENDMENT

Historically, the most common of the formal methods of constitutional change has been the amendment. For reasons of cost, self-interest, political power, or any number of other possible motives, the powers-that-be have usually opted for a piecemeal revision of the state charter by amendment, rather than attempt the more difficult task of full-scale reform. This tendency has frequently served to complicate further and confuse the "fundamental law" of the state and at the same time postpone needed wholesale revision. It also has the important effect of maximizing legislative control over the substantive content of state constitutions.

With only one exception, every state requires that two steps be completed before an amendment reveives constitutional status. The first stage involves initiation, which is followed in all states except Delaware, with some form of popular ratification. The initiation of a constitutional amendment can take three forms: (1) legislative action, (2) state convention or commission, and (3) popular initiative.

All constitutions today provide for some method of legislative initiation of amendments. The particular requirements vary from state to state, but common to virtually all are restrictions that provide that "unusual" majorities and/or successive majorities of the legislature must pass the proposed amendments. Thirty states provide that the proposal pass the legislature with a 60 percent or greater majority; 15 states require, or make it likely, that a proposed amendment must pass in two successive legislative sessions. These types of requirements reflect the belief that pervades U.S. political culture that constitutions are superior to statutory law and should be harder to change. One can argue that the unusual requirements to

initiate and ratify amendments keep much of what is not
fundamental out of constitutions; at the same time they
also make it more difficult to achieve desirable constitutional changes.

Constitutional conventions and commissions are usually
thought of as institutions for accomplishing wholesale
constitutional reform. This fact should not obscure their
frequent role in the amendment process. In New Hampshire,
for example, until very recently a convention was the only
constitutional way to initiate amendments. The procedure
for calling a constitutional convention and setting up
commissions requires authorization by legislature, which
usually specifies the mandate for the body. Whatever
changes are recommended are then subjected to ratification
by the electorate.

A final method of initiating an amendment that is
authorized today in 14 states is through popular initiative. Petitions with signatures of from 3 percent to 15
percent of either the total electorate or the number of
votes cast in the last biennial election are required.
Once initiated, the amendment goes directly on the ballot,
thereby avoiding any consideration by the state legislature.
The initiative method has been used with greatest frequency
in California and Oregon, historical seats of the progressive movement, which had such great faith in direct democracy.

Following the initiation of an amendment, it must be
ratified by the electorate in all states except Deleware,
which provides that amendments take effect after approval
by two-thirds of the legislature in two consecutive legislative sessions. Forty-seven states require a majority
vote for ratification. Rhodes Island requires a three-
fifths vote and New Hampshire a two-thirds vote for ratification.

Table 1.1, which has been adapted from Sturm's analysis of constitution-making, reports the frequency with
which amendments have been proposed and adopted by the
various methods to accomplish this task. Sixty-three percent of all the amendments submitted to the electorate
have been adopted. Most amendments have originated through
legislative initiations. Amendments coming from constitutional conventions are the least common but have met with
the greatest success at the polls. The initiative has not
been a very effective way to introduce amendments in that,
once proposed in this manner, they have met with relatively
little success at the polls.

TABLE 1.1

Amendments to State Constitutions

	Totals to January 1, 1969		1950-68	
	Number	Percent	Number	Percent
All Methods				
Total amendments pro-				
posed to the voters	7,761	--	3,507	--
Total amendments adopted	4,883	63	2,495	71
Legislative Proposal				
Total amendments pro-				
posed to the voters	6,873	--	3,313	--
Total amendments adopted	4,503	65	2,377	71
Constitutional Initia-				
tive				
Total amendments pro-				
posed to the voters	498	--	97	--
Total amendments adopted	161	32	35	36
Constitutional Conven-				
tion				
Total amendments pro-				
posed to the voters	284	--	97	--
Total amendments adopted	194	68	83	82

Source: Adapted from Albert L. Sturm, Thirty Years of State Constitution-Making 1938-1968 (New York: National Municipal League, 1970), pp. 29-31.

CONSTITUTIONAL STUDY COMMISSIONS

The most common way to begin the official process of constitutional revision in the states is to establish a constitutional revision commission. There are three meth- ods by which these commissions come into being: statutory law, legislative enactment, and executive order. The first requires the endorsement of both the legislature and the governor; the latter methods need only the sanction of one branch of government. Sturm reports that during the period from 1939 to 1968, there were 62 recorded revision commissions in 35 states. Thirty of them were created by statute, 16 were established by governors, and 16 owe their existence to legislative resolution.

Technically the commissions can be classified into two types. The most common type is the study commission (50 of the 62 were of this type). Their tasks have varied considerably from state to state, ranging from a limited study of particular sections of a charter to the drafting of a completely new constitution. The recommendations of the commissions are advisory in nature in that they must be submitted to the governor and/or legislature for further action. In some cases the commissions have recommended the calling of a constitutional convention to update the constitution. In other states they have prepared a series of amendments or even a whole new document for official study. The responses of officialdom to the reports of study commissions have been varied. Many of the reports are hastily considered, and no subsequent action occurs. In other states the recommendations are submitted directly to the voters for popular approval. The revision of the Florida constitution (1969) was the result of the specific recommendation of its study commission. A new constitution prepared by the Kentucky Constitutional Revision Assembly was rejected by voters in that state in 1965.

The second type of constitutional commission is the preparatory commission. Its function is to assist in preparations leading up to a constitutional convention by arranging physical facilities for the convention, filling key staff positions, and undertaking substantive studies of major issues. The preparatory commission is usually created before a referendum to call a convention has been approved and thus is frequently a vehicle to publicize the need for constitutional reform. The Maryland Constitution Revision Commission, for example, was appointed by Governor Millard Tawes in 1965. It recommended the calling of a constitutional convention and also issued a report that included a completely new draft constitution with extensive explanatory comments. The report was intended to educate the public about the deficiencies of the existing charter and later provided the basis of discussion for the work of the convention. The commission was unusually relevant to the convention in Maryland since H. Vernon Eney, prominent Baltimore lawyer and constitutional scholar, headed both bodies.

Although the work of a commission has provided the impetus for constitutional reform in some states, the overall track record for commissions is not one of uniform success. In some states, legislatures have authorized a commission as a symbolic response to give the appearance of action and to relieve themselves from pressure imposed by "good-government" reform groups. When a report is made by the commission, the legislature frequently takes no action. In addition, as a mechanism, the commission is an ideal device to ensure legislative control over constitution-making. Nothing the commission recommends can go into effect without legislative and voter approval.

In addition, some argue that because commission members are appointed, a commission is not a democratic method to alter the basic law. One assessment of the commission method concludes with the observation that "the commission lacks the strong legal position and the dynamic character and drama of a convention. Notwithstanding the contributions of a number of excellent commissions, the commission is no substitute for a convention."[13]

WHOLESALE CONSTITUTIONAL REFORM

Attempting constitutional reform more extensive than that afforded by issue-by-issue interpretation or by single amendments sets into motion a complicated political process. The potential stakes are escalated from alignments on one issue to potential gains or losses for all of those institutions, officials, groups, and individuals who are affected in one way or another by the existing basic document. Since constitutions prescribe the structural arrangements for government, all operations and branches of state government are potentially affected by an open, total review of constitutional provisions. If the constitution is a long one, with many statutory-type provisions, then many interest groups, from utilities to educational institutions to conservationists to religious elements, may be concerned. If suffrage or tax questions are involved (as they almost always could be), then the entire state public, as opposed to specialized attentive publics, is at least potentially mobilizable to a level of attention and concern.

Because so many arrangements, rules, and customary ways of conducting politics, as well as existing protections of position and power, are built into any existing document at any point in time, wholesale revision, not surprisingly, requires painstaking effort. Those seeking change have to work to bring into being that institution that has the potential to bring about thorough constitutional change: the unlimited convention. Bartley points out that "pressure for revision must build up to the point where those preventing change have no alternative but to grudgingly give way."[14]

12

The constitution-making process is inextricably linked with the question of political power, and revising a constitution risks upsetting the power positions of any interests to whose advantage it is to retain the status quo. Constitutional provisions contributing to rural dominance in state government up until 1962 preserved legislatures that, it was argued, distributed state resources in such a way that underrepresented urban areas received less in the way of state goods and services than they were entitled to.[15] Business interests that fear the potential modernization of government under strong governors have traditionally fought vigorously against constitutional revision. Associations of minor governmental officials—sheriffs, justices of the peace, registrars of wills—have opposed a revised constitution for fear their position will be denied constitutional status. Because of the role self-interest plays in politics, it is only natural that any interest group that throughout the life of a constitution has had protections built into the document will work in opposition to any wholesale reconsideration of the state's basic law.

We have indicated that reapportionment and the resulting housecleaning that took place in many legislatures in the 1960s marked a considerable breakthrough in the logjam holding up attempts at constitutional reform. During the last decade, 32 of the 50 states made some effort to consider the adequacy of their constitutions. These efforts generally took two forms: the constitutional study commission and the constitutional convention.

Constitutional conventions are a U.S. invention, and they represent the only method of constitutional revision provided for by all 50 states. Forty states provide for the convention method in their basic law. In the remaining states judicial interpretation and practice have dictated that the power to call a convention flows naturally from the power of the people. Throughout the history of the United States, approximately 221 state constitutional conventions have been held.

The convention method is distinguishable from the commission method in that it represents more directly the voice of the people. Delegates elected by the citizenry for the specific task of considering the question of constitutional revision give to a convention the aura of legitimacy that a commission frequently lacks. A convention is considerably more independent from the legislature and other agents of state government.

However, even a convention cannot be totally free from the influence of the legislature. In all but a few states

13

that provide for the automatic consideration of a convention call over a specified period of time, the legislature
must vote to place the question on the ballot. Should the
voters approve, the responsibility for passing the necessary enabling legislation lies with the legislature. A
number of key decisions that significantly influence the
type of action taken by a convention are made at this
juncture. The legislature must determine whether the convention will be limited to certain articles or topics, or
whether it will have unlimited authority to reconsider all
parts of the constitution. Of the 30 constitutional conventions held in the United States since 1938 there have
been 12 that were limited and 18 that were unlimited. In
some states the limited convention has proven to be a useful device to eliminate legislative opposition to constitutional revision by excluding from the convention's work
controversial provisions, which if altered might undermine
legislative power. For example, the New Jersey Convention
of 1947 was not allowed to revise the legislative apportionment provisions of that constitution. The conventions
that provide the basis of our study are all of the unlimited
variety.

Enabling legislation establishes the rules for the
selection and apportionment of delegates, the length of
time the convention can meet, and the date of the popular
referendum on the convention's work. Whether the convention is partisan or nonpartisan, whether delegates are
elected from single- or multimember districts, whether the
convention has adequate time to undertake a thorough revision, and whether the revised constitution is submitted in
a general or special election are all crucial questions
the legislature must answer. Controlling these characteristics of a convention gives the lawmakers considerable
influence over structure, scope, and perhaps even the
make-up of the constitution-making assemblies.

Thus, anyone considering the process of constitutional
revision in the American states must keep in mind that virtually all of the methods are to one degree or another controlled by the state legislature. Alterations that would
undermine or threaten legislative power or challenge the
conservative political values that often dominate American
state legislatures have been difficult to achieve.

In other words at the very beginning of any revision
process, political considerations arise and important calculations have to be made. For those who conceive of the
constitution-making process as somehow outside politics,
what we have just indicated may be a jolt. But if that is

14

so, it will be the first of many, because the politics of
the preconvention, convention, and postconvention phases
of the revision process are the subject of inquiry in our
study, and, as the data at all phases will indicate, there
is no way to avoid considering constitution-making without
analyzing the regular state political process. What is
most intriguing about studying constitution-making is testing propositions that allow us to specify just where this
process is unique and where it taps customary dimensions
of political behavior.

SEVEN STATES IN SEARCH OF NEW CONSTITUTIONS

This volume surveys the efforts of seven states to
revise their constitutions during the period beginning in
1964 and extending through 1970. The sample includes all
the states that held open unlimited constitutional conventions during the period. Confining our study to one
method of constitutional reform was a choice based upon
happenstance, manageability, time, staff resources, and
financial support. The senior authors were drawn into an
interest in conventions through staff roles in Rhode Island, an experience that interested them in the similar
conventions that were taking place, or were on the drawing
boards, in New York, Maryland, Hawaii, Arkansas, New Mexico, and Illinois.

We feel that confining the study to open unlimited
conventions was intellectually defensible and also desirable. All of the states approached the task of constitutional reform in essentially the same manner. The constitution-makers were all popularly elected, and they were
given unlimited authority to revise any part of their
charters. They all functioned in a setting that was very
similar to a legislative-type situation but that also gave
them maximum freedom from legislative control. From a
more practical point of view the deliberations were all a
matter of public record. The leading actors, their activities, and the outcome of the conventions were all highly
visible. Data were readily available. The convention,
like a legislature or a court system, was a rather distinct political subsystem functioning within and in relation to the overall political systems in the seven states.

Although there was much that was common about the way
in which the seven states approached the task of constitutional revision, the political, historical, and constitu-

15

TABLE 1.2

Seven State Constitutional Conventions

State	Dates of Previous Constitutions	Age of Present Constitution (years)	Length of Document	Convention Dates	Referendum Call
Rhode Island	1663, 1843	188	16,000 words, 36 amendments	Dec. 8, 1964–Feb. 17, 1969	Nov. 3, 1964 Yes: 158,241 No: 70,975
New York	1777, 1822, c1846, 1894	77	50,000 words, 168 amendments	April 4–Sept. 26, 1967	Nov. 2, 1965 Yes: 681,438 No: 1,486,431
Maryland	1776, 1851, 1857, 1864	104	40,368 words, 125 amendments	Sept. 12, 1967–Jan. 10, 1968	Sept. 13, 1966 Yes: 160,280 No: 31,680
Hawaii	1950	22	15,000 words, 28 amendments	July 15–Oct. 21, 1968	Nov. 8, 1966 Yes: 119,097 No: 62,120
Arkansas	1836, 1861, 1864, 1868, 1874	98	46,000 words, 60 amendments	May 27–Aug. 21, 1967; Jan. 12–Feb. 10, 1970	Nov. 5, 1968 Yes: 227,429 No: 214,432
New Mexico	1912	60	24,000 words, 73 amendments	Aug. 5–Oct. 20, 1969	Nov. 5, 1968 Yes: 80,242 No: 35,997
Illinois	1818, 1848	102	21,700 words, 14 amendments	Dec. 8, 1969	Nov. 5, 1968 Yes: 2,979,977 No: 1,135,440

State	Preparatory Body	Type and Number of Delegates	Proposal from Convention	Referendum
Rhode Island	Edwards Commission	100 partisan 81 Democrats 19 Republicans	New constitu-tion	Defeated April 16, 1968 Yes: 17,464 No: 68,940
New York	State Commission	186 partisan 101 Democrats 85 Republicans	New constitu-tion	Defeated Nov. 7, 1967 Yes: 1,309,877 No: 3,364,630
Maryland	Constitutional Convention Commission	142 nonpartisan	New constitu-tion	Defeated May 14, 1968 Yes: 284,033 No: 367,101
Hawaii	None	82 nonpartisan	23 amendments	Nov. 5, 1968: 22 of 23 amendments passed. 18-year-old vote re-jected.
Arkansas	Constitutional Re-vision Study Commission and Constitutional Convention Ad-visory Com-mission	100 nonpartisan	New constitu-tion	Defeated Nov. 3, 1970 Yes: 231,000 No: 312,000
New Mexico	Constitutional Re-vision Commis-sion	70 nonpartisan	New constitu-tion	Defeated Dec. 9, 1969 Yes: 59,685 No: 63,387
Illinois	Constitutional Study Commission	116 nonpartisan	New constitu-tion	December 15, 1970. Main package and two of four propositions passed.

Source: Compiled by the authors.

tional settings that characterized the states and their
conventions offered much in the way of diversity. Table
1.2 identifies some of the salient background data about
each of the states, their constitutions, and their conventions. From a geographical point of view all sections of
the country are represented: New York and Rhode Island
from the East, Maryland from the Middle Atlantic states,
Arkansas from the South, Illinois from the Midwest, New
Mexico from the Southwest, and Hawaii from the Far West.
Consequently we were able to examine constitution-making
and processes of political change in the context of a variety of state and regional political cultures.

The historical background and the nature of the existing constitutions of the states varied considerably. Arkansas had been governed by five different constitutions
during her history; New Mexico and Hawaii were operating
with their original charters. The Rhode Island constitution was 123 years old, while Hawaii's charter was not
even 20 years old. New York had the longest and most
amended constitution (50,000 words and 168 amendments);
the Hawaii constitution had only 15,000 words and Illinois'
basic law had been amended only 14 times.

The organization and procedure for the conventions
varied from state to state. The number of delegates ranged
from 186 in New York to 70 in New Mexico. In two of the
states, Rhode Island and New York, the delegates were
elected with partisan labels. Nonpartisanship characterized the selection process in the other states. The length
of the conventions varied from over 4 years in Rhode Island
to 10 weeks in New Mexico. Three states submitted their
revised constitutions to the voters in special elections;
four included the product of the convention on referenda
in regular biennial elections. In two states the efforts
to revise the constitution met with success; in the other
five, the revised documents were defeated by the voters.

Purely by accident then, we managed to encounter a
sample of conventions that offer the student of constitution-making an extremely varied and interesting group of
case studies from which to generate and test a number of
hypotheses about the politics of constitutional change.
Before outlining the theoretical perspectives that guide
our study, a brief summary of the specific background considerations that caused the calling of conventions in the
seven states will be useful to the reader.

Discussion of the need for constitutional reform had been brewing for a long time before the legislature finally authorized a convention call in April 1964.[16] The advisability of constitutional reform, the appropriate method to revise the charter, and the method of delegate selection were all very much a part of the state's partisan politics. Because they suffered from a malapportioned legislature, the Democrats had argued for an open convention since the early 1930s. During the 1950s, however, when they began to win majorities in both houses of the legislature with considerable regularity, their enthusiasm for constitutional reform waned. The press and reform groups like the League of Women Voters replaced the Democrats as the leading proponents of constitutional reform. In 1961 Democratic Governor John A. Notte with legislative consent finally authorized a commission to study the constitution. While the Edwards Commission was meeting, the Supreme Court handed down its decision in Baker vs. Carr. Faced with the necessity of reapportioning the state legislature and spurred by the recommendation of the Edwards Commission that an open unlimited constitutional convention should be convened, Notte directed the commission to prepare appropriate enabling legislation for the calling of a convention.

No such legislation had been passed when Republican John Chafee was elected governor in 1964. The changing of the guard at the state capital meant that the way constitutional reform was achieved was a crucial political question. The Democrats in the legislature believed it essential that they control the constituent assembly. A long period of complicated maneuvering ensued in which both parties tried to seek advantages for themselves in arrangements for delegate choice and in the ultimate work of the convention itself.

Democrats were fearful of an unlimited convention and wanted the delegates elected on a partisan basis, which would virtually ensure that Democratic legislators would control the body. Republicans favored an unlimited convention with nonpartisan delegates. The plan that finally passed in the legislature, over the governor's veto, called for an unlimited convention made up of 100 partisan delegates, thus ensuring a Democratic-controlled convention. The leading paper in the state, Providence Journal, denounced the whole scheme in no uncertain terms: "With shameful cynicism spawned by arrogance of power, the Democratic Party of Rhode Island has prostituted its 1962

19

pledge of support for an open constitutional convention into a sickening exercise in the cheapest ward politics." The convention was never able to shed this image.

New York

States differ rather dramatically in the traditions they develop in the area of constitution-making. Some, like Rhode Island, are governed under brief charters that have little to say about matters of substantive policy. Under this condition, constitutional revision may be rare —no major attempt at constitutional reform took place in Rhode Island between 1841 and 1964. Other states, however, have a fairly well developed tradition of constitution-making and constitutional revision. New York is the prime example of this type of state.[17]

Constitutional conventions have been called nine times in the history of the Empire State.[18] The most recent convention preceding the 1967 conclave was held in 1938.[19] A very partisan body, it submitted a package of 13 recommendations to the electorate in New York, most of which were defeated by the voters. In retrospect, however, the convention was not a complete failure. Many of the provisions that were not approved in 1938 were added in the form of individual amendments proposed by the state legislature in the nearly three decades before the 1967 convention. This fact calls attention to an important constitutional tradition in New York—legislation by constitutional amendment. Between 1938 and 1966, some 95 amendments were proposed, and 82 of these were approved by the voters and added to an already swollen constitutional document.

The ease with which constitutional change has taken place in New York has precipitated the development of a special tradition. Constitutional change is integrated into the overall political process much more fully and explicitly than in the other states. Politicians and interest groups approach the task of constitutional reform with considerably greater awareness of its potential impact upon policy and political power questions than political actors in states with different constitutional traditions. Partisanship has long been a prominent feature in the politics of constitutional reform in New York.

After 1938, the first attempt to consider wholesale constitutional revision in New York occurred in 1956, when the Democratic-controlled legislature placed the question of calling a new convention on the ballot. At the same time, they also created a temporary 15-man commission, headed by Nelson Rockefeller, to formulate proposals for simplifying the constitution. The call for the convention was defeated in 1957, but the "Rockefeller Commission" was given a more permanent status and was asked to propose a series of amendments to the constitution. The commission was not effective and during 1962 went out of existence. Shortly thereafter renewed efforts at calling a convention were made. Among those putting pressure on the legislature to place the question on the ballot were the League of Women Voters, the Liberal Party, and the New York *Times*, through a series of editorials examining the specific deficiencies in the state charter.

When the New York State courts overruled a redistricting plan passed by the "lame-duck" legislature in 1964, additional pressure was exerted for the calling of a new convention, if only to discuss the issue of reapportionment. In 1965 the legislature, responding to considerable pressure from a variety of individuals and groups, placed the question of a new convention on the ballot with a provision for the election of delegates in 1966 and convening of the convention in 1967. The convention was approved by the voters by a very narrow margin, 186 partisan delegates were selected, and a Temporary Commission on the State Constitutional Convention was named to help prepare for the convention.

Maryland

During the early 1960s the combination of a court-imposed reapportionment of the legislature and the electoral success of a new liberal reform element within the state Democratic Party in Maryland seemed to provide the impetus for reformer efforts to call a constitutional convention.[20] In response to Baker vs. Carr (1962), a 1964 reapportionment in Maryland cleared the way for the election in 1966 of a liberalized, more urban General Assembly. In the same period insurgent Democrats ousted entrenched party machines in Montgomery and Prince George's counties, while reform Democrat Joseph Tydings won election to the U.S. Senate. The Tydings organization gave the progressive element within the party a virtual statewide base.

The mood for reform, which seemed to have settled over a segment of Maryland's political elite, provoked Democratic Governor Tawes to ask authorization from the legislature in 1966 to appoint a constitutional commission.

Acting in response to reform pressure from within the
party, the governor explained that he had experienced some
of the shortcomings of Maryland's governmental structure,
especially with the limitation of his own powers and in
dealing with an archaic court system. He was not discouraged when the state senate balked at his proposal. On his
own authority and with executive funds, he appointed a
27-member constitutional convention commission.

The "blue-ribbon" commission, under the leadership
of H. Vernon Eney, a former president of the Maryland Bar
Association, included 19 lawyers, 4 educators, an invest-
ment banker, a labor leader, a public utility head, and
the chairman of the Urban League. The initial finding of
the group was that the Maryland constitution was sorely in
need of revision and that a constitutional convention would
be the logical and most efficient instrument to accomplish
that objective. To aid such a constituent assembly, the
commission subsequently prepared a revised draft constitution for Maryland that resembled very closely the Model
State Constitution drafted by the National Municipal League.

In response to the commission's recommendation the
General Assembly agreed in early 1966 to place the question of a convention call on the ballot at the statewide
primary election in September of that year. The convention call was approved by a vote of 160,280 to 31,680.
However, it was left to the newly apportioned General Assembly of 1967 to provide the enabling legislation for the
convention.

Unlike the pattern that emerged in Rhode Island and
New York, the conditions under which the convention was
organized in Maryland brought universal praise from reform
groups. The enabling legislation provided that 142 delegates be selected on a nonpartisan basis and chosen from
the same multimember districts as the members of the House
of Delegates. In addition, a four-month time limit was
imposed upon the life of the convention, and a special
election for ratification was scheduled for May 12, 1968.

Hawaii

The fact that Hawaii had drafted and ratified a constitution in 1950 at the time of statehood that was well-
praised by political analysts and practitioners made it
seem unlikely that the state would have another convention
as early as 1968. Although it was the reapportionment
question that drew attention to the constitution, it was

through what one observer has called "political ineptitude" that a constitutional convention had to be called to solve the redistricting problem.[21] Neither the Democratic Party under the leadership of Governor John A. Burns nor the International Longshoremen's and Warehousemen's Union, the two most powerful political forces in the state, wanted a convention. Both groups argued that reapportionment was the only constitutional question that needed attention and that this could be handled adequately by the state legislature. After the state attorney general ruled that the Hawaii legislative apportionment violated the Supreme Court ruling in Reynolds vs. Sims, Burns submitted a revised apportionment scheme to a special session of the legislature. The rather obvious effect of the plan would have been to enhance both the Democratic Party's and the governor's control over the politics of the state. When neither house of the legislature could agree on the substance or procedure for reapportionment, the legislature adjourned without taking action.

After specifically ruling in 1965 that the apportionment of Hawaii's Senate was invalid, the Federal District Court specified that the question of calling a constitutional convention was to be placed on the ballot. A provisional reapportionment plan was passed by the legislature, but the court ruled that a constitutional convention was necessary to implement a permanent plan. The state politicians failed in their attempts to maneuver the convention question off the ballot, and in November 1966 the convention call was approved by Hawaii voters. Though many incumbent state legislators were elected delegates to the convention, the selection of delegates injected some new faces into the state politics, individuals who tended to view the convention as an opportunity to make a name for themselves. The newcomers resisted the efforts of the established politicans in the convention to confine the work of the convention to reapportionment. The effect was that the whole Hawaii constitution was subjected to a rather complete review just 18 years after its adoption.

New Mexico

The circumstances behind the calling of the New Mexico Constitutional Convention in 1969 were somewhat different from the other states in this study because there was no single incident or crisis that led to the call. One delegate noted that the convention came about after 17 years

of talk, study, and agitation, during which time the population of New Mexico grew in significant proportions. The
increase in population caused a fundamental change in the
character of the state. A once completely rural and agricultural territory had gradually been transformed into a
state that was more highly urbanized and educated. By
1968 the original "revised" constitution of 1910 had been
amended 73 times and was no longer suitable for New Mexico.
    The first formal step toward the calling of a consti-
tutional convention occurred in 1963, when the New Mexico
Constitutional Revision Commission was established. The
commission was in existence from 1963 to 1968, during
which time it formulated a revised constitution for New
Mexico. The publication of this report in 1967 and the
continuing agitation of "good-government" groups was the
stimulus that caused the convention call to be placed on
the ballot in November 1968. The convention call passed
rather easily, and in 1969 the state legislature passed
an enabling act that provided for the nonpartisan election
of 70 delegates, a convention that would meet for no more
than 60 calendar days, and a referendum that would take
place in a special election within 45 to 60 days after the
convention adjourned. Delegates were elected on June 17,
1969, and the convention was convened on August 15, 1969.

                            Arkansas

    The opposition to constitutional reform in Arkansas
had been sustained by a legislature that was significantly
malapportioned in favor of the rural sections of the state
and by a series of governors who owed their election to
the voters from these rural areas.[22] Only once since 1874
had the constitution come under the scrutiny of a convention. In 1918 Arkansas voters overwhelmingly defeated a
revised constitution prepared by the 1917 convention.
    By 1967, however, Arkansas like many of the states in
the old confederacy began to change. A liberal Republican,
Winthrop Rockefeller, ousted conservative Democrat Orval
Faubus from the state house. Reapportionment increased
the representation of the urban sections of the state and
caused a turnover in membership in the Arkansas House of
Representatives of almost 50 percent. A new brand of urban Democrats, anxious to change the reactionary image
their party had received in the 1966 election began to
plead the cause of constitutional reform and the need for
a constitutional convention. Republicans under Rockefel-

                            24

ler's leadership also saw the need for revision of the
state's basic law but preferred that a constitutional study
commission be created. Unable to secure enough support
for a convention, the Democrats temporarily acceded to the
request for a commission. The Arkansas Revision Study
Commission met during 1967 and recommended that the need
for general revision of the constitution could best be met
by a constitutional convention.

The commission's recommendation was generally accepted
by the political leaders of the state, but there ensued a
long battle over how the convention was to be organized.
The cleavages that were to confront the efforts at reform
were evident in the preconvention maneuvering. In particular there was considerable controversy over whether the
delegates should be elected from the newly apportioned
districts of the House of Representatives or from the old
malapportioned districts. Status-quo forces were still
strong in the legislature. However, a coalition largely
consisting of freshmen Democratic representatives with the
support of the governor managed to secure the passage of
a bill calling for a convention of 100 delegates from newly
apportioned districts. The future course of constitutional
reform did not seem encouraging when Arkansas voters approved the convention call by an extremely narrow vote in
the general election in November of 1968.

Illinois

The background of the constitutional reform movement
in Illinois was similar to the pattern that characterized
the efforts in other states.[23] Attempts to generate support for a constitutional convention had been made by reform groups and governors of the state since the early
1940s without much success. The need for a convention was
undermined somewhat by the passage in 1950 of the Gateway
Amendment, a provision that relaxed the somewhat rigid
constitutional restrictions to amending the state constitution. Gateway allowed for the amendment of three articles instead of one in any legislative session and eased
the majority requirement for legislative passage from two-
thirds of the General Assembly to two-thirds of those voting on the question. The Gateway Amendment served for the
time being to placate constitutional reformers.

By 1959 the League of Women Voters had renewed their
efforts to initiate wholesale constitutional reform. Influential legislators in the state, however, still clung

25

to the belief that piecemeal revision was the appropriate
and best way to reform a constitution. The amending of
the judicial article in 1962 by this method gave added
support to this argument. But growing discontent with the
constitution and in particular the failure to amend an in-
flexible revenue article caused the state to establish a
Constitutional Study Commission in 1965. The commission
made no recommendation for specific changes but did recom-
mend that the legislature authorize the calling of a constitutional convention.

As the revenue crisis in Illinois became more severe,
a number of legislators who had resisted the call for a
convention began to see it as the only alternative to save
the state from financial crisis. The Commission on State
Government, which had been established during the 1967 legislative session, flooded the legislature with over 20
proposals for constitutional change. Overwhelmed by the
immensity of the task set before them, the legislature
authorized a convention call. Another Constitutional Study
Commission was created to help prepare substantive and
procedural guidelines for the convention. The call for a
constitutional convention was approved by the voters of
Illinois by a wide margin in November 1968.

This review of the immediate circumstances surrounding the call for constitutional conventions in the seven
states that comprise this study suggests that many powerful
elements in state politics are reluctant to undertake
wholesale constitutional reform. Despite the continuing
efforts of the League of Women Voters, the National Municipal League, and other reform groups, it almost always takes
some stimulus from outside state politics or some crisis
from within the state to generate legislative and voter
support necessary to call a convention. The Supreme Court's
decisions concerning reapportionment opened the flood-
gates for wholesale constitutional reform in the 1960s.
The court's pronouncements not only called attention to
one major deficiency in contemporary state constitutions
but resulted in the election of a new breed of legislators
who were not as tied as their predecessors to the interests that were protected by the existing constitutions.
The new legislators were free to experiment with wholesale
constitutional change.

Like virtually all aspects of democratic politics,
however, compromise plays a key role in the constitution-
making process. The key decisions that are made in determining whether or not to place the convention call on the
ballot and how such a convention should be structured gen-

26

erate political conflicts between the advocates of reform
and the opponents of change. As a matter of fact, we
think the whole constitution-making process, from the first
efforts at considering the type of reform to undertake
until the final voter referendum, is a struggle between
the reformers and the stand-patters in state politics.
This proposition, as well as who wins the struggle and why
they win, is a main subject of this volume. In the next
chapter we will outline some theoretical constructs and
propositions about constitution-making in a systematic way.
We will also describe our research methods and the data we
collected.

NOTES

1. See Jack L. Walker, "The Diffusion of Innovations
among the American States," American Political Science Review 63, 3 (September 1969): 880-99.
2. See Terry Sanford, Storm over the States (New
York: McGraw-Hill, 1967).
3. See M. Kent Jennings and Harmon Zeigler, "The
Salience of American State Politics," American Political
Science Review 64, 2 (June 1970): 523-35.
4. Commission on Intergovernmental Relations, A Report to the President for Transmittal to the Congress
(Washington, D.C.: Government Printing Office, 1955), p.
37, cited in Albert L. Sturm, Thirty Years of State Constitution-Making 1938-1968 (New York: National Municipal
League, 1970), pp. 2-3.
5. Sanford, op. cit., p. 189, cited in Sturm, op.
cit., p. 4.
6. Duane Lockard, Politics of State and Local Government (New York: Macmillan, 1963), p. 94.
7. The authors and all students of state constitution-making are indebted to Professor Albert Sturm for
his life-long work in the area of state constitutions.
Much of the material for this review of methods of state
constitutional revision was culled from Sturm, op. cit.
8. The Connecticut constitution was amended for the
first time in 1970 to provide for annual sessions of the
General Assembly.
9. Lockard, op. cit., p. 94.
10. See the League's publications: Robert S. Rankin,
State Constitutions: Bill of Rights (1960); Bennett M.
Rich, State Constitutions: The Governor (1960); Robert
B. Dishman, State Constitutions: The Shape of the Document

(1960); Gordon E. Baker, State Constitutions: Reapportionment (1960); Ferrel Heady, State Constitutions: The Structure of Administration (1961); John P. Wheeler, Jr., ed., Salient Issues of Constitutional Revision (1961); Charlotte Irvine and Edward M. Kresky, How to Study a State Constitution (1962); and Model State Constitution, 6th ed. (1963).

11. Albert L. Sturm, Major Constitutional Issues in West Virginia (Morgantown, W. Va.: Bureau of Government Research, West Virginia University, 1961), p. 10.

12. Ernest Bartley, "Methods of Constitutional Change," in W. Brooke Graves, ed., State Constitutional Revision (Chicago: Public Administration Service, 1960), p. 23.

13. Bennett M. Rich, "Revision by Constitutional Commission," in Graves, op. cit., p. 99.

14. Bartley, op. cit., p. 30.

15. The political science literature suggests that the causal impact of malapportionment was not as great as popular opinion would have it, at least insofar as quantitative methods could measure it. Thus, Thomas R. Dye concluded that "On the whole, the policy choices of malapportioned legislatures are not noticeably different from the policy choices of well-apportioned legislatures. Most of the policy differences which do occur turn out to be a product of socioeconomic differences among the states rather than a direct product of apportionment practices." See his Politics, Economics, and the Public (Chicago: Rand McNally, 1966), p. 280, and in general, pp. 270-81. In addition Brian R. Fry and Richard F. Winters did not find that malapportionment had a significant impact on redistribution at the state level; see their "The Politics of Redistribution," American Political Science Review 64, 2 (June 1970); 508-22. On the other hand, Walker, op. cit., found malapportionment was significantly related to the speed of state adoption of new programs.

16. For a detailed study, see Elmer E. Cornwell, Jr., and Jay S. Goodman, The Politics of the Rhode Island Constitutional Convention (New York: National Municipal League, 1969).

17. For an interesting study of the relationships between interest groups and state constitutions, see Lewis A. Froman, Jr., "Some Effects of Interest Groups in State Politics," American Political Science Review 60, 4 (December 1966): 952-62.

18. For a complete study, see Leon S. Cohen, Elmer E. Cornwell, Jay S. Goodman, and Wayne R. Swanson, "The Politics of the New York Constitutional Convention" (New York: National Municipal League, forthcoming). For a

specialized treatment of the New York convention, see Donna Shalala,

19. For a very sophisticated study of this convention, see Vernon A. O'Rourke and Douglas W. Campbell, Constitution-Making in a Democracy: Theory and Practice in New York State (Baltimore: Johns Hopkins Press, 1943).
20. See John P. Wheeler, Jr. and Melissa Kinsey, Magnificent Failure: The Maryland Constitutional Convention of 1967-1968 (New York: National Municipal League, 1970); and Wayne R. Swanson, Elmer E. Cornwell, Jr., and Jay S. Goodman, Politics and Constitutional Reform: The Maryland Experience, 1967-68 (Washington, D.C.: Washington Center for Metropolitan Studies, 1970).
21. For very thorough studies see Norman Meller, With an Understanding Heart: Constitution-Making in Hawaii (New York: National Municipal League, 1971); and Sean A. Kelleher, "The Politics of the Hawaii Constitutional Convention," unpublished doctoral dissertation, Brown University, Providence, R.I., 1973.
22. For a complete description and analysis, see Calvin Ledbetter, George Dyer, Robert Johnston, Wayne R. Swanson, and Walter H. Nunn, Politics in Arkansas: The Constitutional Experience (Little Rock: Academic Press of Arkansas, 1973); and Walter Nunn, The Arkansas Constitutional Convention, 1970 (New York: National Municipal League, 1973).
23. See Charles A. Pastors, Jay S. Goodman, and Elmer E. Cornwell, Jr., "The Politics of the Illinois Constitutional Convention" (forthcoming).

2

METHODOLOGICAL
AND THEORETICAL
PERSPECTIVES

We have outlined in the opening chapter some of the basic characteristics of state constitutional change in general and the seven states we studied in particular.[1] In this chapter we shift to a more analytical and less descriptive focus. Our concern is to discuss our methods for studying constitution-making in the states and to indicate what broad hypotheses and specific propositions we feel such a comparative inquiry should undertake. In some ways our research ventures onto new ground. The empirical study of constitution-making as a political process has been quite limited, although some excellent work has been done.[2] On the other hand, although comparative studies of constitution-making were virtually nonexistent, we could draw upon the theoretical insights and methods that a generation of scholars in the field of comparative state politics had developed.[3] Thus, in thinking about our political science audience, we hope our study provides a unique contribution, the behavioral analysis of constitution-making, to the already solid area of comparative state studies. As for our general audience of officials, activists, and citizens, we try throughout, and especially in our conclusions, to indicate the implications of our findings for those whose duties in life go beyond the classroom and into solving real problems in the real world.[4]

STUDYING CONSTITUTION-MAKING: AN
ECLECTIC RESEARCH DESIGN

Our interest in the many aspects of constitution-making began when two of the senior authors were associated with the Rhode Island Constitutional Convention in a staff capacity.[5] From this beginning there evolved one of the most complicated research projects ever undertaken in state politics, generously supported by the Carnegie Corporation of New York and in cooperation with the National Municipal League.[6]

Our data came from many sources. We collected the standard primary and secondary source materials: complete newspaper clipping files for each state, including not only major dailies but also weeklies in many instances; virtually complete daily journals and records of deliberations and votes for all the conventions; and our own notes and those of other observers in each of the states. We also have now the seven one-state monographs to draw upon for this volume.[7]

In addition, we collected an extensive set of behavioral research data. We conducted interviews before and immediately after the convention in six states. In two states, Rhode Island and Kentucky, where there was a constitutional revision commission, we did one interview. Our completion rate was 93 percent of the 846 delegates. The project could never have proceeded without this exceptional cooperation from the many delegates who helped us in their individual and often in their leadership capacities as well. We are very grateful for their assistance. Nor could such a study have been conducted without the help of scholars in each state.[8] The end result is the largest interview data archive on state political activists in the country.

The interviews each lasted 45 minutes to one hour and collected four kinds of information: demographic material, experiences with and attitudes toward the convention process, sociometric data, and attitudes about politics and conventions in more general terms. In the last section we included various liberalism-conservatism, personal efficacy, and idealism-realism items. By interviewing the delegates both before and after the convention, we are able to report their preconvention expectations about the process and measure the impact of the convention experience on their attitudes.

The interview data are presented in various formats. Chapter 3 on the delegates as constitution-makers draws upon the demographic and attitudinal material. The discussion of leadership and group interaction in the conventions in Chapter 4 relies upon the sociometric data. Our section on the delegates' evaluation of the convention also relies upon the interview material. Delegates' rankings of

the importance of different cleavages also appear, along
with voting material in Chapter 4. And delegate rankings
of the importance of issue areas appear in Chapter 5.

In addition to the interview data, we collected all
the recorded roll-call votes and analyzed them by a method
known as factor analysis, explained in the section on blocs
in Chapter 4. The method is a neutral, deductive system
for objectively characterizing internal voting alignments
and, as such, provides a good technique for testing the
validity of our many propositions about our a priori identified delegate types. Finally, by collecting data by
county in each state on socioeconomic, political, and
county employment indicators, we were able in Chapter 6 to
use correlation and multiple-regression analysis to test
patterns of support and opposition for the final document.

While our methods may seem to some to be very heavily
behavioral, we have not eschewed traditional analysis and
find, rather, that in many instances it is the only way
to offer a coherent explanation of particular happenings.
We are wedded less to any single research method than to
a basic goal—that is to uncover whatever comparative uniformities can be found in the process of constitution-making, so as to be able to say something about this relatively rare political process and also about state politics.
Where we do not find uniformities, we hope to be able to
say something about the uniqueness of sets of states, individual states, or subaspects of constitution-making.
At the price of some purity of technique, we cast a wide
methodological net. We feel the catch is worth the costs.

STATE CONSTITUTIONAL CONVENTIONS:
SOME THEORETICAL PERSPECTIVES

State constitutional conventions pose a particular
theoretical challenge. They do not occur often. They are
legislative bodies but are unlike legislatures in many
ways. They do not have continuity and established patterns
of internal structure and socialization. They do not have
continuing constituency ties. Their major subject matter
is supposed to be the structural composition of state government and thus concerns the alignments of priorities and
power relationships among institutional units, rather than
day-to-day issues. Yet in some conventions, the conflict
over such day-to-day issues may escalate to a top rank of
concern simply because the convention is an authoritative
body and has the potential power to act. Uniquely, the en-

tire substantive product of a state constitutional convention is put before the voters for approval. In the following section of this chapter we will outline a model and some theoretical propositions. We will offer a few examples and data to illustrate how constitution-making may be analyzed as a political process.

THE CONVENTION AND THE STATE
POLITICAL SYSTEM

Certain basic questions must underpin any overall view of conventions. Of prime importance is the relationship of the convention to the larger state political system. What are the crucial variables in initiating conventions and selecting delegates? What propositions seem most useful in predicting the internal functioning and power alignments of conventions? How do the ratification campaigns link what has gone on in the convention bodies to the politics of the states?

There are three models that relate constitution-making to state politics and provide propositions that address themselves to the questions listed above. The "statesman model" embodies an idealized view about how conventions should and do operate. This model is put forth most explicitly in the reform/good-government literature about conventions and constitution-making. The statesman model holds that constitution-making is a special process, above ordinary politics. Delegates have the duty to draft a "higher law document" and should behave as impartial law-givers, above the normal loyalties, interests, and conflicts of everyday politics. They should carefully and abstractly weigh the issues of constitutional revision, with the end goal being the creation of an ideal document subtly attuned to the needs of the state.

The statesman-model perspective is shared, we postulate, by reform groups in the population, by a certain number of delegates, and by elements in the attentive public. How many delegates hold to the statesman view depends upon a number of other variables. The attentive public elements that support this perspective are likely to be newspapers and civic groups whose socioeconomic base are the same as the reform groups.

Two interesting theoretical questions flow from the statesman model. How well does it describe how constitutions are actually made in the conventions? What impact does it have, as myth or ideology, on the perceptions of

delegates and electorate? Even if the statesman model
does not explain what happens, it may have a powerful influence on the outlooks of delegates, voters, or both.
In a situation, where the statesman view is more "myth"
than reality, depending upon the substantive output of the
convention, the scene could be set for substantial disen-
chantment with a convention. The significance of the
statesman model goes beyond its explanatory power and into
its impact as an independent variable. In other words, it
could affect how delegates and voters feel about whatever
is produced, because of the way it shaped their original
expectations about how a convention should function.

The second model is a "political model" of convention
activity. It posits that conventions are political bodies,
subsystems within the larger state political system and
connected to that larger system in a variety of ways. This
approach owes much to studies of the 1961-62 Michigan convention. Speaking about that body, Professor Robert S.
Friedman challenged the "higher law" view of constitution-
making:

> Stated simply, this proposition is that political
> forces within a state will support the organiza-
> tional structure likely to enhance the achieve-
> ment of their goals. This proposition is based
> on the assumption that constitution-making, al-
> though not a frequent phenomenon, is nevertheless
> an integral part of the political process.[9]

Although the second model takes a political view of
constitution-making, it recognizes that the substance of
the conventions has a unique quality: The emphasis is upon
the structural aspect of government. Thus, in our version
of this model, we postulate that the essence of convention
politics is conflict between supporters of structural reform versus those who want to preserve the status quo.
While conventions are political, they are not a mirror
image of the partisan politics of the state nor would
they necessarily reflect an ideological liberal-conservative split.

What convention conflict boils down to is whether the
document, together with the established relationships, perquisites, and group advantages accumulated by its existing
terms, shall remain the same, or whether the terms and arrangements shall be changed. If the latter happens, inevitably there will be new patterns of relationships among
institutions and actors in state politics and new advantages
and disadvantages will be created.

The political model can be tested in much the same way as the statesman model—that is, at two levels. We can test how well it explains what occurs within conventions, the degree to which the reform-status-quo cleavage is pre-eminent. We can also test the degree to which a "realistic" perspective characterizes the attitudes of the delegates, as ideology about how conventions should be run, and what they should produce. We would expect that the political model would be subscribed to by sophisticated politicians and officials, and especially state legislators, who are more likely than other delegates to perceive the stakes involved.

The third model is a variation of the second. It takes a political view of convention behavior but assumes that conventions are direct extensions of state politics. This "partisan-legislative model" assumes that political parties would play the same role in the convention that they play in the politics of the state generally, and specifically in the operation of the state's legislature. Party leaders will obviously be in important formal or informal convention leadership positions. In fact, the same persons may occupy legislative and convention spots.

In addition, the partisan-legislative model assumes that the subject matter of the convention is likely to be largely the same as that of the legislature: the hottest issues of the day. Thus the convention agenda as well as its personnel would replicate the legislature, and the outcome would be legislative politics fought out temporarily in another arena. In the end, the most distinctive feature of the process would be that, unlike the legislature's, the convention's results would come before the public.

To test which of the models has the greatest validity, we start with the second model and elaborate from it an extensive set of propositions. Whether it applies to all conventions, some conventions, or no conventions and to what degree it applies is an empirical issue. It seemed to us a priori to be a fertile starting point, based upon our initial experience in Rhode Island and the written commentary upon the earlier Florida and Michigan conventions.[10]

It is possible to reduce the political model to its specific components in schematic form. The accompanying figure identifies the major variables involved in our study of constitution-making. Lines of representation and influence trace the process of constitutional revision from the initial input stage through the ratification process.

FIGURE 2.1

Model of Constitutional Convention

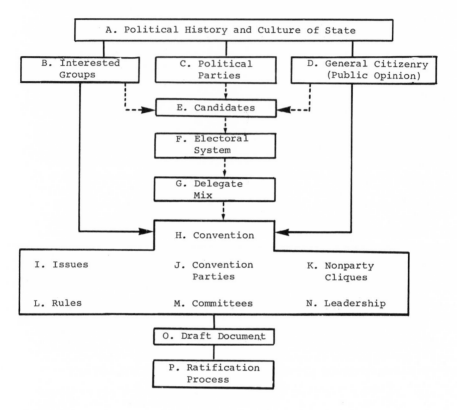

Lines of:

Representation -----
Influence   _____

Source: Compiled by the authors.

We feel that the most crucial elements are the electoral system (F), the delegate mix (G), and the ratification process (P). The electoral system is the process through which candidates (E) are filtered into the convention by the parties, interest groups, and citizenry (B, C, D). The delegate mix is the actual composition of the convention body produced by the electoral system. The draft document (O) as well as the operations of the convention (H-N) will be influenced to a large extent by the backgrounds, experiences, motivations, and issue concerns of the delegates. Accordingly, we devote much of Chapter 3 to examining how the electoral system shapes the delegate mix, and the configuration of experiences and attitudes the delegates who are chosen bring along with them.

Of equal interest is the ratification process (P). At this point, the product of the convention comes before the public. In the ratification campaign, public and group attention focuses on the constitution as a policy "output." There are some unusual circumstances in this situation. As we will demonstrate, an all-or-nothing choice of a multi-item constitution places a power premium in the hands of those groups with intense opposition to individual provisions where the majority may be mildly receptive to the whole.

A basic point of inquiry is whether those groups who support initiation of the convention are the core supporters of the final document. The ratification process becomes especially important when we realize that in the seven states—Rhode Island, New York, Maryland, Hawaii, New Mexico, Arkansas, and Illinois—the new constitution won approval only in Hawaii and Illinois. Indeed, when confronted with such a high record of final failure, explanation of the ratification result has to become a major part of a comparative study. For those who participated in the conventions especially, the pattern of defeat has been very disappointing. And for those engaged in purely intellectual inquiry, the reasons for the defeat of constitutional reform raise many fascinating issues about leaders and mass electorates and stability and change in state politics.

We have organized our research to test the political model, and especially the breadth of the reform/status-quo cleavage that we postulate to be at its core. As we proceed, however, we keep the statesman and the legislative-partisan models in mind, searching for ways in which they apply to parts of the constitutional process within individual states, or, indeed, may best describe the overall process in some of the states. Thus, although the work is organized around one model, it is intended to be a test of all three.

INITIATING CONVENTIONS AND
SELECTING DELEGATES

All observers of the state constitutional revision process have noted the strong initiating role of reform-oriented "good-government" groups. In an early theoretical article, William C. Havard suggested that reformers could muster the strength to get a convention called, but there was no certainty they could dominate the process or win ratification.[11] Norman C. Thomas studied three convention calls and one ratification campaign in Michigan between 1958 and 1963.[12] He concluded:

> Support for constitutional revision will initially
> be strongest among voters with higher levels of
> education and socio-economic status. As the drive
> for revision mounts, interest groups and other
> non-partisan forces are likely to influence refer-
> endum voting, especially if the issue is cast in
> terms of a traditional mode of conflict in the
> state political system.[13]

It is our hypothesis that Havard and Thomas are right: A special thrust to initiate conventions does come from middle- and upper-class reformers with a good-government orientation. There are two ways to test this view. At one level, we can examine, state by state, which groups took the lead in bringing the conventions into being. For example, in Illinois the impetus appears to have come from good-government and reform organizations who finally got their chance when it appeared that revenue reform could only be brought about by a convention.[14] In Maryland, the good-government forces found an ally in Governor Tawes and a temporarily strong reform wing of the Democratic Party. This combination brought the convention call to a vote.[15] In almost all of the states the conventions have been preceded by blue-ribbon study commissions whose membership and outlook fit the "reform" orientation we have referred to. The descriptive one-state monographs, which are part of our overall convention study project, tend to document the recurring initiating role of reformers.

There is another way to test the connection between starting conventions and the reform movement. Almost all

38

treatments of the reform/progressive movement in American state and local politics note the high socioeconomic status (SES) of the reformers. Thus, thinking about the bases of support for reform in the general public, we would postulate that increasing support for convention calls is correlated with increasing socioeconomic status. This proposition can be tested by common correlational methods, which we have done; we have reported the findings in Tables 2.1 and 2.2.

Table 2.1 contains 11 contextual variables from state social, economic, and political life in simple correlations with the "yes" votes on the calls. The data are by county. In Arkansas, Maryland, Illinois, and New York, socioeconomic and political variables are highly correlated with "yes" votes on the calls. In Arkansas and Illinois, the pattern seems to be high SES support plus high Republican support. In Maryland and New York, especially in the latter, the pattern that emerges includes high SES support plus high Democratic support. In New Mexico, the picture is less clear, but there appears to be a combination of some high SES support, particularly in the variability of population change (mobility), plus heavy association with Democratic Party support. For Rhode Island, the only statistically significant variable is the 1962 Democratic gubernatorial vote, but it is clear from that, plus the direction of the socioeconomic variables, that the convention call (on the ballot in the landslide Democratic presidential election of 1964(was supported by the Democrats' basic low SES constituency. For Hawaii, there are no statistically significant correlations (the N is only 4).

In Table 2.2 we present a stepwise multiple regression of votes on the calls, using first the socioeconomic variables alone, second the political variables alone, third the two combined, and fourth the two combined with variables on county expenditures. The stepwise analysis indicates that for Illinois and New York, the most important individual variables accounting for support for the calls are socioeconomic. In Illinois it is education (62.0 percent) and income (5.0 percent). In New York it is percent owner-occupied dwelling, which is a negative relationship, thus meaning that renters predominate. For Arkansas, the most important single variable is the 1966 vote for governor (19.7 percent), a negative correlation with the Democratic vote, meaning therefore support for Republican Winthrop Rockefeller. For Maryland, the most important single variable is education, accounting for 34.7 percent of the variance, followed by county expenditures, with 13.5 percent. The latter is a negative relationship, meaning that coun-

TABLE 2.1

Simple Correlations Among Contextual Variables and "Yes" Votes on Convention Calls

Type Variable	Arkansas (N = 75)	Maryland (N = 23)	Illinois (N = 101)	New York (N = 62)	New Mexico (N = 32)	Rhode Island (N = 5)	Hawaii (N = 4)
Socioeconomic Variables							
Median income	0.26[a]	0.57[b]	0.71[b]	0.27[a]	0.34[a]	-0.49	0.13
Median education	0.29[b]	0.59[b]	0.79[b]	0.05	0.14	-0.64	-0.91[a]
Percent owner-occupied dwelling	0.002	0.06	-0.39[b]	-0.56[b]	-0.18	-0.11	0.07
Percent urban	0.31[b]	0.48[a]	0.43[b]	0.44[a]	0.29	-0.68	0.28
Population change (1960–70)	0.28[b]	0.53[b]	0.62[b]	0.09	0.46[b]	0.40	0.17
Political Variables							
Democratic presidential vote							
1960	-0.25[a]	0.27	-0.25[a]	0.54[b]	0.50[b]	0.50	0.39
1964	0.05	-0.01	-0.29[b]	0.45[b]	0.52[b]	0.74	-0.64
Democratic gubernatorial vote							
1959	—	—	—	—	—	—	—
1960	—	—	0.09	—	—	—	—
1962	-0.24[a]	0.65[b]	—	0.48[b]	0.38[a]	0.96[b]	0.43
1963	—	—	-0.30[b]	—	—	—	—
1966	-0.44[b]	-0.30	—	0.19	-0.25	-0.41	0.75
1967	—	—	—	—	—	—	—
County Employee/Expenditure							
Employee	0.46[b]	0.05	0.09	0.22	-0.19	—	—
Expenditure	0.11	-0.11	-0.07	-0.25[a]	-0.23	—	—

[a] significant at the 0.05 level.
[b] significant at the 0.01 level.

Sources: Data from following sources: socioeconomic variables by counties from County and City Data Book, Bureau of the Census, 1967; county expenditures from Census of Governments, 1967, vol. 4, no. 3, Bureau of the Census, and Census of Governments, 1967, vol. 3, no. 1, Bureau of the Census; political data by counties from Richard M. Scammon, America Votes, 4-8 (Pittsburgh: University of Pittsburgh Press, 1962, 1964); Congressional Quarterly, 1966, 1968, 1970.

TABLE 2.2

Stepwise Multiple Regression Analysis of "Yes" Votes on Convention Calls

State	Socio-Economic Variables	Political Variables	Socioeconomic and Political Variables	All Variables
Arkansas				
R	0.38	0.45[b]	0.53[a]	0.56[b]
Percent of total variance accounted for	14.7	21.9	29.0	31.9
Most important variables and percent variance of each				
Percent urban	9.5			
Education	2.9			
Percent population change			4.1	4.1
1966 gubernatorial		19.7	19.7	19.7
1964 presidential		1.0		
Maryland				
R	0.61	0.74	0.83	0.88[a]
Percent of total variance accounted for	37.9	54.8	68.9	78.9
Most important variables and percent variance of each				
Education	34.7		34.7	34.7
Income	1.1			
Expenditure (percent)				13.5
1962 gubernatorial			9.6	
1960 presidential		21.1		
1964 presidential		19.4		
Illinois				
R	0.84[b]	0.46[b]	0.85[b]	0.85[b]
Percent of total variance accounted for	71.6	21.2	73.3	76.6
Most important variables and percent variance of each				
Education	62.0		62.0	62.0
Income	5.0		5.0	5.0
1960 gubernatorial		10.5		
1964 gubernatorial		9.2		
New York				
R	0.62[a]	0.65[a]	0.68[b]	0.68[b]
Percent of total variance accounted for	39.2	42.6	46.7	47.5
Most important variables and percent variance of each				
Percent own dwelling	31.6		31.6	31.6
Percent population change	7.3		7.3	7.3
1966 gubernatorial		8.3		
1960 presidential		29.5		
New Mexico				
R	0.57[a]	0.74[a]	0.85[b]	0.86[b]
Percent of total variance accounted for	33.0	55.3	73.0	74.4
Most important variables and percent variance of each				
Education	6.9			
Percent population change	21.2			
1966 gubernatorial		23.7	23.7	23.7
1964 presidential		27.4	27.4	27.4

[a]Significant at 0.05.
[b]Significant at 0.01.

Source: Compiled by the authors.

ties that spent less offered greater support for the call. For New Mexico, the most important variable was the 1964 Democratic presidential vote, accounting for 27.4 percent of the variance. Next was the 1966 vote for governor, a negative relationship, meaning Republican support, accounting for 23.7 percent.

In an interpretive sense, analyzing both the simple and the stepwise multiple regressions, several features of support for convention calls emerge. In some states socioeconomic variables in the predicted direction play the main role. In other states, both socioeconomic and political factors are important in the patterns of support. Maryland is a good example, where increasing SES is significant, and, in the simple correlations, so is 1962 support for Democratic governor Millard Tawes. Tawes played a major part in the constitutional revision movement during his term. In Arkansas, in the stepwise analysis, the influence of Governor Winthrop Rockefeller also shows up. In the New Mexico case, socioeconomic variables have less impact than political variables; the vote on the call appears to be connected primarily to political alignments.

Cumulatively, the analyses seem to provide substantial but certainly not absolute support for our proposition about the relationship between reform movements and stronger support for calls among higher socioeconomic elements in the general public. The data suggest that patterns of voting support for the calls are more complicated than the elements the one proposition includes and that there are important state-to-state individualities. This brief exercise also illustrates the utility of quantitative techniques for testing propositions about constitution-making.

THE SELECTION OF DELEGATES

Electoral systems are decision rules that rarely affect all citizens and interests in identical ways. Questions of who can vote, what hours the polls will open, whether the contest overlaps a general election or is held at a special election, whether districts are small single-member or more inclusive at-large, whether victory is by winner take all or by proportional representation, whether the election is partisan or nonpartisan--none of these are purely abstract questions.[16] Indeed the reform movement in U.S. municipal politics has had as a main part of its program concern with electoral rules, and the relationship of these rules to the movement's concern about who should hold office and what should be done is often explicit.[17]

Accordingly, we have hypothesized about the likely impact of six different systems on the selection of convention delegates, from the perspective of the reform versus status-quo cleavage. Figure 2.2 outlines in schematic form the predicted impact. The accuracy of this schema is tested in the next chapter. We believe that each produces a distinct type of delegate mix.

The systems can be viewed as lying on a continuum. Type A, the partisan small-district system, maximizes the representation of party activists, current officeholders, and interest-group leaders, all of whom would be most likely to be bent on preserving the institutional status quo. Type F, the nonpartisan at-large system, maximizes the representation of "blue-ribbon" "disinterested" types seeking structural reform. We hypothesize that the other systems will produce a more heterogeneous delegate mix weighted according to their proximity to either pole.

The reasons the electoral system is likely to have this impact are simple. In a partisan election with a small district, local leaders can use their party or group ties to influence who will be nominated, and then, on election day, to get out the vote and to provide, through the party label on the ballot, electoral cues for the voters. A system organized this way is most likely to replicate the legislature. Indeed, the electoral process most resembles state legislative contests.

On the other hand, in the Type F electoral system, the guidance of party cues and party organization are minimized. The influence of notables with high status and recognition —"blue-ribbon" types—is maximized, especially since the media, which are likely to treat this type of person very favorably, will be major cue-givers in the nonpartisan and at-large context. The criteria for choice can be presented as the disinterested ones of the civic reformer and the do-gooder. It may be that what we have labeled Electoral Systems A and F are ideal types. In the next chapter we shall examine who was chosen and how.

We can indicate here, however, how we think the choice of initial system influences the eventual output of the convention. Our observations have suggested to us that several types of delegates exist in a convention. Different electoral systems will produce different mixes of these types of delegates. The types are identifiable a priori as units that will behave in reasonably predictable ways in relation to convention issues and outcomes.

FIGURE 2.2

Hypothesized Relationship Between Convention Selection System, Delegate Mix, and Output

Delegate Mix

Lobbyists, Party Politicians,   Nonpolitical "Blue-Rib-
and Elected Officials   bon" Delegates

                ←————————————————————————→

Selection System

A.	B.	C.	D.	E.	F.
Partisan	Partisan	Partisan	Nonpartisan	Nonpartisan	Nonpartisan
Small	Multimember	At Large	Small	Multimember	At Large
District	District		District	District	

Output

Standpat   Reform
Document   Document

    ←——→

Source: Compiled by the authors.

A TYPOLOGY OF DELEGATE TYPES

Reflecting on what we have said so far about conventions and our observation of early ones, we were led to a series of general comments about delegates and, from that, to a more systematic typology of delegate types. The initial questions were, What kinds of people are likely to be present? What are their motives? What sorts of outlooks are they likely to bring with them?

Reformers will certainly be there, impelled by motives whose satisfaction will be found, if at all, in the actual work of constitutional revision and change. They seek such change, at least in their conception of themselves and in their rhetoric, for idealistic reasons. They try to fit the popular ideal of selflessness. At the other extreme, guardians of existing institutional or group interests certainly will be there to protect the status quo. The existing structures may give them advantages vis-à-vis challengers. At the minimum, the existing way is a known way. At the maximum, the reformers may be out to take away the constitutional protection for their jobs.

Still others may be there with no definite goals in mind but because delegate positions are part of the opportunity structure of state political life. While their one-shot nature means conventions cannot become political careers in themselves, nonetheless they do fit into the ambition-career system.[18] For some, being a delegate may launch a career. For others it may be the high-status capstone to a lifetime in politics. Still others may see even a broader opportunity, especially through the medium of convention leadership, in being the "father of the constitution."

Consider some possibilities of this sort. A candidate for convention delegate may run at the behest of a party or group of officeholders, who see proposed reforms as threats to their jobs. Or, he may run as a fledgling politician who wants to parlay delegate election into later election to the city council, a legislative seat, or minor political office. Or, if he is an established politico, with rising expectations at the state level, he may, as George Romney did in Michigan, turn convention leadership into gubernatorial election. Aging politicians whose careers have culminated in high judicial office, or who have retired from the political wars, may seek no more than recognized association with successful constitutional reform. In short, convention roles are compounds of individual perceptions or their relation to convention outcomes, plus career expectations deriving from convention participation.

45

With these kinds of ideas in mind, we developed a
six-category delegate typology based on the two interre-
lated dimensions of (1) motivation for entering the convention and (2) attitude toward innovation. The types, which
may be ranged on a continuum between the status quo and
reform poles, include the following:

Standpatters are officeholders at middle or upper-
middle levels of state or local government (legislators,
judges, state bureaucrats) who enter the convention to protect a present position in the governmental structure.
They are sufficiently far along, in age and in career development, to perceive change as threatening.
    Their behavior on issues is likely to be a consistent
opposition to change in the existing arrangements.
    Stand-ins are older individuals who hold low public
office or some small party position and who seek neighbor-
hood recognition and notoriety. They enter the convention
to satisfy these ego needs. Selection to the convention
is a reward for various kinds of political loyalty and is
given to the stand-ins by local political magnates or officeholders who find it inadvisable to seek the office
themselves. The stand-in, whose presence depends upon
partisan district electoral arrangements, is expected to
follow the advice of those who provide him with the nomi-
nation--for whom he is a "stand-in."
    They are likely to be supporters of the status quo,
backing the antireform positions of the standpatters.
    Statesmen have held positions in high public office
(governors, judges, congressmen) or in some cases presently
hold "terminal" judicial positions or the like. They enter
the convention for the public prestige of capping prior
careers through being constitution-makers. Because of their
past positions statesmen may generate some following in the
convention, but this will be restricted by their lack of
present political power.
    Their behavior on issues is likely to be fluid, with
some potential for reform support.
    Chieftains are individuals with a large existing power
base in state politics, or great and immediate potential
for achieving such a position. They enter the convention
for career advancement. Because they have such a base
outside the convention (as governors or potential governors, legislative leaders, mayors), they are in a position
to exercise considerable internal convention leadership.
    Although their behavior on issues is likely to be
fluid, there is considerable potential for reform support.

Aspirants are young professionals, often lawyers, on the political make. Many have held some party or civic position prior to convention office; the convention is a stepping-off point to further political activity—their motive for entering is therefore career advancement.

Their voting behavior is likely to be fluid, but they go preponderantly in the direction of whatever is the majority bloc in the convention. Thus there is both stand-pat and reform potential here.

Reformers often have been active in civic organizations including citizen's commissions and the League of Women Voters, though few have held office in government. They are likely to be highly educated professionals from middle and upper-middle social strata who enter the convention to change the established order.

On issues they will vote uniformly for change in the direction of "good government" provisions.

We have attempted to make each category operational by rigidly specifying the characteristics of each delegate type and outlining a series of testable propositions about each type's predicted attitudes toward, and behavior in, the convention. Classification of delegates was made on the basis of (1) biographical data on the age, education, occupation, party, elective, and appointive offices held, and interest group and civic activities of the delegates, and (2) evidence gleaned from a preconvention interview that revealed the delegates' general orientation toward the convention process.* Two judges classified each delegate as belonging to one of the six types. Disagreements were resolved in discussion with a third judge.

Utilization of typologies of this sort is common in legislative research. Thus Wahlke et al., Matthews, and Barber, to name a few, have employed typologies to explain, clarify, and classify various aspects of legislative behavior.[19] In some cases their typologies were developed prior to data collection and then tested for empirical utility. In other instances, their typologies emerged af-

---

*For example a young lawyer in the lower echelons of a political party who indicated he ran for the convention as a means to further his political career is categorized as an aspirant. Similarly, an older man who had had considerable experience in local party affairs and who indicated that the city chairman of his party had requested him to run is categorized as a stand-in.

terward, as a way of organizing data that had already been collected. We followed the first method--specifying in advance what seemed to be reasonable categories and then testing them throughout the research.

THE INTERNAL OPERATIONS OF CONSTITUTIONAL CONVENTIONS

From our general model of the constitution-making process as already outlined and from accepted knowledge about legislative behavior, we can offer some propositions about the internal operations of conventions.[20] We predict that the primary cleavage will be the reformers versus the defenders of the status quo. We anticipate bloc cohesion on voting questions where this fundamental cleavage is clear-cut but more random voting on other issues. Wherever there is party organization in a convention, we would expect greater voting bloc cohesion.

We predict that most conventions will organize their work in ways roughly similar to the closest familiar model, the legislature, but with some differences. In bodies of this one-shot nature, we would not expect standing committees with the influence of those in Congress--with their tradition, hierarchy, socialization systems, and well-defined clientele relationship. Rather, committees will be less important. Behind-the-scenes activity organized on an ad hoc basis, and even floor debate, will be more important. Because of the absence of prior experience and the uncertainty of future relations between the institution and the public, it would be surprising if the body quickly found the key to perfectly smooth public relations with potentially affected constituencies. Indeed, we would expect uncertainty, mistiming, and perhaps even a lack of awareness among many potentially affected interests and citizens, simply because of the uniqueness and unfamiliarity of organized constitution-writing.

In terms of internal leadership, we anticipate that the usual bases will hold--that is, leaders will be sought out on the basis of some combination of charismatic and positional qualities. We also expect leaders and followers in the conventions to demonstrate considerable attitudinal and ideological congruence. Leadership has a formidable challenge, and also an opportunity, because the one-shot quasi-legislative format, minus socialization, tradition, and powerful standing committees, means that conventions will be like early U.S. legislatures. They will have the

rules and parliamentary procedures of legislative bodies
and the need for group decision-making but without the
heavy weight of senior members and past traditions to
structure how they go about it.

NEW CONSTITUTIONS AND THE PUBLIC: SUBSTANTIVE ASPECTS OF THE RATIFICATION PROCESS

The ratification of a new constitution is a complicated process and the public may react on the basis of a
large number of potential cues--the substance of the proposed changes, the image of the convention as a political
institution, the signals of important community leaders
or of party organizations, private calculations of gains
or losses, or even the opportunity costs of casting a vote.
Since we are looking at new constitutions in seven states,
it is important to have some standard comparative formula
to measure total outputs. This standardized measure can
then be supplemented with a description of those individual issues that appeared to arouse particularly intense
reactions in individual states.

There is no absolute standard as to what a new con-
sitution should be or what should be included in an "ideal"
state constitution. However, the National Municipal League's
Model State Constitution[21] probably comes the closest to
setting the standard that reformers think a state constitution should meet. Reproduced as Table 2.3, it gives us
a unit against which to measure both existing state constitutions before revision, and also the revised documents,
the outputs of the revision process.

To measure the reform content of each of the seven
constitutions, we constructed a reform index by awarding
each of 29 selected constitutional provisions and sections
a specific number of points on the basis of substantive
proximity to the reform model standard of The Model State
Constitution. Two points were awarded for a provision
that met the reform standard; one point was earned by a
semireform standard, one that in part approximated the
Model; and no points were given to before or after provisions that had no reform content. Chapter 6 presents the
reform index in detail.

Since we did not do state-by-state public opinion
surveys, we cannot measure precisely how the public reacted
to the total amount of reform content in a new constitution
or to the distance the new constitution traveled from the

TABLE 2.3

Provisions of Model State Constitution: Reform Ideal

Provision	"Model State Constitution"
Preamble	"Succinct statement of constitutional purpose"
Declaration of Rights	"Sparse," modeled after federal Constitution
Enumeration of Powers	"Explicitly stated that constitution is a grant, not a limitation on state"
Suffrage and Elections	
Voting age	18
Residence requirements	Minimal, three months
Legislature	
Form	Unicameral
Size	Set by statute
Term of office	Two years, lower house; six years, upper house
Type districts	Single-member
Compensation	Set by statute
Sessions (length)	Flexible
Procedure	Unspecified
Apportionment	Mandatory--every 10 years
Postaudit	Specifically under legislative control
Executive	
Time of election	Odd-numbered years
Term	Four years, no limit
Elected state offices	None
Administrative organization	Consolidated
Succession	Explicitly provided for
Judiciary	
Organization	Unified
Selection	Missouri plan type
Administration	Centralized
Minor officials	Eliminated from constitution
Finance	Borad local autonomy
Education	Specific grant
Intergovernmental relations	Free from obstacles to cooperation
Civil service	Specific grant
Constitutional change	Liberal, rather than cumbersome procedure

Source: Model State Constitution (New York: National Municipal League, 6th ed., 1963).

old one in terms of amount of change. Similarly, we recognize the importance of particular controversies in many of the states, whose impact we have gleaned primarily from their reflected coverage in the media and the statements of activists (although also to some extent in voting data). Such stand-out single issues included the conduct of the convention itself in Rhode Island, the portrayed threat of new taxes in Maryland and Arkansas, and the Blaine amendment, which prohibited state aid to parochial schools until the convention eliminated it, in New York.

THEORETICAL AND QUANTITATIVE ASPECTS OF THE RATIFICATION PROCESS

There are at least two ways to look at the ratification vote. First, we have developed a game-theory-type analysis, which illustrates the inherent complexities of ratification in an all-or-nothing response to a multi-item document. Second, we have some propositions about likely support and opposition that can be tested quantitatively against the county data on the ratification the same way we examined support for the call. In all of these analyses, the search for the causes of the defeat of revision efforts remains a prime goal, both as an intellectual end in itself and as a possible help to those who might want to undertake such efforts again sometime in the future in the states.

One factor that may account for some of the defeats is the all-or-nothing manner in which six of the eight constitutions were presented to the voters. Only in Hawaii and Illinois, where provisions were voted on separately, did the new documents pass. No U.S. legislature ever faces such a total public evaluation of its policy decisions. Local or state ballots with multiple referenda contain only a portion of the output of the city council or state legislature; even these items, however, are considered separately by the voters. One might therefore suggest that this all-or-nothing mode of presentation makes it difficult, inevitably, for a draft constitution, whether it be reformist or stand-pat, to secure majority support.

The hostility engendered to specific provisions may lead many individuals to vote "no" on the whole document. The cumulation of specific "no's" then spells defeat for the document even when there is generalized feeling that, on balance, the revised draft is a good one. What the ratification process provides is another example of what political scientists know as Arrow's theory of voting. The substance of this theory is that "with three or more alternatives and three or more voters it may happen that, when the alternatives are placed against one another in a series of paired comparisons, no alternative emerges victorious over each of the others."[22]

Table 2.4 presents a much simplified explanation of the implications of the "no"-vote thesis to the constitutional referendum. Given a hypothetical universe of six voters and four choices, the table demonstrates that on an individual basis each of the four provisions was favored by a majority of the voters. However, when compounded by the "no" votes generated by particular provisions, a majority chose to reject the entire constitution in the "all-or-nothing" framework in which it was presented.

The electoral environments in which the draft constitutions were competing was often extremely difficult. We will examine how many of the major external and internal blocs supported the drafts in each state. Suffice it to say by way of theoretical introduction that the creation of composite anticonstitution majorities made up of offended minorities was a possibility in almost all of the states. For example, in Rhode Island, opponents, led by the Republican governor of the state, focused on the legislative pay provision and the deletion of a prohibition on state lotteries. In Maryland, provisions such as 19-year-old vote and a strong antidiscrimination provision drew heavy attack. In Arkansas opponents focused on possible tax increases.

TABLE 2.4

"No" Vote on Hypothetical Constitutional Referendum

Voter	19-Year-Old Vote	Legislative Pay Increase	Court Reform	State Lottery	Final Vote
Voter A	Yes	Yes	Yes	Yes	Yes
Voter B	Yes	Yes	Yes	No	No
Voter C	Yes	Yes	No	Yes	No
Voter D	No	No	Yes	Yes	No
Voter E	No	No	No	Yes	No
Voter F	Yes	Yes	Yes	No	No
Total	(4-2)	(4-2)	(4-2)	(4-2)	(1-5)

Source: Compiled by the authors.

It would seem that almost any issue in a constitution can potentially generate a percentage of "particular no votes." Getting such votes is probably facilitated by the presence of a substantial "alienated" constituency in state and local politics, one used to voting against various state and local referenda, which cumulatively have done less and less well in recent years. When the people opposed to particular provisions are combined with those generally suspicious of wholesale constitutional change, it is not hard to understand how, in theoretical terms at least, the deck may be stacked from the start against ratification of revised constitutions.

Having outlined some of the conditions in which revised constitutions come before the public, let us list some specific propositions derived from the reform versus status-quo cleavage of the political model. Several propositions come immediately to mind as worth examining against data-- for example, where high socioeconomic support backs the call and the convention appears to produce results in accord with the goals of these strata, does the ratification vote reflect the same divisions? If the convention produces a document with low reform content, do high socioeconomic groups turn upon it and vote against it? How do the parties come into play in their attitudes toward ratification, and what is their impact upon ratification voting patterns?

In a comparative sense, are there uniformities in the vote on the ratification across the states, or at least broad patterns? If there are no uniformities or patterns, we should conclude that responses to each constitution are unique to each state. Then, while there may be uniform aspects of constitutional reform in the states on other parts of the process, the response of the public to the documents is not part of that uniformity. All of these propositions and other related ones will be tested through simple correlation and multiple regression analyses on the ratification votes in Chapter 6.

This chapter has outlined a number of theoretical considerations and propositions about the process of constitution-making by conventions. In the next chapter we begin our systematic test of these propositions, analyzing the characteristics and attitudes of the delegates.

NOTES

1. We also studied the Kentucky Constitutional Revision Assembly, a commission appointed by the governor,

which proposed an entirely new constitution and acted, in effect, as an appointed unlimited convention. At various points in the text, we insert data from Kentucky for comparative purposes.

2. See, for example, Albert L. Sturm, Constitution-Making in Michigan, 1961-1962 (Ann Arbor: Institute of Public Administration, 1963); Robert S. Friedman, The Michigan Constitutional Convention and Administrative Organization: A Case Study in the Politics of Constitution-Making (Ann Arbor: Institute of Public Administration, 1963); and also Vernon A. O'Rourke and Douglas W. Campbell, Constitution-Making in a Democracy: Theory and Practice in New York State (Baltimore: Johns Hopkins Press, 1943).

3. For a review of these developments, see Herbert Jacob and Michael Lipsky, "Outputs, Structure, and Power: An Assessment of Changes in the Study of State and Local Politics," Journal of Politics 30 (May 1968): 510-38.

4. The authors of this volume have written a special "cookbook" of applied lessons emerging from the larger research project, aimed specifically at those who might have to participate in such conventions in the future. See Elmer E. Cornwell, Jr., Jay S. Goodman, and Wayne R. Swanson, Constitutional Reform by Convention (New York: National Municipal League, 1973).

5. Cornwell was director of research; Goodman was assistant research director. For the story of this convention see their The Politics of the Rhode Island Constitutional Convention (New York: National Municipal League, 1969).

6. Neither institution is responsible for the data and opinions offered in this volume.

7. See notes 16-23 in Chapter 1.

8. See note 10 in Chapter 1.

9. Friedman, op. cit., p. 134.

10. See Cornwell and Goodman, Politics of the Rhode Island Constitutional Convention; Sturm, op. cit.; Friedman, op. cit.; and William C. Havard, "Notes on a Theory of State Constitutional Change: The Florida Experience," Journal of Politics 21 (February 1959): 80-104.

11. Havard, op. cit.

12. "The Electorate and State Constitutional Revision: An Analysis of Four Michigan Referenda," Midwest Journal of Political Science 12 (February 1968): 115-29.

13. Ibid., p. 129.

14. See Charles Pastors, Jay S. Goodman, and Elmer E. Cornwell, Jr., "The Politics of the Illinois Constitutional Convention, 1969-1970" (forthcoming).

15. See Swanson, Cornwell, and Goodman, Politics and Constitutional Reform: Maryland Experience.

16. For the classic treatment of this subject, see Douglas W. Rae, The Political Consequences of Electoral Laws (New Haven, Conn.: Yale University Press, rev. ed., 1971).

17. For a good review of this literature and a test of many aspects of it as they relate to local government, see Robert L. Lineberry and Edmund P. Fowler, "Reformism and Public Policies in American Cities," American Political Science Review 61, 3 (September 1967): 701-16.

18. The now classic analytic treatment is Joseph A. Schlesinger, Ambition and Politics: Political Careers in the United States (Chicago: Rand-McNally, 1966).

19. For the use of typologies in legislative studies, see John S. Walke et al., The Legislative System (New York: John Wiley & Sons, 1962), especially Parts 1, 3, 4, and Appendix 1; Donald R. Matthews, U.S. Senators and Their World (New York: Vintage Books, 1960), pp. 61-67 and subsequently; and James D. Barber, The Law-Makers (New Haven, Conn.: Yale University Press, 1965), which is organized completely around a four-part typology.

20. See Malcolm E. Jewell and Samuel C. Patterson, The Legislative Process in the United States (New York: Random House, 2d ed., 1972); and William J. Keefe and Morris S. Ogul, The American Legislative Process: Congress and the States (Englewood Cliffs, N.J.: Prentice-Hall, 2d ed., 1968).

21. New York: National Municipal League, 6th ed., 1963.

22. William H. Riker, "Arrow's Theory and Some Examples of the Paradox of Voting," in Mathematical Approaches in Political Science, John M. Claunch, ed. (Dallas: Arnold Foundation of Southern Methodist University, 1965), p. 43.

3

THE DELEGATES:
BACKGROUNDS
AND ATTITUDES

The electoral system is the crucial independent variable in the early stages of a constitutional convention for
two reasons. First, it is the initial convention-shaping
choice, which can be affected directly by various interest
groups interested in the process. The shape of the system
is often the first point of conflict among those who will
be concerned with convention outputs--from reform groups
to state bureaucrats. Second, the electoral system deter-
mines in large part the mix of delegates for the convention
by structuring recruitment--that is, the access that different interests and individuals have to the convention
through paths of obtaining nominations and becoming successful candidates.

In discussing what transpires in a constitutional
convention, it is important to keep in mind that the
elected delegates do not simply represent the members of
the community in geographical units but rather that they
represent in varying degrees parties, interest groups,
and other general attitudes and vested interests in the
electorate. Depending, therefore, on whether the electoral
system is partisan or nonpartisan, is susceptible to party
manipulation or not, provides for district or at-large
choices, and so on, it may operate to maximize the representation of certain kinds of groups and attitudes and
minimize the representation of others.[1]

Political activists in U.S. politics, from municipal
reformers to party bosses, have for a long time argued
that the shape of the electoral system would affect their
fortunes at the ballot box. Their perceptions about their
stakes in the structural rules of the games have led to
repeated controversies about the impact of nonpartisan ver-

sus partisan elections and, to a lesser degree, about such provisions as single- versus multimember districts.[2] The reformers who devised items such as the nonpartisan election in the late 19th and early 20th centuries had a number of consequences distinctly in mind: reduction in party activity, increased efficiency in the management of government, and the selection of "better" people for public office. Nonpartisan elections were intended to force voters to concentrate on head-to-head contests between individual candidates, without help from party cues. Emphasis on personal qualifications and credentials was intended to give an advantage to those groups who came from higher socioeconomic strata, like the reformers. The aim was "politics without politicians."[3]

Concern over the type of individuals who should be entrusted with the task of rewriting state constitutions invariably raises the question of the type of selection system that should be used. Arguments for a nonpartisan system have come from individuals who adhere to the "statesmanlike" notion that constitutions are "higher-law" documents. Proponents of the nonpartisan convention believe that nonpartisanship will be more likely to select delegates who are above the normal political struggles in the state and who will be able to make decisions on the basis of rational disinterested choice. Implicit in their argument is the notion that there is apt to be considerably more "reform" potential in a nonpartisan body. The argument also follows that the partisan convention will tend to be an extension of normal legislative politics and will be determined by what is best for the political party or interest group that aided their election. Wholesale constitutional reform will be more difficult to achieve in this context.

The question that we confront here is: Do differences in convention selection systems in fact bring different kinds of people to office and does this have an impact upon the kinds of constitutions that they produce? Political science literature contains little that would suggest the impact of selections systems on recruitment patterns. The literature seems to have focused upon aspects of selection other than the actual characteristics of those chosen.[4]

One empirical study that does present data on those who have been elected to office in the nonpartisan context is Eugene C. Lee's The Politics of Nonpartisanship.[5] Using his own data on 38 councilmen in six California cities and Huckshorn's study of 282 Los Angeles councilmen, Lee found the nonpartisan systems resulted in the elections of disproportionately fewer people from certain elements of the population: women, persons in low-status jobs, and individuals from poorer neighborhoods. Local nonpartisanship seemed to favor disproportionately those who were otherwise affiliated with the minority party in the state. Lee concluded that nonpartisan election reduced the representation of minorities of "social, racial, religious, and economic groups in the community."[6] The councilmen elected in nonpartisan elections were more of a "blue-ribbon," high-status group of officials than appeared under partisan systems.

Lee's data and the impressionistic evidence spawned by both academicians and reformers suggest a number of hypotheses relating to the partisan-nonpartisan convention contexts, which might help to explain the politics of constitution-making. The following propositions will be helpful in explaining what happened as seven states attempted to rewrite their constitutions:

1. The nonpartisan convention setting would limit the role of political parties in the recruitment process and result in the selection of delegates with a low rate of prior political experience.

1. The partisan setting would maximize the role of political parties in the recruitment process and result in the selection of a large percent of elected officials and other party activists.

2. The nonpartisan convention would result in the election of a larger proportion of delegates who identified with the minority party in the state than appeared in the state legislature.

2. The partisan convention would result in the election of assembly whose partisan balance would approximate the balance in the state legislature.

3. Demographically, the nonpartisan setting would work to the advantage of individuals from high socioeconomic position and would produce a "blue-ribbon" elitist type body.

3. Demographically, the partisan context would be a more heterogeneous mix and would be more representative of the larger state population.

4. The nonpartisan context would maximize the representation of individ-

4. The partisan convention would maximize the power of status-quo groups

iduals we have labeled   whom we have called the
reformers.   stand-patter and stand-
                                ins.

Another structural factor that may influence the type
of delegate selected to a convention is how the districts
are structured. Some districts are of the single-member
type--that is, one representative is selected from each
geographic area. There are multimember districts in which
more than one representative is elected from a geographic
area. There are also at-large elections where the whole
state elects all or part of the assembly.

The type of district--single-member, multimember, or
at-large--is important because it is assumed that the
smaller the district, the more representative are the individuals selected. To put it more succinctly, the smaller
the district is, the more demographically homogeneous it
is, with the result that the person(s) selected are more
apt to mirror the characteristics of the district. Con-
versely, the larger the district is, the more heterogeneous
it will be, and the greater is the likelihood that representatives from high-status or wealthy parts of the district
will dominate the selection process.

A final factor concerning the selection process that
is important for our study concerns whether the delegates
are appointed or elected. The major portion of our study
deals with states in which the delegates were elected to
their positions. However, some states use an appointed
commission to revise their constitutions. For illustrative
purposes, we have gathered demographic data from the Kentucky Constitutional Revision Commission appointed by the
governor in 1964.

In Table 3.1 we have placed the selection systems of
the seven conventions and one commission along a continuum
according to their degrees of representativeness (assuming
our hypotheses are in fact correct about selection systems
and degrees of representativeness). The eight selection
systems can be differentiated on three broad dimensions:
(1) partisan or nonpartisan; (2) elected or appointed; and
(3) single-member district, multimember district, at-large,
or a combination thereof. Thus, two selection systems were
partisan and six were nonpartisan. Seven were electoral,
and one was appointed. Two selection systems were based
on small or medium-sized single-member districts. Three
focused on large multimember districts and two combined
single-member districts.

TABLE 3.1

Eight Convention Selection Systems by Level of Representativeness

Most Representative ──▶ Least Representative

Rhode Island	New York	New Mexico	Arkansas	Hawaii	Illinois	Maryland	Kentucky
Partisan; small* single-member districts	Partisan; large multimember districts; some elected at large statewide	Nonpartisan; medium single-member districts	Nonpartisan; medium-size single-member districts except in Pulaski County (Little Rock) where a delegate was selected from a multimember district	Nonpartisan; 36 small single-member districts; some at-large single-member districts; some multimember districts	Nonpartisan; large multimember districts	Nonpartisan; large multimember districts	Nonpartisan; appointed not elected; large districts; some chosen at large statewide

*Small, medium, and large districts may be put into clearer perspective by noting that in Rhode Island, Arkansas, and Illinois each district respectively had 8,600, 17,860, and 289,000 in population.

60

Delegates to the Rhode Island constitutional convention (1964-68) were selected on a partisan basis from 100
small single-member districts identical to those for state
representatives. Delegates to the New York convention
(1966-67) were elected from partisan, large multimember
districts, three from each senatorial district. Fifteen
delegates were also elected at large statewide from party
lists. In New Mexico (1969) delegates were elected on a
nonpartisan basis from 70 medium-size single-member state
representative districts. The delegates to the nonpartisan
Arkansas convention (1969-70) were chosen from medium-size
single-member house districts reapportioned in 1965 on a
one-man, one-vote basis--other delegates were selected
from a multimember district in Little Rock. Voters selected
82 delegates to the nonpartisan Hawaii constitutional convention (1968) from 43 single-member districts and 11 multimember districts. Delegates to the nonpartisan Illinois
convention (1969-70) were chosen from 58 large two-member
senatorial districts. In Maryland, delegates to the 1966-68
convention were elected on a nonpartisan basis from large
multimember districts identical to those for the House of
Delegates. Finally, in Kentucky (1964-66) the governor
appointed a Constitutional Commission of 50 members including the seven living ex-governors, five delegates chosen
at large statewide, and one delegate from each of the
state's 38 senatorial districts.

All of these selection systems would seem to vary in
the degree of representativeness they should produce.
The partisan Rhode Island and New York selection systems
should, if our assumptions are correct, produce a more
representative delegate mix than the nonpartisan New Mexico
and Arkansas constructs. Similarly, the nonpartisan but
single-member systems of New Mexico and Arkansas should
produce a more representative delegate mix than the multimember district selection structures of Illinois and Maryland. Kentucky's Constitutional Commission should produce
the least representative delegate mix because of its nonpartisan, appointed selection format. In sum, as we move
away from the more representative selection systems the
delegate mix should become less like the larger population
and more "blue ribbon" in character.

We have chosen to test our hypotheses on three broad
classificatory dimensions: social difference, public participation experience, and party representation. We will
also look at the differences in the distribution of delegate role types among the eight constitution-making assemblies.

SELECTION SYSTEMS AND THE SOCIAL
COMPOSITION OF THE CONVENTIONS

Table 3.2 contains data comparing the eight conventions by the five most commonly accepted indicators of social status--sex, age, race, education, and occupation. The states are arranged on the table according to their hypothesized degree of representativeness. The most representative selection systems appear at the left of the table; the "least" representative systems are on the right.

Many who have studied the decision-making processes in U.S. politics have argued that an "elite" or series of "elites" dominate the political power structure in the United States.[7] The "elites" who rule are almost always found to be atypical of the masses they govern. The social characteristics of political decision-makers invariably underrepresent women, young people, blacks, and other minorities, and persons from the lower socioeconomic strata of society. The concerted attempt by the major political parties during their most recent national conventions to ensure a more representative group of delegates has dramatically called attention to the unrepresentative nature of most political decision-making bodies in the United States.

The first conclusion that one can draw from the data in Table 3.2 is that the makeup of the eight constitutional conventions for the most part conforms to the traditional "elitist" pattern. The conventions were dominated by men, middle-aged and older persons, whites, the highly educated, and persons from prestige occupations. The high percentage of lawyers serving as delegates also conforms to a pattern that is familiar in American legislative bodies.

The data in Table 3.2 seek to compare differences in the kinds of individuals chosen under different selection systems with the institution held constant: the constitutional convention. It is important to make convention-by-convention comparisons to uncover the similarities and differences among delegates in the assemblies. But in addressing the question of "representativeness," we must be careful not to overlook the possible influence of the intervening variable of differences among state populations. Since the state populations are not identical for all variables considered, there is always the possibility that differences in delegate characteristics are a result of differences in state populations rather than in convention selection systems.

TABLE 3.2

Social Differences Among Convention Delegates
(percent)

	Rhode Island (N = 100)	New York (N = 186)	New Mexico (N = 70)	Arkansas (N = 100)	Hawaii (N = 82)	Illinois (N = 116)	Maryland (N = 142)	Kentucky (N = 50)
Sex								
Male	90	95	87	92	90	87	87	96
Female	10	5	13	8	10	13	13	4
Age								
Under 35	16	11	16	22	11	20	24	0
35-60	64	71	55	59	83	70	61	67
Over 60	20	18	29	19	6	11	15	33
Race								
White	100	94	100	99	--	89	94	98
Black	0	6	0	1	--	11	6	2
Occupation								
Lawyer	40	69	23	36	31	40	50	72
Other high-status	19	18	33	17	33	39	29	33
Low status	41	13	44	37	36	21	21	5
Education								
High school	30	6	20	11	20	7	13	0
College	18	17	38	38	26	24	20	15
Law school	44	69	23	46	36	49	50	72
Post-college	8	8	19	12	18	20	17	13

Source: Compiled by the authors.

63

To guard against this error and identify the recruitment system as an independent variable only when it is one, we have devised an index of representativeness to neutralize state differences in each category and to facilitate a visual comparison of the relative degrees of representativeness of the conventions. Table 3.3 indicates the extent to which each group is either under- or overrepresented in the convention.

Each index figure is obtained by subtracting the percentage of the category as found in the state's population from the percentage of that same category found in the delegate group. For example, 49 percent of the Rhode Island population is male, but 90 percent of the delegates are male. Subtracting 49 from 90 gives an index of +41. By the same token, subtracting the 51 percent females in Rhode Island from the 10 percent female delegates provides an index of -41. These indexes can be read as a +41 overrepresentation of males, and a -41 underrepresentation of females in the delegate group as compared with the population of the state. (Obviously, if 49 percent of the delegates were male and 51 percent female, this would be perfect proportionate representation in the convention, and both indexes would be 0.) Since each index figure is the percentage range between the population category and the same category among delegates, state-by-state comparisons, holding population differences constant, are possible.

The two questions we need to explore in examining the data in Tables 3.2 and 3.3 are, first, are the conventions different in terms of the social characteristics of the delegates? Second, do different selection systems produce "more" or "less" representative delegate mixes? Despite the conclusion that the conventions were substantially "elitist" in make-up, the data reveal that on all of the social variables there were differences of varying proportion among the delegate populations. The percentage of women, for example, varied from 5 percent in New York to 13 percent in Maryland, New Mexico, and Illinois. There were no "young" persons selected to serve on the Kentucky Revision Commission while almost one-quarter of the Maryland delegates were under 35 years of age. Eleven percent of the Illinois delegates were black; no blacks were elected in either Rhode Island or New Mexico. The percentage of lawyers in the conventions varied from 23 percent in New Mexico to 72 percent in Kentucky. Levels of education also varied considerably; 31 percent of the Rhode Island delegates had not attended college; all of the Kentucky commission members had received college training.

64

TABLE 3.3

Representativeness of Convention Delegates in Relation to State Population

	Rhode Island	New York	New Mexico	Arkansas	Hawaii	Illinois	Maryland	Kentucky
Sex								
Male	+41	+47	+37	+38	+43	+36	+38	+46
Female	-41	-47	-37	-38	-43	-36	-38	-46
Age								
21-35	-26	-20	-30	-8	-9	-21	-12	-34
35-60	+21	+27	+42	+26	+18	+11	+17	+26
60+	+5	-7	-12	-13	-9	+10	-5	+8
Race								
White	+2	+2	--	-1	+21	+2	+11	+5
Black	-2	-2	--	+1	-21	-2	-11	-5
Education								
No college	-56	-77	-64	-77	-78	-57	-70	-89
College	+56	+77	+64	+77	+78	+57	+70	+89
Occupation								
High status	+41	+65	+42	+60	+56	+31	+57	+79
Low status	-41	-65	-42	-60	-56	-31	-57	-79

Source: Compiled by the authors.

65

When we compute the differences between the total state populations and the convention delegates in the eight states (Table 3.3), the results on the full spectrum of tested variables do not fall into a consistent pattern of confirmation or rejection of the predictions for "more representative" versus "less representative" selection systems. Thus we cannot generalize for all variables. It is necessary to consider separate conventions, because in some instances the results confirm the listed hypotheses; in others, the findings are ambiguous; and, in still others, outcomes seem to deny expectations.

On the positive side the Kentucky appointive system would appear to confirm almost all of the theoretical expectations about appointment as a less representative system of selection. Note that Kentucky differs significantly from the other states in more drastically underrepresenting youth, women, and blacks and in overrepresenting high-status occupations and those in the population with higher educational attainment. Without question the appointive system produced the most "blue-ribbon" delegate mix.

When we add the variable of public election of delegates, however, the results are far from conclusive. For example, the so-called less representative systems used in Maryland and Illinois did significantly overrepresent high socioeconomic status individuals on the one hand, but women and young people also did very well. On the race variable, Maryland with a relatively high percentage of blacks among the population underrepresented that minority in the convention. Illinois, on the other hand, had a higher percentage of blacks in the convention than in the general population.

The hypothesized "most representative" systems (New York, Rhode Island, and New Mexico) also provide both support for and rejection of the "representative" hypothesis. Rhode Island and New Mexico were the two most representative conventions from a demographic point of view, particularly on the education and occupation variables. New York, however, resembles the pattern that we found in Kentucky more than it does either the Rhode Island and New Mexico pattern. The fact that, when delegates were elected to their positions, a somewhat haphazard distribution of social characteristics appears leads us to reject or at least qualify the notion that the differing selection systems produce a predictable social mix of delegates. Social characteristics are only one dimension of a delegate's preconvention experiences, however; the extent to which the delegates had participated in public affairs and party activities will also influence their attitudes about state constitutions.

SELECTION SYSTEMS, PUBLIC PARTICIPATION,
AND PARTY REPRESENTATION

The data in Table 3.4 compare public participation
differences among delegates in the eight conventions.
Three dimensions of public participation are considered:
political party activity, elective positions held, and
present or previous legislative experience. Section IV of
the table compares the partisan make-up of the convention
with the branch of the state legislature most closely resembling the convention selection system. Our hypotheses
are that the less representative systems, particularly the
nonpartisan systems, will discriminate against party activists and elected officials and also result in the election
of more members who identify with the current minority
party in the legislature.

With some interesting exceptions the evidence generated by the data confirm the hypothesis that fewer experienced party politicians are selected in the nonpartisan
convention context. Nearly twice as many party activists
(about two-thirds of the total delegate mixes) were selected
in the partisan conventions in Rhode Island and New York
as appeared in the nonpartisan Maryland, Illinois, and Arkansas assemblies. New Mexico, the nonpartisan convention
most closely linked on the "representative" continuum to
the partisan conventions, fell midway between the two ex-
tremes. The tendency for nonpartisan conventions to discriminate against party activists was also confirmed by
the open-ended portions of our interviews with the delegates. When we asked them how they happened to become
candidates, in the partisan conventions most delegates reported that they had been asked to run by the party organization or one of its leaders. In the nonpartisan setting, however, the delegates tended to be self-recruited
and motivated to run because of a sense of civic duty and
a desire to reform state government.

Kentucky and Hawaii proved to be exceptions to the
nonpartisan pattern. Although on a demographic basis the
Kentucky Commission was decidedly "blue ribbon" in its social composition, many of the appointees came from a political "elite" as well. Seven former governors, four U.S.
senators, seven judges, and ten individuals with experience
in the state legislature served on the commission. Nonpartisanship, when accompanied by appointment rather than
election, thrust a number of persons with political experience at high levels of state government into the commission. Presumably most of these individuals would have been

TABLE 3.4

Public Participation and Party Representation in Eight Constitutional Conventions
(percent)

	Rhode Island	New York	New Mexico	Ar- kansas	Hawaii	Illi- nois	Mary- land	Ken- tucky
I. Party experience								
Yes	64	62	57	33	78	33	33	56
No	36	38	43	67	22	67	67	44
II. Elective experience								
Yes	43	36	46	40	64	30	33	39
No	57	64	54	60	36	70	67	61
III. Legislative experience								
Present legislature	8	6	4	2	45	2	6	2
Past legislature	15	16	17	8	7	8	2	18
Nonlegislator	77	78	79	90	48	90	92	80
IV. Partisan make-up* (percent Democrat)								
Convention	81	55	47	70	70	94	75	73
Legislature*	76	57	34	81	63	96	82	76

*The branch of the legislature most resembling the convention structure.

Source: Compiled by the authors.

unwilling to campaign for election to these posts in smaller districts of the state.

The situation in Hawaii was very much linked to the circumstances surrounding the call of the convention, to which we alluded in the first chapter. Although the "unwanted" convention was nonpartisan, election districts were structured very closely along the lines of the lower house of the Hawaii General Assembly. In a majority of districts a number of hopefuls, including the incumbent legislator, filed for office. The recognition factor of the incumbents gave them an advantage in the election and despite the outcry that the politicians were trying to control the convention, the vast majority of those who were elected had had previous party experience, including 52 percent with legislative experience. The spirit of nonpartisanship, which to one degree or another discouraged party activists from becoming involved in the other nonpartisan convention, was not allowed by the parties to permeate the electoral context in Hawaii. The Hawaii and Kentucky conventions illustrate an important factor in the constitution-making process--namely, that a nonpartisan structural format does not necessarily assure that politicians and political leaders will not become involved.

With the exception of Hawaii the differences that appeared on the party activist variable all but disappear when we compare the percentages of delegates with experience in elected positions. In each of the seven other conventions, between one-third and two-fifths of the delegates had had prior elective experience. Thus all of the conventions, both partisan and nonpartisan, produced a large number of veteran state officials, many of whom were probably participating in their final activity in state politics. We found that the convention setting served equally well as a capstone to and the beginning of many political careers.

It is interesting, however, that when we compared the conventions in terms of the number of delegates with legislative experience, the pattern we found on the party activity dimension reappears. In other words, the conventions that attracted the greatest number of party activists also elected the greatest number of incumbent and ex-legislators. This fact is significant because legislators and party officials are the two groups of delegates who will have the most to lose from a major overhaul of the state constitution.

Finally, we find in Table 3.5 that there is little evidence to support the hypothesis that fewer members of

TABLE 3.5

Percentage Distribution of Delegate Types Among
Conventions

State	Stand-patter	Stand-in	As-pirant	Re-former	States-men	Chief-tain
Rhode Island	26	20	36	11	8	0
New York	29	16	23	15	11	6
New Mexico	43	10	19	24	3	1
Arkansas	42	3	27	29	2	0
Hawaii	28	7	23	28	4	9
Illinois	37	12	23	28	--	--
Maryland	25	6	29	29	10	2
Kentucky	38	--	18	28	13	3

Source: Compiled by the authors.

the minority party are selected in nonpartisan conventions.
In none of the eight states does the distribution of party
strength vary significantly from the legislature to the
convention.

The conclusion that we would draw from the political
experience data is that, more than on the social variable,
we begin to see some differences in the "political" composition of the conventions. Despite the common social
status of delegates to the respective conventions, nonpartisanship may in fact produce a different type of elite
mix than the partisan setting. Although their social status
may be comparable, the wealthy lawyer-ward-healer from the
Bronx will not approach the task of rewriting the state
constitution from the same perspective as the college professor from the suburbs of Washington, D.C. In other
words, as we argued in the preceding chapter in presenting

our delegate typology, the specific kinds of life experiences that a delegate has had will influence his attitude toward the convention process. The delegate role typology may be the most effective way to capture these differences in motivation.

DISTRIBUTION OF DELEGATE TYPES

Table 3.5 reports the distribution of delegate types in the eight conventions. If the data are to support our hypothesis that electoral systems affect the delegate mix, then certain predictable patterns will be present. In the first place, we expect that two groups will be represented more or less similarly in a convention, whatever the electoral system: aspirants and standpatters. Any convention will attract a substantial number of individuals who see it as an initial step up the political ladder; any convention will, because of its potential impact on the status quo, also attract a number of present beneficiaries and officeholders bent on preserving their stake in things as they are. We have already noted this tendency in the data on prior elective experience.

As Table 3.5 shows, standpatters were substantially represented in all of the conventions and their proportion of the delegate mix bore very little relationship to the type of selection system used. In fact, the largest percentage of standpatters appeared in New Mexico and Arkansas, two nonpartisan systems. Aspirants were also distributed among the conventions at rates averaging about 25 percent and ranging from 19 percent in New Mexico to 36 percent in Rhode Island.

The real impact of the electoral system we would expect to find in relation to the reformers and stand-ins. Party control of the electoral system would seem to maximize the representation of stand-ins at the expense of reformers. The opposite would likely occur in the nonpartisan system. So it proved in the eight states under consideration. Twice as many reformers were elected in the six nonpartisan systems as appeared in Rhode Island and New York. In the latter states, the proportionate number of stand-ins far exceeded their representation in the nonpartisan conventions.

Although these tendencies may not seem to be of dramatic proportions, they are important. In many ways it is the ratio of stand-ins to reformers that establishes the balance of power within the convention. If the standpat-

ters have enough stand-ins to bolster their ranks, it may
be relatively easy for these status-quo groups to dominate
the agenda of the convention. Such proved to be the case
in Rhode Island and New York. The election of a larger number of reformers in the nonpartisan conventions makes it
more difficult for established policies to dominate the
deliberations. We will discover later that in at least
one state, Maryland, the reformers actually controlled the
convention.

SUMMARY

The reader might conclude on the basis of the data we
have presented that some propositions about the demographic
effects of differing selection systems need to be recon-
sidered. We would agree that both reformers and students
of electoral systems, who have insisted that structural
arrangements determine selection outcomes, may have over-
estimated their importance. Given provisions for popular
election of some sort, the delegates comprised an elite
group who were not representative of the populations at
large. There seemed to be little consistent confirmation
of the hypothesis that partisan systems were any more representative than nonpartisan systems.

The differences between partisan and nonpartisan conventions did begin to show up in the political experiences
of the delegates. Generally speaking the partisan convention recruited more veterans of state politics than their
nonpartisan counterparts. When these differences were
fixed on the delegate role typology, we found that despite
the similarity in delegate mixes, the nonpartisan convention produced the most balanced representation between
reform and status-quo forces. This will become a very important factor in explaining both the style of individual
conventions and their output. A convention dominated by
either reformers or standpatters will in all likelihood
be unrepresentative of statewide sentiments on the constitutional issues and reform in general. Thus, such a convention may have difficulty producing a document acceptable
to a majority of the voters.

ATTITUDES OF CONSTITUTION-MAKERS

When we compare the process of constitution-making
in eight states, it may prove even more useful to examine

72

the delegates' attitudes about their task than to look at
their social and political experience. Our interviews with
the delegates measured a number of attitude dimensions.
Three aspects of the delegates' attitudes discussed below
include (1) the delegates' perceptions of the relationship
of the convention to regular state political processes,
(2) the representational focus and style of the conventions, and (3) the role of political parties and interest
groups in the convention process.

THE "STATESMAN" AND "POLITICAL" MODELS

We noted in Chapter 2 that there were conflicting
ideas about the manner in which constitutional conventions
should be conducted. One notion, and the one that pervades
much of the prescriptive literature on constitutional conventions, we have called the "statesman" model. This conception embodies the "idealized" view of how conventions
do or should operate that is shared by the "good-government" proponents and by the attentive public generally.
It is sustained by the belief that a constitution is a
"higher-law" document designed to propagate "neutral"
principles.

The assumption underlying the second conception of conventions, the "political" or "realistic" model, argues that
conventions are more accurately described as mere extensions of normal politics. Despite the infrequency with
which conventions are held, the delegates come to the convention wedded to a distinct set of interests that they
desire to see reflected in the revised constitutions. They
are receptive to the notion that interest groups, political
parties, and political leadership should work to support
the structural apparatus most likely to enhance their own
goals.

Which of these conflicting role expectations more accurately describes the way in which constitution-makers
approach their job? The only empirical study to date that
examined this question was a study of delegate role perceptions in the Michigan constitutional convention of 1962.[8]
Robert Friedman and Sybil Stokes concluded from their findings that the prevailing "myths" about constitutional conventions, the essence of which are described by the statesman conception, shaped the role perceptions of the delegates.
Even though the Michigan convention was organized in a partisan manner, the authors hypothesized that "statesmanlike"
myths were more important in determining delegate attitudes

than were the formal structure and process by which the delegates performed their task.

The limitations of the Michigan study were twofold. First, the authors themselves recognized that any generalizations drawn from their findings had to be qualified by the fact that only one political system was involved. Comparative data could conceivably yield contradictory results. Second, and perhaps more important, the Michigan survey was administered before the real work of the convention began. It was only speculation to argue that "myths" are more important than structure and process in determining attitudes if the delegates have not yet experienced the full effects of that structure and process.

Our approach was to interview the delegates both at the beginning of the convention and again at the conclusion of the deliberations. Thus not only were we in a favorable position to measure the delegates' preconvention orientation but also we were able to detect any changes in attitudes that might have taken place during the convention.[9] We were concerned with the delegates' perceptions of the convention process in relationship to the "statesman" and "political" models, and also with the socialization effect of convention participation upon their attitudes.

Table 3.6 reports the aggregate responses of delegates in six conventions to two attitude questions that elicited delegates' reactions to the relationship of constitution-making to regular political processes. (We did not ask these questions and completed only one round of interviews in Rhode Island and Kentucky.) Data are included for both preconvention and postconvention surveys. We coded responses as "idealistic" if the delegates accepted the "statesmanlike" notion that the convention was special and above ordinary politics. If the delegates viewed the conventions as an extension of normal state politics, we registered a "realistic" response. The reader should consider the data from at least two perspectives. First, is there any single pattern that characterizes the responses across the six conventions to sustain the hypothesis that "statesmanlike" notions shaped delegate perceptions? Secondly, is there any evidence to suggest the extent to which the attitude pattern may reflect the structural characteristics and political style of individual conventions?

The data from the preconvention interviews do lend some support to the Friedman-Stokes hypothesis. With only one exception, on the two items included in Table 3.6, the majority of the delegates in six states perceived the convention in "idealistic-statesman" terms. The conventions

TABLE 3.6

Persistence and Change in Delegate Attitude Patterns
(percent)

	New York	Illinois	Maryland	Hawaii	New Mexico	Arkansas	Totals
Constitutional Conventions Are as Political as Anything Else							
All delegates							
Realist (both interviews)	35	38	20	28	9	20	26
Idealist to realist	37	29	8	16	11	11	20
Realist to idealist	6	8	18	17	7	11	11
Idealist (both interviews)	22	25	54	39	73	58	43
Attitude-changers only							
Percent changing	43	37	26	33	18	22	31
Idealist to realist	86	69	31	49	50	39	64
Realist to idealist	14	31	69	51	50	61	36
Constitutional Conventions Are Special and Above Politics							
All delegates							
Realist (both interviews)	44	49	23	18	10	42	33
Idealist to realist	24	35	12	21	19	20	21
Realist to idealist	22	7	20	17	8	1	12
Idealist (both interviews)	10	9	45	44	63	37	35
Attitude-changers only							
Percent changing	46	42	32	38	27	21	33
Idealist to realist	53	83	37	55	70	95	64
Realist to idealist	47	17	63	45	30	5	36

Source: Compiled by the authors.

were looked upon as something special and above ordinary
politics and not as political as anything else.

Despite the uniform direction of the responses in the
first round of interviews, there were still significant
differences in the rate of idealism among the delegate
populations. Delegates in Illinois and New York, in particular, exhibited less of a tendency to support the
"statesman" view. We will show in the next chapter that
the Illinois convention, ostensibly nonpartisan, generated
cleavages that reflected the traditional division in Illinois politics between Chicago Democrats and downstate Republicans. To some observers of the highly partisan New
York convention, it may be surprising that that convention
enhibited any support at all for the "statesman" myth. The
"idealist" sentiment that was expressed is illustrative
of the kind of "above-politics" aura of constitution-making
that Friedman and Stokes found in the preconvention setting
of Michigan's partisan constitutional convention. Thus,
even though the "myth" was reflected in the initial attitudes of the delegates, there is evidence to suggest that
"structure" and "style" had already shaped some of the preconvention responses where the convention had become politicized.

The effect of the style and process of the six conventions is reflected even more in the nature of the attitude change from the preconvention to the postconvention
interview. The idealist view of the convention process
persists in Maryland, Hawaii, New Mexico, and Arkansas.
Attitude change was relatively small and generally moved
to a more "idealist" position. This pattern confirmed
our own and others' observations that these conventions
remained remarkably aloof from partisan state politics.
Note, however, that the attitude shift is much more pro-
nounced in New York and Illinois, where the response pattern moved significantly toward the "realist" position on
all three questions.

Table 3.6 reports a more detailed breakdown of the
nature and scope of the attitude change of the delegates
on the three questions. The data reveal that the percentage of attitude-changers was far greater in New York and
Illinois than in the other states on both propositions.
The majority of those who changed attitudes during the
convention moved away from the "statesman" position. The
preconvention support for the "idealist" image of constitutional conventions in these two highly politicized assemblies was significantly undermined during the convention
deliberations.

In the other states, the tendency was for the attitude change to reinforce the preconvention "statesman" image. Some erosion of this point of view is exhibited in the response pattern to proposition II in Table 3.6. Attitude-changers in three of the states—Hawaii, Arkansas, and New Mexico—were slightly less likely to perceive the convention in "above-politics" terms on the second interview. In none of these states, however, was the rate of change significant on a chi-square test. By and large, data from the four nonpartisan conventions indicate that the delegates' preconvention expectations about the convention were confirmed by their experience as delegates.

Our interviews with constitutional convention delegates in six states confirmed that there exists an awareness of the supposed special "above-politics" quality of conventions. The prevailing myths in U.S. politics about the constitution-making process seemed to be important at the outset of the deliberations in all six conventions. In those states where the organization and style of the convention allowed it to be free of partisan considerations, the "above-politics" quality of the deliberations reappeared in the delegates' postconvention evaluations.

Preoccupation with the "myth," however, ignores the fact that one-third of the interviewed delegates changed their perceptions of the convention process from the preconvention to the postconvention interview. The effect of the attitude change, which occurred primarily in Illinois and New York, was to deny the "statesman" myth. In other words, in those conventions where the degree of politicization seemed to contradict the "myth," the delegates were resocialized into accepting different role expectations.

It seems logical to argue that if it was the organization and style of the conventions that caused the attitude change in Illinois and New York, then it also seems plausible that it was the organization and style of the other conventions that sustained the "idealist" position. Friedman and Stokes's hypothesis that myths are more important than either formal structure and process does have some utility as an indicator of preconvention role expectations. Decision-making elites in all political settings will have preexisting role expectations that actual political experience may or may not prove to be adaptable to the individual's performance. Our data showed that actual political experience, particularly experience that contradicted the delegates' original perceptions, acted as an important socializing agent in restructuring political attitudes. We will be able to show in the next two chapters that the impact of the socialization process also had a crucial bearing on voting behavior in the conventions and upon the documents they produced.

REPRESENTATIONAL ROLE

The organizational configuration of the constitutional convention raises an important question concerning the representational role orientation of its delegates. A notion shared by many students of government is that a major function of an elected representative is to act as a spokesman for the interests of his constitutents. One of the findings to emerge from The Legislative System was that the major factor that orients a legislator toward his district is the "mechanism of political responsibility effectuated by political competition."[10] This type of situation is realized most effectively, however, in a competitive political system where the elected representative is periodically held responsible to his party and constituency for his actions.

In a very real sense this "mechanism of responsibility," which links the representative and the represented, is not present to the same extent in a constitutional convention. First, the convention is a "one-shot affair" of limited duration; few of the delegates are concerned with the possibility of future electoral reprisals. Second, the delegates in five of the states were selected on a nonpartisan basis, which in theory at least allowed them to act independently of local party organizations. The incentives that tend to encourage a delegate to reflect the desires of his constituency are seemingly minimized within the organizational context of the convention.

The data in Table 3.7 seem to support his hypothesis. The consensus of the delegates in all of the states was that their primary role in the convention was to represent the state as a whole rather than their district, region, or party. The dynamics of the convention proceedings did not significantly alter the aggregate representational role perceptions of the delegates from the preconvention to the postconvention interview.

However, when the responses of the delegates are compared with similar findings reported in the Wahlke legislative study, it is interesting to note the marked decrease in the perceived importance of "district" from the legislative to the convention arena. Perhaps equally signifi-

TABLE 3.7

Representational Orientation of Delegates
(percent)

(What is the major representational responsibility
of the delegate?)

	District	State	Combination
New York			
Pre-	16	51	32
Post-	15	46	38
New Mexico			
Pre-	24	55	21
Post-	30	60	10
Arkansas			
Pre-	15	73	12
Post-	11	68	21
Hawaii			
Pre-	10	70	20
Post-	6	72	22
Illinois			
Pre-	18	47	35
Post-	25	44	31
Maryland			
Pre-	3	75	22
Post-	6	82	12
State legislators	45	33	21

Source: Compiled by the authors.

cant is the fact that with the exception of Illinois, the range of support for the district also declines from the partisan to the nonpartisan convention setting. We can conclude on the basis of these findings, then, that both the convention setting and the nonpartisan electoral system acted to weaken the identification of the delegates with their districts.

The type of representational focus expressed by the delegates raises an important question concerning the relationship of the convention to their publics. The convention setting, more than the regular legislative setting, clearly maximizes the freedom of the delegates to decide for themselves what is in the best interests of the state.

There is very little pressure upon the delegates to seek
out constituency opinion on all but a few very controversial issues. However, the freedom that the delegates exer-
cised in writing the new constitutions would come back to
haunt them in many instances during the ratification process. No U.S. legislature ever faces the kind of total
public evaluation of its policy decisions that a constitutional convention does. In a very real sense the fact
that the total work of the convention must be approved by
a majority of the electorate in a state makes it more im-
perative that the delegates not lose sight of district and
group interests. To socialize delegates into believing
that the public will passively accept their "good judgment"
ignores the very real political stakes of any attempt at
restructuring the state constitutions.

PARTY AND INTEREST GROUPS

     Political scientists have demonstrated convincingly
that political parties and interest groups play a critical
role in structuring the activities of most legislative
bodies. The third aspect of the delegates' attitudes that
we sought to measure was their reaction to the activities
of parties and interest groups as they affected the conventions' deliberations. Given the variety of political contexts within which the conventions were staged, the delegate perceptions of party and interest group activity may
help us to distinguish among the different political styles
that characterized the conventions. Our particular concern
was to examine the impact of "party" in the nonpartisan
context.
     Although the delegates to five of the six conventions
for which we have parallel attitude data were selected on
a nonpartisan basis, all but a few of the delegates willingly expressed a preference for a specific political party
during the interviews. Consequently, the survey allowed
us to elicit delegates' descriptions of what role, if any,
they felt called upon to take by virtue of their party
identification. Data from both preconvention and postconvention interviews were available to help capture the dynamic impact or "socialization effect" of the convention
proceedings on the delegates' perception of party activities. At this point in our study, our concern is confined
to delegates' perception of party activity. Whether the
convention itself operated in accordance with these expectations is discussed in the next chapter.

80

The delegates' responses to four items pertaining to "party" are reported in Table 3.8. The questions were designed to determine the attitudes of the delegates toward the role of party as it applied (1) to their perceptions of the political style of the whole convention, (2) to their own individual experiences within the convention, and (3) to their belief about the importance of party in the political system at large.

The pattern that emerges from the data duplicates rather closely the earlier attitude findings. In the four conventions that exhibited the "statesmanlike" quality, the vast majority of the delegates expected, first, that parties would play a weak role in the convention and, second, that they themselves would pay little or no attention to their party's position on the issues. The figures would also seem to belie the assumption that nonpartisanship was a facade that would disappear once the convention got under way. Positive assessments of the role of party became less frequent in the postconvention interviews in these four states.

The attitude data from New York and Illinois point to a different conclusion. In both states at the outset of the deliberations, the role of party was perceived to be significantly more important than in the "statesmanlike" assemblies. What is even more significant, however, is that at the conclusion of the convention, party was an even more important factor in explaining the activities of the convention in the minds of the delegates.

These findings are significant because they dramatize the impact of state political culture in structuring the style of these two conventions. Of all of the states included in the study, New York and Illinois probably are best known for their strong, well-disciplined party organizations. It is not particularly surprising that in New York, which structured its convention along partisan lines, the "above-politics" quality of the convention process did not survive. When an exercise in restructuring the rules of the game in state politics is infiltrated by avowed partisans who are the major contenders for political power in the state, the self-interest of the opposing camps is likely to characterize the deliberations. In this context the question of "reform vs. status quo" will be less important than the effects of proposed constitutional changes on the balance of power within state politics.

The Illinois example is perhaps even more significant because it illustrates the fact that a nonpartisan organizational framework does not necessarily eliminate the en-

TABLE 3.8

Political Parties and Constitutional Convention
(percent)

	New York		New Mexico		Arkansas		Hawaii		Illinois		Maryland	
	Pre-	Post-	Pre-	Post-	Pre-	Post-	Pre-	Post-	Pre-	Post-	Pre-	Post-
Role of party in convention												
Strong	49	77	1	1	4	--	5	9	32	41	7	3
Moderate	34	13	23	9	29	22	35	17	51	41	24	14
Weak	10	4	69	89	59	77	49	72	7	13	63	83
None	7	6	7	1	8	1	11	2	9	5	7	--
Attention to party position												
Great deal	15	23	--	--	--	--	--	--	--	--	0	1
Some	59	43	--	--	--	--	--	--	--	--	10	5
Little	17	19	--	--	--	--	--	--	--	--	5	7
None	85	87	--	--	--	--	--	--	--	--	8	15
"Party loyalty strongly influences voting"												
Agree	53	75	17	5	7	2	17	8	41	75	12	3
Disagree	47	25	83	98	93	98	83	92	59	25	88	97
Individuals Act Independent of Party												
Agree	27	17	--	--	--	--	--	--	--	--	46	43
Disagree	73	83	--	--	--	--	--	--	--	--	54	57

Source: Compiled by the authors.

82

trenched state party organization from the activities of the convention. In the case of Illinois the political culture and tradition was able to overcome the "obstacle" imposed by nonpartisanship. The extent to which the Chicago Democratic machine managed to influence a significant portion of the convention agenda frequently turned the convention into a contest between the city Democrats and downstate Republicans. In retrospect, however, the element of partisanship that was introduced into the Illinois convention setting may have helped to influence the convention to produce a document that would be acceptable to a majority of Illinois voters. This point will be developed in more detail in subsequent chapters.

The differences that emerged among the conventions in their perceptions of the significance of political party activity did not appear when we inquired about the impact of interest groups (Table 3.9). The overwhelming proportion of the delegates in all of the conventions approved of lobbying activity as it applied to the convention and also indicated that the activities of interest groups affected outcomes at the convention. The evaluation of interest groups did not vary significantly from the preconvention to the postconvention interview.

The data are useful in that they illustrate that, at least in the minds of the delegates, even the "statesmanlike" conventions were not conducted in a political vacuum. There was an opportunity for interest groups to make their attitudes known and also a recognition of the fact that the delegates frequently might need the type of "expert" input that these groups could provide. It was our observation, however, that one reason so many new constitutions were not ratified was that in actuality there was not enough contact between the constitution-makers and the groups with a stake in the product.

What seemed to happen was that by trying to take "politics" out of a very political exercise, the conventions were often isolated from major groups in society. The willingness of the delegates to listen to interest groups was less important than the fact that in many of the states, channels of communication were never established between the conventions and the wide range of interest groups who played an important part in everyday politics. Constitution-making remained a very special exercise in state politics for many groups, and it was only when the conventions had finished their work that some realized how they were affected by the process. It was unfortunate that neither the convention and its leaders nor the groups

TABLE 3.9

Interest Groups and Constitutional Convention
(percent)

	New York		New Mexico		Arkansas		Hawaii		Illinois		Maryland	
	Pre-	Post-	Pre-	Post-	Pre-	Post-	Pre-	Post-	Pre-	Post-	Pre-	Post-
Lobbying in Convention												
Approve	76	85	80	66	76	92	69	85	80	88	81	88
Tolerate	18	9	14	17	15	2	25	6	14	4	15	8
Disapprove	3	6	6	14	9	7	6	9	5	4	4	4
Interest Groups Affect Convention Outcomes												
Agree	84	77	87	80	89	89	77	71	87	90	90	74
Disagree	16	23	13	10	11	11	23	29	13	10	10	26

Source: Compiled by the authors.

themselves did much to activate channels of communication during the time the convention was doing its work.

To raise this last subject is to introduce the problem of the linkages between the data of this chapter--characteristics and attitudes--and actual behavior in the convention. A serious critique of other studies of legislative role has been that they do not establish the connections between attitudes and actual behavior in any systematic way.[11] We have tried to overcome this legitimate objection in our work, and in the next chapter we move to two crucial aspects of behavior--leadership and voting.

NOTES

1. For our earlier treatment of this problem, see Jay S. Goodman, Wayne R. Swanson, and Elmer E. Cornwell, Jr., "Political Recruitment in Four Selection Systems," Western Political Quarterly 23, 1 (March 1970): 92-103.

2. See Richard S. Childs, Civic Victories (New York: Harper, 1952); Charles R. Adrian, "A Typology for Nonpartisan Elections," Western Political Quarterly 12 (June 1959): 449-58; Charles R. Adrian, Governing Urban America (New York: McGraw-Hill, 1955), pp. 56-63; and John Porter East, Council-Manager Government: The Political Thought of Its Founder, Richard S. Childs (Chapel Hill: University of North Carolina Press, 1965). See also various articles in the National Municipal Review and the National Civic Review from 1911 to the present.

3. Richard S. Childs, "500 'Non-Political' Elections," National Municipal Review 38 (June 1949): 282.

4. See Oliver P. Williams and Charles R. Adrian, "The Insulation of Local Politics under the Nonpartisan Ballot," American Political Science Review 53 (December 1959): 1052-63; Robert H. Salisbury and Gordon Black, "Class and Party in Partisan and Nonpartisan Elections," American Political Science Review 57 (September 1963): 584-92; Eugene C. Lee, The Politics of Nonpartisanship (Los Angeles: University of California Press, 1960); Samuel Eldersveld, Political Parties: A Behavioral Analysis (Chicago: Rand McNally, 1965); Charles E. Gilbert, "Some Aspects of Nonpartisan Election in Large Cities," Midwest Journal of Political Science 6 (November 1962): 345-62; Gerald Pomper, "Ethnic and Group Voting in Nonpartisan Municipal Elections," Public Opinion Quarterly 30 (Spring 1966): 79-98; and Charles R. Adrian, "Some General Characteristics of Nonpartisan Elections," American Political Science Review 46 (September 1952): 770-71.

5. Berkeley and Los Angeles: University of California Press, 1960, pp. 50-59.

6. Ibid., p. 181.

7. See Thomas R. Dye and L. Harmon Zeigler, The Irony
of Democracy (North Scituate, Mass.: Duxbury Press, 1970,
1972); Peter Bachrach, The Theory of Democratic Elitism
(Boston: Little, Brown, 1967); and E. E. Schattschneider,
The Semi-Sovereign People (New York: Holt, Rinehart, 1961).
For an analysis of alternative models, see Robert A. Dahl,
Democracy in the United States (Chicago: Rand McNally,
1972).

8. Robert S. Friedman and Sybil Stokes, "The Role of
Constitution-Maker as Representative," Midwest Journal of
Political Science 9 (May 1965): 148-66.

9. For our earlier treatment of some of these issues,
see Wayne R. Swanson, Sean A. Kelleher, and Arthur English,
"Socialization of Constitution-Makers: Political Experience,
Role Conflict, and Attitude Change," Journal of Politics
34, 1 (February 1970); 183-98.

10. John C. Wahlke et al., The Legislation System:
Explorations in Legislative Behavior (New York: John
Wiley & Sons, 1962), p. 292.

11. See the criticisms of The Legislative System advanced by Wayne L. Francis in his "The Role Concept in
Legislatures: A Probability Model and a Note on Cognitive
Structures," Journal of Politics 37, 3 (August 1965): 567-
85.

4

**DYNAMICS OF
CONVENTION BEHAVIOR:
VOTING AND
LEADERSHIP**

The crucial stage of the convention decision-making process comes when delegates' proposals will be included in the revised constitutions they will submit to the voters. Our concern in this chapter is with these decisions, especially as they are reflected by internal cleavages among groups of delegates. Two propositions we advanced at the onset of this study generated questions about the behavior of convention delegates during the deliberations. First, to what extent did the basis of conflict that divided the delegates reflect a reform/status-quo cleavage as opposed to party, regional, or other types of divisions? Did the convention conform to the "statesman" view of constitution-making or was the "realistic" model a more accurate view of the constitution-making process? Second, did the actual behavior of the delegates lend support to the a priori group typology developed in Chapter 2? Thus, we are interested in exploring those aspects of the convention process that will help to explain the types of constitutions that were produced and also the political cleavages that characterized the decision-making processes.

Three kinds of data are utilized in this chapter to study the conventions at work. We have already introduced attitude data that help to explain the delegates preconvention perceptions of the convention process, as well as changes in attitudes that took place during the convention. Throughout the study we found that both closed and open-ended interview data proved to be revealing indicators of convention styles and operations. In this chapter we will continue to make use of the delegates' attitudes and perception of various aspects of the internal operations of the conventions.

Social scientists have demonstrated that the internal functioning of formal organizations is conditioned to a large extent by "informal" behavior patterns. Students of legislatures, in particular, have responded to the notion that informal interaction patterns are important in explaining the dynamics of legislative behavior.[1] To identify interaction and leadership perception patterns within the seven conventions we generated sociometric data by asking the delegates to indicate the other delegates whom they sought out and looked to for advice and leadership during the convention.

Probably the most revealing indicator of internal convention cleavages comes from roll-call analysis. The votes of legislators, judges, or representatives of any political body provide the researcher with hard data of such precision that they can be subjected to a variety of statistical measurements. However, we are mindful of the warning that voting data are selective and that some important decisions never reach the roll-call stage.[2] Admittedly the registering of a "yea" or "nay" response is only one part of the interaction of ideas and individuals in complex decision-making processes. Yet the fact remains that the results of roll-call analysis yield a variety of information about the nature of the output of political units, as well as clues to the behavior of the individuals who make up these bodies.

DELEGATES PERCEIVE THE CLEAVAGES

One method to test the proposition that the basic cleavage within a convention would be between the reformers and delegates desiring to protect the status quo was to ask delegates about the internal divisions that emerged within their respective conventions. Such a test rests on the usual assumption that what the delegates perceived to be real was likely to be real in its consequences. We read each delegate the following statement. "There are always conflicting opinions in an assembly. How would you rank these particular conflicts of opinion in order of importance here in _____?" The items on the list were drawn up with observers in each of the states, and delegates were permitted to suggest other cleavages that did not appear on the list. Table 4.1 reports the number and percentages of first choices received by each of the items.

It is clear from the data that the reform/status-quo conflict was the most crucial division in five of the seven

TABLE 4.1

Delegates' Perceptions of Convention Cleavages

Cleavage	New York		Rhode Island		Illinois		New Mexico		Maryland		Arkansas		Hawaii	
	Num-ber	Per-cent	Num-ber	Per-cent	Num-ber	Per-cent	Num-ber	Per-cent	Num-ber	Per-cent	Num-ber	Per-cent	Num-ber	Per-cent
Reformers versus those who want to preserve status quo	12	9	37	43	22	24	43	75	91	72	58	63	40	65
Cities versus remainder of state	60	44	8	9	52	55	13	24	22	18	22	25	1	2
Republicans versus Democrats	62	45	5	6	9	9	--	--	--	--	1	1	1	1
Legislators versus nonlegislators	--	--	35	41	--	--	--	--	6	5	--	--	9	15
Governor supporters versus opponents	--	--	1	1	--	--	--	--	4	3	6	7	11	17
Judges versus non-judges	3	2	--	--	11	12	1	1	3	2	--	--	--	--

Source: Compiled by the authors.

89

conventions. In four of the states, Maryland, New Mexico, Arkansas, and Hawaii, the delegates overwhelmingly perceived their deliberations in these terms. This pattern confirms the attitude data presented in the previous chapter that indicated that these four conventions were most free of partisan influences. We suggested earlier that the reform/status-quo conflict would be most likely to dominate in conventions free of partisan divisions.

The data from the New York, Illinois, and Rhode Island conventions suggest that the political struggles in these states were somewhat different. In Rhode Island the reform/status-quo conflict received the most first choices, but it was closely followed by a legislator/nonlegislator cleavage. In the New York and Illinois conventions the reform/status-quo division was not the first choice of the delegates. In New York the primary conflict was between the parties, followed by two variations of a rural/urban division. In Illinois the urban/rural cleavage was by far the most significant division; this would suggest that at least in the minds of the Illinois delegates a Chicago/downstate cleavage was responsible for much of the conflict of opinion.

While this type of information is very suggestive of the types of conflicts that shaped the seven conventions, attitude data alone cannot sufficiently explain the nature of political conflict within legislative bodies. Political scientists have for a long time expressed reservations about the utility of political attitude studies that do not make some attempt to show the relationship between demographic characteristics, political attitudes, and actual behavior. In his analysis of the concept of "role" as it is used by the authors of The Legislative System, Wayne Francis argued that "many political scientists have developed data on political attitudes, but few have achieved a convincing technique for predicting behavior on the basis of attitude measurement."[3] The challenge that Francis offers is a significant one. In the next section, we will examine the actual political behavior of convention delegates on roll calls in relationship to their attitudes, as well as to their demographic profiles as they were reflected by our classification of convention participants into six delegate types.

An important question in analyzing the roll calls was to select a method that would facilitate a cross-convention comparative analysis of voting behavior and one that could handle the large number of votes available. Our analysis of voting behavior does not include the Hawaii convention, for which roll calls were limited to about 15 "final passage" items that revealed very little division of opinion.

Another factor in determining the choice of method for analyzing the roll calls was the nonpartisan setting of four of the conventions. To our knowledge, one other study has subjected the votes of a nonpartisan legislative body to systematic analysis.[4] The great majority of recent legislative roll-call studies has analyzed partisan legislatures by enlarging upon the pioneering efforts of A. Lawrence Lowell, Stuart Rice, and Julius Turner, which utilize the more conventional deductive techniques to uncover the structure of legislative voting.[5] This type of analysis requires that the voting patterns to be looked for (party, constituency, region) be specified prior to analysis; rates of cohesion are computed, and the hypothesized voting relationships are either confirmed or denied.

Most legislative voting studies have confirmed that the existence of party, factional, and regionally organized groups within legislatures give the legislator a significant array of reference groups to focus upon during the decision-making process. When large numbers of legislators take cues from relatively stable sources of leadership, such as a political party, considerable consistency and predictability in aggregate voting patterns occurs. Voting behavior in this situation can be described as highly structured. Uniformity in voting has been shown to decline, however, as the importance of party and other factional groupings declined.[6] It would seem to follow that by consciously suppressing and/or eliminating these sources of voting cohesion, as in the case of the nonpartisan constitutional convention, the decision-making process would become unusually unstructured.

One of the propositions we will test in this chapter is that voting behavior in a nonpartisan legislative setting is less structured and more random than in partisan legislatures. However, there is no compelling reason to assume a priori that party, constituency, or any of the other reference groups that are said to cue legislators as they vote will or will not shed much light on voting behavior within the nonpartisan convention setting. By limiting an interpretation of convention voting to a preselected number of possible variables, our analysis might overlook very meaningful voting relationships that cannot be anticipated by deductive inquiry. It would seem that this handicap is especially applicable to nonpartisan legislative bodies wherein, if our hypothesis is true, voting may be less structured and more random than in partisan bodies.

A number of political scientists have resorted to methods devised by psychologists and sociologists to come up with an "open-ended" or inductive method to examine roll-call votes. Factor analysis proved to be one method that could handle a large number of roll calls and would reliably identify, without prior specification, all of the significant voting blocs within a legislative assembly. In the first application of factor analysis to bloc voting in a state legislature, John Grumm confirmed the importance of "party" as a major determinant in structuring the votes of Kansas legislators.[7] Similarly in a somewhat different type of legislative setting, Bruce Russett was able to identify six significant nation/state voting blocs during the 1963-64 session of the UN General Assembly.[8]

In more precise terms, factor analysis is a statistical measurement that uses correlation measurements to identify common factors underlying various sets of responses, without prior indication of the nature or number of factors to be identified. When it is applied to voting behavior in a constitutional convention, its ultimate function is to identify the groups of delegates whose voting records were similar. The particular application of factor analysis adopted for use in this study represents the so-called "Q-technique."[9] This approach differs somewhat from the more commonly used "R-technique" in that the former method treats individuals (delegates) as variables, while holding the responses (roll calls) as observed constants; in the "R-technique," roll calls become the variables, while delegates are observed. The purpose of "R" analysis is to isolate groups of issues that evoke a common response; the "Q" test identifies groups of delegates who voted alike.

In the processing of the data, all of the roll calls on which at least 10 percent of the delegates were in a voting minority were abstracted from convention journals. (The exception to this pattern occurred in Illinois, where 49 was used as the cutoff point.) The inclusion of votes on which the minority is very small is known to distort significantly the product-moment correlation coefficients used to compute the weight of possible factors.

The data in Table 4.2 summarize the results of the factor analysis for the six conventions. The conventions are listed according to the degree to which their voting was structured as indicated by the average percent of the predicted variance accounted for by each significant bloc. Structure is used in the context to mean those situations where the number of significant voting groups is small and is inclusive of large numbers of delegates and where the

TABLE 4.2

Voting Behavior in Six Constitutional Conventions

State	Delegates	Organization	Number Roll Calls	Significant Voting Blocs[a]	Delegates Included in Significant Voting Blocs	Total Variance[b] (percent)	Predicted Variance[c] (percent)	Average Percent Predicted Variance Each Sign Bloc
New York	186	Partisan	126	2	181 (97%)	55.9	77.1	38.5
Rhode Island	100	Partisan	113	2	73 (73%)	44.6	72.3	36.1
Illinois	116	Nonpartisan	237	3	83 (72%)	55.6	76.4	25.5
New Mexico	70	Nonpartisan	139	3	38 (54%)	47.2	65.8	21.9
Maryland	142	Nonpartisan	377	4	105 (73%)	33.5	70.1	17.5
Arkansas	100	Nonpartisan	1,052	5	45 (45%)	29.2	66.2	13.2

[a]A bloc was significant if it accounted for 5 percent of the predicted variance or greater.

[b]Total variance includes the percentage of the total convention voting behavior accounted for by the significant voting blocs.

[c]Predicted variance includes the percentage of the variance of the 15 most important factors identified by the rotated factor analysis accounted for by the significant voting blocs.

Source: Compiled by the authors.

93

interrelationship among the groups is well-defined. Thus, structure is the function of the number of significant clusters that emerge as well as the percent of the voting variance those clusters collectively explain. A perfectly structured relationship would exist in a situation where one bloc of delegates accounted for 100 percent of the variance--in other words, where all members voted alike on all issues. As voting becomes more random, structure declines.

The conclusion that seems to emerge from a comparative analysis of convention voting is that the partisan organized conventions were also the ones that were the most structured in their voting. In both New York and Rhode Island, only two significant voting blocs appeared, and the percent of the variance accounted for by those blocs was high. The Illinois convention exhibited the most structure of the nonpartisan conventions, followed by New Mexico, Maryland, and Arkansas. Another indicator of voting structure is the percentage of delegates who cluster above the 0.555 level on the individual factor loadings for the significant blocs.* Note that the percentage of delegates included in the significant blocs is much greater for New York, Rhode Island, and Illinois than for the other conventions.

Once delegate voting blocs have been identified by the factor analysis, the nature of each bloc must be uncovered. To understand voting behavior, we need to know which attributes or characteristics that are common to the delegates who comprise each of the major blocs might explain their tendency to vote together. In each instance the blocs were labeled, first, by pinpointing the particular characteristics that distinguished each voting group from the other delegates and, second, by analyzing the nature of the response of bloc members to the specific issues that confronted the conventions.

To examine the composition of each voting group, the members of the voting blocs were compared with all other convention delegates on several important demographic characteristics, including their group typology. Table

*In those conventions in which the number of delegates included in the significant blocs fell below 50 percent, we included those delegates with factor loadings between 0.400 and 0.499 as block members. For the unstructured conventions, it seemed to make sense to modify the criteria somewhat.

4.3 identifies the "group distribution" for each of the
significant blocs within the six conventions. To derive
some indication of the "issue content" of bloc voting behavior, a sample of the most important roll calls in each
convention was constructed. The roll calls included in
the sample were those perceived by the delegates to be the
most important at the conclusion of the convention as well
as those selected on the basis of a rather thorough analysis of newspaper coverage of each convention. Virtually
all of the issues that confront a constitutional convention represent a question of reforming the constitution
or maintaining the status quo. Table 4.4 indicates the
percentage of sample issues on which blocs of delegates
voted for the reform or status-quo position, and the percentage of issues on which bloc voting did not appear.
Our discussion of these findings will be divided into
three sections: the "partisan" conventions (Rhode Island
and New York), the "semi-structured" conventions (Illinois
and New Mexico), and the "unstructured" conventions (Maryland and Arkansas).

THE PARTISAN CONVENTIONS: RHODE
ISLAND AND NEW YORK

In both New York and Rhode Island only two significant voting blocs appeared. In New York, all but five of
the delegates clustered into the two groups, which proved
to be the highest percentage of delegates to cluster in
the significant blocs for the six conventions. As one
might easily have predicted, the voting blocs in New York
were highly partisan, one made up entirely of Republican
delegates and the other of Democrats. Partisanship in
New York was so powerful that it eliminated almost every
other possible competitor as a basis for systematic delegate behavior. Nowhere in the functioning of the New York
convention does its resemblance to the legislature emerge
more clearly than in these voting patterns.
Because of the importance of party voting, we found
very little indication that delegates in New York responded
to the questions of constitutional reform on the basis of
the demographic characteristics we had predicted would be
important. Most of the issues that dominated the convention were cast in reform or status-quo terms, but no clear
reform-status-quo pattern between the parties emerged.
The tendency seemed to be for the Democrats to take a
reform stance, while the Republicans were inclined to sup-

TABLE 4.3

Voting Blocs Identified by Group Types

State and Bloc Name	Number Delegates	Stand-patters (percent)	Stand-ins (percent)	States Chief (percent)	Aspirant (percent)	Reformer (percent)	Total (percent)
New York							
Democratic bloc	99	16	25	24	21	13	100
Republican bloc	82	45	6	9	20	20	100
Rhode Island							
Democratic legislative bloc	49	35	24	4	37	--	100
Reform Republican bloc	24	8	21	12	33	25	100
Illinois							
Chicago Democratic bloc	34	32	32	--	24	12	100
Independent Democratic reform bloc	22	9	5	--	18	68	100
Republican downstate bloc	27	54	4	--	26	16	100
New Mexico							
Status-quo bloc	16	62	19	--	7	12	100
Spanish-American bloc	15	33	7	7	46	7	100
Reform bloc	7	14	14	--	14	58	100
Maryland							
Reform bloc	36	8	5	5	34	48	100
Moderate reform bloc	23	26	18	4	18	34	100
Moderate status-quo-rural	19	37	6	16	16	31	100
Status-quo bloc	27	45	7	11	33	4	100
Arkansas*							
Reformers	31	22	3	--	23	52	100
Moderates	40	44	5	2	29	20	100
Standpatters	23	70	--	4	22	4	100

*The Arkansas bloc represents a modification and a combination of the factor analysis blocs. Their derivation is described in the section discussing Arkansas voting.

Source: Compiled by the authors.

TABLE 4.4

Issue Content of Convention Voting Blocs

State Bloc	Number Roll Calls	Reform Response (percent)	Random Response (percent)	Status-Quo Response (percent)
New York	25			
Democratic bloc		56	32	12
Republican bloc		16	24	60
Rhode Island	10			
Reform bloc		90	10	--
Status quo		--	--	100
Illinois	39			
Chicago Democrats		15	6	79
Republican downstate		56	28	16
Independent-Democrat-Reform		72	28	--
New Mexico	32			
Standpatters		--	25	75
Spanish-American		40	25	35
Reformers		81	19	--
Maryland	25			
Reformers		88	12	--
Status quo		8	32	60
Bipartisan Republican		72	20	8
Rural		36	48	16

Note: Because of the extremely fragmented pattern that emerged in Arkansas, another method was used to identify issue positions. The findings are discussed below.

Source: Compiled by the authors.

port the status quo. That is not an unfamiliar pattern
in New York politics. However, on two of the issues in the
sample survey, the ones advocating a four-year term for
state senators but not assemblymen and the establishment
of a State Criminal Justice Department, the opposite pattern occurred: Republicans supported the reform position,
while the Democrats defended the status quo.

It would seem from this pattern that partisan advantage largely determined the rate of support for reform.
Republican ability to control the State Senate in New
York and their control of the executive branch was a strong
motivating force in the "reform" response. Simarily, the
Democrats would appear to have more to gain than Republicans by lowering the voting age, easing property qualifications, and increasing the power of the Assembly.

Although it did not reach a level of significance on
the factor analysis, even in New York we did find a degree
of support for our group typology. On a few of the issues
to confront the convention there emerged from within the
ranks of the Democrats a cluster of about 28 delegates
who aligned themselves against the other Democrats and
Republicans. All of the at-large elected Democrats were
included in this group, as well as a number of individuals
who had received the endorsement of the Liberal Party in
New York. That 10 of the 14 Democrats we had classified
as "reformers" and a number of "aspirants" and "statesmen"
comprised this group tends to confirm our belief that underlying the partisan cleavage in New York was a reform/
status-quo split.

The "reform" Democrats split away from their party in
significant proportions on approximately 16 of the 126 convention votes included in the analysis. The 16 votes en-
compass three general substantive areas that concerned the
convention: judicial reform, the establishment of the
State Department of Criminal Justice, and aid to nonpublic
schools. By supporting judicial reform, the "maverick"
Democrats were in effect endorsing the recommendations of
the then junior senator from New York, Robert F. Kennedy,
and opposing virtually all "regulars" from both parties,
including most of the 22 past or present judges sitting
in the convention. In supporting the consolidation of
criminal enforcement in the state, the "reformers" joined
then Governor Nelson Rockefeller and a number of convention Republicans in an effort to create a Criminal Justice
Department in the executive branch. In opposing the repeal of the ban on aid to nonpublic schools, the "reformers" and a relatively small number of allies from the larger

98

voting clusters were soundly defeated in their attempt "to preserve the separation of church and state."

It is very difficult to assess the impact of the "reform" Democratic faction on the convention because on no issue on which they defected did they come out on the winning side. That is not to say, however, that their presence in the convention and in particular their ability to act as a "swing" bloc on close votes was not responsible for moving the convention in a liberal direction. One newspaper account, for example, reported that a number of "reform" Democrats were about to support the Republican-sponsored amendment providing for four-year terms for state senators but two-year terms for assemblymen. By promising to liberalize the reapportionment scheme in the constitution, President Anthony Travia was alleged to have "won back" the votes of the "mavericks" to defeat the Republican bill.

That this division did not become more prominent during the deliberations can be attributed to the need for tight party discipline in a body in which the balance between the parties was relatively close. The Democratic leadership needed the support of the "liberal" element from among its ranks to win on almost all convention votes.

Rhode Island's partisanship was of a somewhat different kind--less strictly party-oriented than in New York. Actually, the familiar reform/status-quo cleavage emerged as the basic line of demarcation. There might have been some partisan line of division, but it was muted by the fact that roughly four-fifths of the delegates were Democrats and only one-fifth were Republicans. In contrast, New York's delegate body was quite evenly divided, with the Democrats only enjoying enough of a margin to claim partisan control.

Our factor analysis when applied to the Rhode Island delegates turned up two blocs that included all but 28 of the 100 delegates. The first, of 49, or just under half of the convention, was clearly status-quo-oriented. All of its members were Democrats, except for one lone Republican. Its more interesting characteristic was the heavy proportion of the previously identified status-quo-oriented delegates in this bloc, 29 of the 46. Sixteen of the convention's 21 legislator delegates also clustered within status quo. (Seven more of the status-quo delegates ended up in the other bloc, and the rest had sufficiently variable behavior to land in the group, which did not cluster to a significant degree at all.) On the issue survey, this group of delegates also voted as a bloc in a status-quo direction on each of the 10 sample items.

The second of the two Rhode Island blocs, we called the reform bloc. This was justified by the fact that it contained 17 of the 20 Republicans (most of whom had a generally reform bent) plus 6 of the 13 preidentified reformers. The remaining seven reformers fell in neither bloc. On 9 of the 10 sample issues, this group of delegates cast their vote for the reform position. In short, it became clear that though the party division seemed (and was) of considerable importance in explaining the make-up of the two blocs that emerged from our voting analysis, the reform/status-quo cleavage was more important and was the key to analyzing the behavior of the convention as a whole. This point is further underscored by the fact that 26 of the 28 delegates unaccounted for were Democrats, showing that it was not so much the party as such that made up the status-quo bloc, but rather a legislative faction plus its allies.

"SEMI-STRUCTURED" CONVENTIONS:
ILLINOIS AND NEW MEXICO

In none of the nonpartisan conventions was the voting behavior as structured as it was in New York and Rhode Island. In this section we will discuss the two nonpartisan conventions that seemed to exhibit the most structure. In both Illinois and New Mexico, three significant blocs of delegates were identified by the factor analysis.

In Illinois the three blocs that emerged encompassed 83 of 116 delegates. The largest cluster of delegates was heavily Democratic and Chicago-oriented. Thirty-three of the 34 delegates were Democrats; 32 represented the city of Chicago. In addition, 22 of our preidentified standpatters and stand-ins also clustered within this bloc, which we labeled the Chicago-Democratic bloc.

The second largest cluster was heavily Republican: 25 of its 27 members indicated a preference for the GOP. Geographically its members were drawn heavily from downstate (20 of 27), with most of the remaining members coming from suburban Cook County. Since 15 of the delegates had been identified prior to the convention as "status quo" types, this bloc also appeared to be "standpat"-oriented. We called this group the downstate-Republican bloc.

The third bloc had a very different composition. It had eight Democrats, nine Republicans, and five independents; it contained 15 of the 33 previously categorized reformers in the convention, and its members were scattered geographically with nine from downstate, six from suburban Cook County, and seven from Chicago. On the basis of its group membership, it appeared to be a reform-oriented cluster.

On the attitude survey discussed at the outset of this chapter, Illinois delegates expressed the view that the most important cleavage within their convention was between the interests of Chicago and the remainder of the state. Because the existing constitution in Illinois had something of a pro-Chicago bias in the sense that most major reforms would tend to undercut the power of Mayor Richard J. Daley's Chicago machine, it was not surprising that the general pattern of voting in the convention found the Chicago bloc opposed to the other two. Thus, what appeared to happen was that the Republican bloc, which ordinarily would seem to have a status-quo bias, frequently aligned itself with the reformers when the issues seemed to involve the power of the city of Chicago in Illinois politics.

An analysis of 39 roll calls that comprised the final vote on various parts of the completed document found that on 21 of the 39 at least three-fourths of the members of the reform and Republican blocs were lined up against at least three-fourths of the Chicago bloc. The discipline within the Chicago cluster is evidenced by the fact that on 19 of these 21 votes the bloc cohesion exceeded 90 percent. The subject matter of these hotly contested and divisive roll calls often dealt with matters of legislative or judicial selections, issues that posed severe challenges to the power of the Chicago Democratic Party organization within Illinois.

The Illinois case falls somewhere between the extreme case of partisanship in New York and the Maryland extreme of complete nonpartisanship, discussed below. In one sense the most important dividing line in Illinois may have been between reformers and supporters of the status quo, but across that line cut another division that separated urban Democrats from downstate, suburban, small-town, and rural delegates who were heavily Republican, both reform and status quo and who not infrequently coalesced against the Chicago "machine."

This finding underscores in a significant way points made earlier about the nature and extent of partisanship perceived in the Illinois convention and exemplified in the operation of the delegate selection scheme. In each instance the pattern reflected was that of a blend of partisanship and nonpartisanship, in the selection of candidates, in the working of the convention generally, and now in the mingling of status-quo/reform, and urban-Democrat/downstate-bipartisan voting.

The strong party organization in the state and a rural-urban conflict that overlay patterns of party competition minimized the impact of nonpartisanship to give the convention a rather partisan image, especially when crucial questions of political power were debated and voted upon.

The voting behavior in the New Mexico convention was similar to that in Illinois in that three significant blocs appeared and an important strain in the state's political culture manifested itself in the voting. The strength of the voting bloc relationships was not as strong in New Mexico as it was in Illinois. The three significant blocs accounted for 47 percent of the total variance and only 54 percent of the delegates clustered significantly within the three blocs. Yet it was quite clear from both the preconvention classification and an analysis of 32 of the most significant votes that a rather strong reform/status-quo split divided two of the groups.

In one bloc of 16 delegates (22 percent of the convention), 13 of the delegates were categorized as standpatter or stand-ins and on 24 of the 32 sample roll calls they voted as a bloc for the status-quo position. On none of the sample issues did this group vote for the reform position. A smaller group of seven delegates (10 percent of the convention) was clearly aligned against the standpatters. It was dominated by "reformers" and voted as a bloc for the reform position on 26 of the 32 issues. On 60 percent of the sample issues these two groups voted as a bloc in the opposite direction. It is interesting to note that on these issues the status-quo group won on 11 votes while the reformers won on 8. This finding lends support to the view expressed by the majority of the New Mexico delegates that the major cleavage that characterized the convention was that between reformers and those who wanted to keep things the same.

The second largest cluster of delegates consisted of 15 individuals who as a group seemed indistinguishable from the rest of the convention on a variety of standard demographic variables, including the distribution of preclassified group types. The one characteristic that was common to all members of the group, however, was their Spanish-American heritage. The New Mexico population consists of 28 percent Spanish-Americans; they constitute the major ethnic group within the state. In the convention itself an analysis of delegate surnames suggests that approximately

23 percent of the delegates were of Spanish-American background. The fact that a voting bloc consisting solely of Spanish-Americans emerged at the convention suggests that there was a Spanish-American interest represented at the constitutional convention.

On the sample issues the voting response of the Spanish-American bloc was haphazard. They voted as a bloc as reformers on 13 of the issues and as standpatters on eight issues. On the other 11 issues, they voted randomly. A comparison of the issues on which the Spanish-Americans voted as "reformers" or "standpatters" suggests that on items relating to court structure, individual rights, aid to parochial schools, college loans, 19-year-old vote, they were reformers. On items that would have curbed the power of the legislature, made several elective offices appointive, introduced a merit system, and provided for unicameralism, the Spanish-Americans supported the status quo. This behavior might be explained by the fact that members of the group had made some inroads into the legislature and bureaucracy in New Mexico, which might be threatened if the convention tampered with electoral and structural arrangements. On the other hand, they still viewed services provided by state government, the franchise, the courts, and the Bill of Rights as crucial ingredients to improving their lot in the economic, political, and social life of New Mexico. Constitutional reform in these areas seemed more desirable.

The conclusion one derives from the voting in Illinois and New Mexico is that although both conventions were ostensibly nonpartisan, in neither body did the delegates manage to free themselves completely from the kinds of partisan divisions that characterized the normal day-to-day politics in the states. We have argued throughout this study that constitution-making is an exercise in which questions of the distribution of political power will inevitably come to the forefront. The Chicago Democratic machine and the downstate Republicans in Illinois and the Spanish-Americans in New Mexico were of sufficient strength and organization to make their influence felt in the voting patterns. Thus, within the reform/status-quo context, which seemed to underlie both conventions, important strains in the political cultures of the respective states introduced a measure of structure and predictability in the voting patterns. The two states whose convention seemed to avoid this kind of division, Maryland and Arkansas, are considered in the next section.

THE UNSTRUCTURED CONVENTIONS:
MARYLAND AND ARKANSAS

The factor analysis leaves little doubt that the voting behavior in the Maryland and Arkansas conventions were the least structured of the six conventions. Four blocs appeared in Maryland and five in Arkansas; the percent of delegates who clustered significantly within those blocs was below 50 percent in both states. When compared with the other conventions, none of the conditions that tended to introduce structure into the voting in those bodies was present in either Maryland or Arkansas. Both the Maryland and Arkansas conventions were nonpartisan. In neither state was the balance between the parties in terms of delegates' expressed party affiliation close; Democrats had clear majorities in both states. Neither state had a strong rural-urban or ethnic conflict conditioning its partisanship, and in both states the myth that constitution-making was above politics seemed to permeate the debate about constitutional reform. Each of the factors helped to keep the conventions unstructured and introduced voting patterns that were often unpredictable and random.

The interesting point to observe about the unstructured conventions is that they seem to generate what might be called a "permissive atmosphere," which results in more random voting, to be sure but also allows the reform/status-quo cleavage to operate in an almost pure form. This was particularly true in Maryland.

The Maryland delegates did not sort themselves out into a neat two-bloc pattern. Rather, four blocs emerged, in addition to a group of 37 delegates who failed to cluster within any of the blocs. The first and largest of the four blocs (36 delegates), when examined for its salient characteristics, showed unmistakable "reformist" dimensions. It substantially overrepresented the various groups in the convention that one would normally associate with reform attitudes: urban delegates, blacks, Jews, women, and the younger members of the convention. In terms of our group typology the bloc was comprised almost entirely of reformers and supporting aspirants.

The second largest bloc consisted largely of male, non-Jewish Democrats with prior political experience. It also was dominated by our standpatters. The third and fourth blocs were more difficult to pinpoint from a demographic analysis because they represented in their membership a cross-section of the overall convention membership. But the third did overrepresent Republicans and in fact broke about half and half by party preference (in a convention that was 74 percent Democratic), which appeared to give it somewhat of a bipartisan orientation. The fourth cluster to emerge from the factor analysis was especially interesting in light of some of our earlier assertions about general convention alignments. Its salient characteristic was its very substantial overrepresentation of delegates from the rural parts of the state.

The issue analysis gave a rather clear picture of the orientation of the respective blocs. The figures bear out the identification of the first two blocs as, respectively, reform- and status-quo-oriented. The reformers went right down the line in favor of change, casting "bloc" votes on 22 of the 25 roll calls tabulated and giving a majority of their support to the reform position on all of the 25 issues. The status-quo bloc was somewhat less consistent but did cast status-quo-bloc votes on 16 of the 25 roll calls. They were won over to change twice to the extent of casting a bloc vote against the status quo, suggesting that they were less against change of any kind than they were intent on protecting elements in the existing document that were important to them or the groups and constituents they represented. Thus, despite its relative unstructured appearance, we can still observe in the two largest convention blocs an extremely clear division between reformers and the proponents of the status quo.

The bipartisan bloc was a swing bloc to a significant extent. It went with the reformers much of the time but did diverge from them on occasion. Bloc III's most important characteristic was that it votes the way the whole convention voted on all but one of the 25 roll calls. The nature of this bloc illustrates where the center of gravity of the convention was, how reform-oriented the assembly was, and, further, how extreme the reform position taken by reformers actually was. The rural bloc seems to have been mildly reformist, but in light of the point just made, was actually quite status quo, as one would have expected, in the context of the overall convention pattern. Some of the issues of reform that gained heavy rural bloc opposition were unicameralism, eliminating the elective comptroller and elective attorney general, and a provision that would have stripped counties of a guarantee of at least one district judge.

Our inability to explain adequately the two smaller blocs that emerged in Maryland as clearly as we had been able to pinpoint the nature of the "third" blocs in Illinois and New Mexico directed us to some further analysis of the data and an interesting finding. In addition to the 25 issues that dealt with matters of structural reform, we were also able to identify three roll calls designed to test how liberal or conservative the delegates were on questions relating to the scope of the role of governmental activity (for example, in promoting economic security of its citizens) and five more to test how liberal they were in the area of personal rights (for example, a provision to prohibit racial discrimination). Without going into the specific issues, we found that the pattern of bloc voting on "role of government" issues was different from that cast on "structural" votes. In a word, the reform and status-quo blocs were completely random in their response in this issue area but the rural bloc cast three clear bloc votes against an expanded role of government.

From this, we concluded that there is no necessary correlation between support for the status quo in the matter of the structure of government and a liberal or conservative attitude toward what government should do in solving social problems. The same sort of finding came out on the personal liberty votes, only here the reformers were also liberal, quite consistently, in their positions. But so too were the status-quo-bloc members on some of the roll calls, suggesting the general conclusion that political liberalism and an antipathy toward such innovations as unicameralism, single-member districts, and the elimination of political patronage positions did not appear to be contradictory responses to a number of delegates who composed the status-quo bloc.

Turning now to the Arkansas voting behavior as revealed by the factor analysis of roll calls in that convention, we discover a pattern of almost total fragmentation. Five blocs collectively accounted for only 29 percent of the total variance and included only 45 of the 100 delegates at factor loadings greater than 0.500. To guard against the possibility that the inordinate number of roll calls in Arkansas (1,052) had generated the fragmented pattern, we selected 40 of the most important votes and subjected them to a separate factor analysis. The results did not vary significantly on the second test.

Confronted with five rather small voting blocs ranging from 7 to 21 delegates and 10 less significant clusters with anywhere from 2 to 6 members in each, an analysis of bloc voting behavior proved to be an especially difficult task. We observed that within the most significant clusters there was a tendency for preclassified reformers to appear in one bloc and standpatters to cluster in another.

The fact suggested that despite the fragmented pattern, the reform/status-quo conflict was important in Arkansas.

With this fact in mind, we selected 10 of the most important roll calls to see what patterns of voting were revealed and what relationship the votes on these 10 issues bore to the factor analysis findings. The process of sifting out significant issues confirmed that the major portion of the policy agenda of the convention could be categorized in reform/status-quo terms. On the basis of the response of individual delegates to the sample items, we divided the delegate population into three groups: reformers, moderates, and status-quo delegates.*

The distribution of delegates on the reform index corresponded in a significant way to the groups identified by the factor analysis. Twenty-six of the 31 reformers on the 10-item index came from four of the blocs identified by the factor analysis, while 20 of the 23 status-quo delegates clustered with five other blocs. We plotted the issue-oriented delegate types against our preconvention typology (Table 4.2) and also noted a tendency for preclassified reformers to support the reform position and standpatters to endorse the status quo.

The conclusion suggested by the data is that Arkansas, like Maryland, was a convention patterned on the pure "statesman" model, the ideal of what conventions presumably ought to be. As in Maryland, party had been pretty effectively suppressed as a factor in deliberations and voting. It seems clear that the random pattern that emerged in the Arkansas convention was the result of the absence of party organization, the one-party Democrat nature of the convention, plus an absence of the kind of reform majority that obtained in Maryland. In Arkansas, on the other hand, no group was in a position to control the convention, and in fact no group was large enough to become the same kind of focus around which the decision-making process could orient itself, as the reformers became in Maryland.

All of this is not to say that the reform/status-quo division did not appear in Arkansas. Our investigations,

---

*The votes of the delegates on the 10 issues were recorded as either "reform" or "status quo." By scoring a +1 for each reform vote and a -1 for each status-quo vote, we could construct a reform index score for each delegate. Delegates scoring between +10 and +4 were labeled reformers; those individuals falling between +3 and -2 were called moderates; delegates scoring between -3 and -10 constituted the status-quo bloc.

using 10 selected roll calls as a means of categorizing voting roughly on reform, standpat lines, did produce groupings of reformers, status-quo delegates, and a middle group we called moderates. These patternings corresponded closely with our preidentified categories of reformers and status-quo-oriented delegates. They also displayed predicted characteristics whereby reformers were disproportionately Republican, independent, young, female, and urban. The status-quo delegates were disproportionately from southern and eastern Arkansas, the most rural, conservative and Southern-oriented areas of the state.

Thus in Arkansas, we did find that the status-quo/reform cleavage was present and was the only cleavage that could be systematically identified, though it was much less salient than in Maryland. The lesson of Arkansas, probably, is that the pure-statesman, idealized convention model does not work very well in the real world. Some kind of catalytic agent is important around which patterns of delegate behavior can develop. A further and closely related moral is that a high level of representativeness is not enough either, without such a catalytic agent. It may even compound the problem. As in Arkansas, voting and hence decision-making become too random and unstructured, and the body had too little ability to "mass" its membership.

VOTING: SOME CONCLUSIONS

The question of reform or keeping things the same was almost always the major consideration. In certain types of convention, this cleavage emerged in almost pure form, in which case the voting seemed to be unstructured and unusually random. In other conventions the reform/status-quo conflict was subsumed under other kinds of divisions, which usually resulted in much more structured voting patterns. From our investigation, four forces seem to be particularly significant in determining whether a convention tended toward the structured type assembly or conformed to a more fragmented pattern:

1. Those conventions that were organized in a partisan manner had structured voting patterns, usually along partisan lines in which two voting blocs appeared. On the other hand, conventions that were organized in a nonpartisan manner generated unstructured voting patterns that resulted in three or more significant voting blocs, which accounted for a smaller percentage of the voting behavior.

108

2. Those states whose politics was characterized by an intense urban-rural conflict or by other unusually strong strains in their political cultures evidenced more structured voting than in those states that lacked these divisions.

3. Conventions that were either partisan or nonpartisan in organization and where the balance between the parties were close were more apt to coalesce around structured bloc relationships than conventions in which one party dominated.

4. States that were able to sustain the view that constitution-making was above politics were likely to avoid the kind of structured bloc-voting relationships that appeared in conventions that operated under the assumption that constitution-making was more like an extension of everyday politics.

Table 4.5 attempts to portray graphically how each of the states fits into the pattern on each of the four factors. Despite the fact that one factor may have influenced another and that the table treats all factors as equally important to the total results, we do come out with findings that closely parallel the pattern revealed by the factor analysis. New York exhibits the qualities of a partisan structured convention on all four variables; Maryland and Arkansas fall perfectly into the unstructured category. The other states score in approximate proportion to the degree to which the factor analysis reported structured voting. For example, we can see from the table reasons why nonpartisanship may not have taken hold in Illinois as it did in other states and also why a convention like New Mexico, which on the surface seemed "above politics," fell into its own unique pattern. We do not have any pretensions that the same results would prevail in every state constitutional convention, but we do feel they contribute to an understanding of the kinds of dynamic behavior that are apt to influence convention decision-making.

LEADERSHIP

Another important aspect of state constitutional conventions is leadership. Constitutional conventions are essentially "new games." Traditions and overlapping memberships do not provide the body with any large degree of continuity, and therefore the "leadership structure" that governs the convention is theoretically more fluid than in the ordinary legislative context. The term "leadership struc-

TABLE 4.5

Factors Influencing Voting Behavior in Six Conventions

State	Partisan Organization	Heterogeneous Political Culture (major division that reinforces partisanship)	Close Balance Between Parties in Convention[a]	Partisan- or Legislative-Type Convention Image[b]	Total Yes
New York	Yes	Yes	Yes	Yes	4
Rhode Island	Yes	Yes	No	Yes	3
Illinois	No	Yes	Yes	Yes	3
New Mexico	No	Yes	No	No	1
Maryland	No	No	No	No	0
Arkansas	No	No	No	No	0

[a]We defined close balance as conventions where the majority party had less than 60 percent of the delegates.
[b]Whether a convention had a partisan or legislative-type convention image was a subjective judgment made by the authors on the basis of our familiarity with convention styles.

Source: Compiled by the authors.

ture" is used here to imply, first, that the leader is not
an isolated individual but is involved with other delegates
in a structure of role differentiation and personal inter-
actions, and, second, that leadership in the conventions
did not reside merely in one delegate but in several delegates representing major groups within the conventions.

To identify the leaders of the convention, an adaptation from sociometry was used to ascertain the delegates'
assessment of the "influence" of their fellow delegates.
"Influence" is defined as a relationship between two individuals in which the bahavior of one is determined in part
by the behavior of the other. It is the contention of this
study that one of the most reliable indicators of "influence" within any group is provided by the perceptions of
the members themselves. Consequently, the delegates were
asked to identify those individuals within the convention
whom they looked to for advice and leadership.

The identity of the leaders was only one part of the
investigation of convention leadership, however. With the
aid of open-ended questions administered during the postconvention interview, information was also gathered about
the nature of the activities that determined whether a delegate became influential.

Four aspects of convention leadership will be considered here. The first section is devoted to the delegates'
assessment of the role of leadership and its impact upon
the conventions. A second section discusses the role of
the convention president. Following an examination of the
general leadership structure in the seven conventions, we
conclude with a case study about the relationship between
voting behavior and leadership in two of the conventions.

DELEGATES' EVALUATION OF LEADERSHIP

At the conclusion of the deliberations of the conventions, we asked the delegates a number of questions about
the leadership in their respective bodies. (In some cases
our interview schedule varied from state to state, and we
do not have exactly comparable data in all instances.)
Table 4.6 reports the aggregate responses of the delegates
to questions about the importance of leadership, the importance of party leaders, and the degree to which power
in the respective conventions was either concentrated or
dispersed. The great majority of the delegates in all of
the states were in agreement that leadership was important
in influencing the course of the conventions' delibera-

TABLE 4.6

Leadership and Power in Seven Constitutional Conventions
(percent)

	New York	Rhode Island	Illinois	New Mexico	Maryland	Arkansas	Hawaii
I. "How important was leadership in the convention?"							
Very important	--	--	31	42	55	63	47
Somewhat important	--	--	28	33	24	21	30
Not very important	--	--	20	7	12	--	20
Not important	--	--	18	18	8	17	3
II. "How important was party leadership in the convention?"							
Very important	65	--	50	2	2	1	6
Somewhat important	19	--	36	12	10	2	15
Not very important	6	--	11	37	31	33	24
Not important	8	--	3	49	57	65	52
III. "To what extent was power concentrated in the convention?"							
Very concentrated	69	23	7	7	20	4	21
Somewhat concentrated	15	34	30	38	19	19	29
Somewhat dispersed	12	19	35	35	22	23	23
Very dispersed	4	23	28	19	36	48	26

Source: Compiled by the authors.

tions. The leadership structure seemed to bear little
relationship to party identification, except in New York
and Illinois, where we have already demonstrated that partisan considerations provided a significant input into the
life of the convention. (We do not have data for Rhode
Island on these questions.)

The question concerning the concentration of power
did not yield any dramatic differences among the various
conventions except that there was a tendency for the delegates in the so-called structured conventions, particularly
in New York, to perceive power to be more concentrated than
dispersed. Similarly, there was an inclination on the part
of delegates in the nonpartisan "unstructured" conventions
to view the power structure as more dispersed than concentrated. The differences are not always consistent across
the range of conventions, nor is there overwhelming unanim-
ity among the conventions about the degree to which power
was concentrated. However, in those conventions in which
the voting patterns were most structured, the delegates
also tended to perceive power as being more concentrated.

Another method of uncovering leadership style in
five states was to ask delegates to express their opinion
on what determined whether a delegate was an influential
member of the assembly. The data reported in Table 4.7
divide the reported influence attributes into two broad
categories--performance attributes and position attributes.
In all cases, but particularly in the least structured of
the assemblies, delegates were more often perceived to be
influential on the basis of their internal activities than
for their reputations or for positions they filled either
before or during the convention. One implication that
might be drawn from this finding is that a convention is
a more open operation than a legislature in the sense that
virtually any delegate with the know-how and ability to
lead can make his influence felt. Because they were not
part of permanent legislative bodies, delegates were not
as inhibited in their activities by the seniority and rules
and traditions that structure the behavior of most legislators.

To illustrate this point further, we note that an attribute that was most frequently cited as a key to understanding influence within the convention context was the
ability to speak and persuade in debate. This finding may
seem surprising to students of the legislative process in
light of the fact that in most legislative bodies formal
debate is often perfunctory in nature. The nature of decentralization that characterizes most legislative bodies

TABLE 4.7

Influence Determinants in Five Constitutional Conventions
(percent)

Influence Determinant	Illinois	Hawaii	Arkansas	Maryland	New Mexico
A. Performance attributes					
Ability to speak effectively and persuade in formal debate	28	11	21	45	--
General ability and intellectual competence	--	24	17	23	--
Subject matter expertise	14	24	16	19	--
Conscientiousness and hard work	--	16	8	10	--
B. Position attributes					
Formal convention leadership position	20	25	4	25	--
Prior reputation and experience	18	24	14	17	--
Follow leaders and favor by "in" group	--	--	--	8	--
Party loyalty	11	--	--	--	--

Note: Figures indicate percentages of delegates mentioning attribute. Multiple responses by delegates were allowed except in Illinois, where delegates' perception of most important attribute was cited.

Source: Compiled by the authors.

114

frequently assigns the bulk of decision-making power to specialized committees and in particular to their chairmen.

However, it was our observation that convention delegates were not as prepared to accept the recommendations of their committees to the same degree as their legislator counterparts. Committee reports frequently received a rather thorough scrutiny in the Committee of the Whole, and it was not unusual for a convention upon reconsideration to reverse a position it had taken earlier. The fact that the revised constitutions were hammered out on the floor of the convention put a particular premium upon the parliamentary and political skills of the various presidents of the conventions.

Although the delegates often cited what we have called "performance" attributes in identifying leadership traits, it was our observation that the individuals who were most often cited for their influence were those individuals who had acquired a preconvention reputation either in politics or some other venture that put their name before the public. An examination of the individuals cited for their influence by the delegates will illustrate this finding. Our first consideration will be with the convention president.

THE CONVENTION PRESIDENCY

Although the men who presided at the seven conventions are individuals in their own right and cannot be neatly categorized, their prior experience and career patterns suggest that they fall into two very broad categories. On the one hand, four of the presidents came to their convention positions on the basis of reputations gained in partisan politics. The three other leaders had acquired a stature in their respective states as established authorities on state constitutional law and had devoted significant portions of their careers to constitutional reform. Table 4.8 lists the presidents and a brief synopsis of their career patterns.

Although we cannot point to any one president or category of presidents as the ideal leader, our observations of the conventions and interviews with delegates uncovered a number of qualities that reveal much about the nature of the convention process and types of direction it requires. We have suggested elsewhere that

The primary qualities that make a good convention president appear to be: stature which makes for

TABLE 4.8

Convention Presidents

State	President	Position Held Before Convention
New York	Anthony P. Travia	Speaker of the House, New York General Assembly
Rhode Island	Dennis J. Roberts	Ex-Democratic governor
Illinois	Samuel W. Witwer	Member, Illinois Constitutional Study Commission and counsel for Illinois Committee for a Constitutional Convention
Hawaii	Hebden Porteus	Republican state representative
New Mexico	Bruce King	Ex-speaker of the House, elected governor after convention
Arkansas	Robert Leflar	Dean, University of Arkansas Law School
Maryland	Vernon J. Eney	Lawyer, chairman of Maryland Constitutional Revision Commission

Source: Compiled by the authors.

respect among his convention colleagues, a relatively non-partisan or neutral position among the various groups that make up the convention membership, skill at compromise and untangling political impasses, unmistakable reputation for fairness, and hopefully some flair for public relations or at least a realization that this is an important role that can probably be played or supervised by the President. Negatively, the President probably should not have any personal objectives of a specific nature in the revision process.[10]

A few illustrations from some of the conventions will shed some light upon the functions of presidential leadership in a constitutional convention.

Partisanship and issue neutrality were serious problems in some states--and most particularly in the Rhode Island convention. Former Governor Dennis Roberts won election to the presidency through a coalition of groups among the delegates who later were to take a generally reformist position, against the candidate of the legislative, status-quo faction. Thus from the start he was identified as a partisan. Furthermore, he had been pushing unicameralism even before the convention met. In light of the divisions that surfaced at this early stage, and in the absence of any potential leader of comparable prestige but greater neutrality, Roberts won relatively easily.

It became abundantly clear as the convention proceeded with its work that his partisanship was undercutting his leadership seriously. He came to occupy more and more the position of behind-the-scenes floor leader of the reform forces and not infrequently passed the gavel to the first vice president so that he could participate in debate on questions relating either to legislative or executive reform. This, so far as any available evidence suggests, ruled out any role as a mediator or compromiser, and pitted the status-quo supporters against the convention chairman as well as against their opponents on the floor. Rather than exerting a moderating influence, the chairman acted wittingly or otherwise to exacerbate some of the divisions. That did not prove to be a viable model for convention leadership.

The problem with the leadership in the New York convention was a broader one than the selection of Anthony Travia, Democratic speaker of the General Assembly. Rather, it was the fact that the convention replicated the legislature so closely, which in turn virtually assured not only that Speaker Travia would be chosen by the partisan Democratic majority but also that the floor leadership system of the legislature, and its personnel, would be transferred to and used in the convention. Thus the leadership problem in the Empire State was less one of personality than the overall partisan pattern into which the body had itself locked.

In Hawaii, a kind of bipartisanship emerged that turned out well for the convention. The convention, though nominally nonpartisan, was in fact controlled, or could have been, by a 68 percent Democratic majority, many of them sitting legislators. Nevertheless, a longtime legis-

117

lator from the Republican side of the aisle, Hebden Porteus, was chosen president and moved decisively to reassure the nonpoliticians among the delegates that it would be an open convention and not a replication of the legislature. Porteus' selection from the minority party stemmed from a Democratic split, which dictated a neutral outside candidate, plus consciousness of the bad image earned by both the Rhode Island and New York conventions. A Republican of stature could do much to avoid this problem, and Porteus was praised for his work. Thus almost by accident Hawaii hit upon a bipartisan leadership scheme that proved eminently successful and largely avoided the kind of leadership problems posed by the strictly partisan or nonpartisan conventions.

The advantages of the nonpartisan president were revealed most clearly in Illinois. President Samuel Witwer came to the leadership of the convention following a deep and active concern with constitutional revision stretching back into the 1940s. To many he was the logical head of the body when it convened, and though challenged by some, his choice was eventually unanimous. He was a Republican and relatively conservative on policy questions but an ardent reformer where state constitutions were concerned. The success of the convention and the acceptance of its handiwork were in no small measure due to him. He took as among his chief concerns, keeping business moving and overcoming major threats to the cohesiveness and hence the operation of the body. That the convention was somewhat partisan in nature also aided Witwer because it relieved him of much of the burden of selling the convention product once the deliberations were completed.

The limitations of a nonpartisan leader are suggested by the Maryland experience. Vernon Eney was a man of enormous ability, a highly successful Baltimore lawyer, and had served as the chairman of the Constitutional Convention Commission. He finally won in a three-way contest with two legislators when it came time to elect a convention president. Generally, his presidency was praised highly. "Without Vernon Eney, the convention would have ended in disaster" was a frequent comment. However, he failed to press a vigorous public information campaign and did not provide the kind of leadership in the ratification campaign that turned out to be so crucial in Maryland. The occasional criticism by convention liberals and others who felt the weight of his iron control over deliberations also clouds the picture somewhat. It is probably true that the Maryland delegate body was so thoroughly atomized and unstructured that Eney's firm control was essential but bound to cause some restlessness in so independent a body. In retrospect the detachment of the nonpartisan leader from "regular" politics can inhibit the relationship of the convention with the body politic. This becomes a particularly crucial problem during the ratification campaign.

There is no question but that the president of the convention is the single most important delegate. In all but one of the conventions, the president was the individual cited most often for his influence by the other delegates both before and after the convention deliberations. In the convention context, a successful president must be a master of procedure and a skillful compromiser rather than the avowed champion of a particular constitutional philosophy. In the ideal sense, he is the manager of the deliberations, the purveyor of the convention image, and the most active defender of the revised constitution. Those presidents who became too involved in particular reform proposals and who failed to understand their role as a link with the general citizenry did not provide the complete kind of leadership the convention required.

GENERAL LEADERSHIP PATTERNS

Convention leadership, however, extended beyond the president. The data in Table 4.9 summarize the findings from our efforts to uncover the scope and distribution of leadership in the seven conventions both at the outset of the deliberations and again at the conclusion of the conventions. Approximately 82 percent of the delegates were nominated at least once by other delegates for their influence prior to the convention. The average delegate was mentioned an average of 8.6 times. By the end of the convention 91 percent of the delegates had been mentioned and the average number of mentions received by delegates had risen to 11.4. In all of the conventions the percentage of delegates receiving leadership nominations and the average number of nominations received by each delegate increased from the pre- to the postconvention interview.

Prior to the convention deliberations, the 10 percent of the delegates in each convention receiving the most nominations accounted for an average of 48 percent of all leadership nominations. In all of the conventions that percentage declined as the convention met and as more of the delegates became known to their colleagues. The data suggest that almost all delegates were "influential" to

TABLE 4.9

Leadership Nominations in Seven Conventions

State	Number Delegates	Preconvention			Postconvention		
		Percent Delegates Receiving Leadership Nominations	Average Number Nominations Received per Delegate	Percent Nominations Received by Top 10 Percent Delegates	Percent Delegates Receiving Leadership Nominations	Average Number Nominations Received per Delegate	Percent Nominations Received by Top 10 Percent Delegates
New York	186	77	9.0	53	88	9.6	42
Rhode Island	100	--	--	--	64	6.5	64
Illinois	116	84	6.0	54	92	11.9	34
Hawaii	82	79	5.7	46	82	9.0	37
New Mexico	70	96	9.3	45	99	10.5	29
Arkansas	100	84	9.3	49	100	12.9	36
Maryland	142	75	13.5	45	87	14.4	43
Average*	--	82	8.6	48	91	11.4	36.7

*The averages for the preconvention interviews exclude Rhode Island, whose survey was taken during the middle of convention deliberations.

Source: Compiled by the authors.

TABLE 4.10

Leadership Stability in Six Constitutional Conventions

State	Number Delegates in Top 10 Percent	Percent Delegates in Top 10 Percent Pre- and Postconvention	Postconvention Top 10 Percent Who Had Been in Top 20 Percent on Preconvention
New York	19	79	95
Illinois	12	67	75
Hawaii	8	50	88
New Mexico	7	71	100
Arkansas	10	90	100
Maryland	14	78	100
Average	70	75	93

Source: Compiled by the authors.

some extent in the convention, particularly at the conclusion of the conventions, and that the leadership structure became less concentrated during the course of the deliberations. Although the leadership structure of the respective conventions became less centralized, the persons most often cited for their leadership ability tended not to change significantly from the pre- to the postconvention interview. Table 4.10 shows that as a group, 74 percent of the delegates who were in the highest 10 percent in terms of the number of leadership nominations received at the outset of the conventions, reappeared in that list at the end of the convention. Most of the delegates who made the top 10 percent list at the end of the convention, who had not been there on the first interview, made only a slight jump in rank from the first to the second interview. Thus, despite the alleged openness of the convention deliberations, the hierarchy of influence in the respective assemblies remained relatively stable.

Our data suggest that "position" may have been as crucial as "performance" in determining who were the most influential delegates in the seven conventions. Table 4.11 identifies the "leaders" in terms of the positions they held in the convention or had held prior to the convention. The list includes the convention president in every convention, most of the vice presidents, large numbers of commit-

121

TABLE 4.11

Positions Held by Individuals Cited Most Often for Their Influence

Position	New York	Rhode Island	Illinois	Hawaii	New Mexico	Arkansas	Maryland
Convention president	1	1	1	1	1	1	1
Convention vice-president	3	--	2	1	2	1	2
Committee chairman, vice-chairman	8	7	5	3	3	3	4
Convention majority leader, minority leader	2	--	--	--	--	--	--
Revision committee members	--	--	--	--	--	3	--
Judge, ex-judge	1	--	--	--	--	--	3
Legislators, ex-legislators	3	1	1	1	--	1	--
Ex-congressmen	--	--	--	--	--	--	1
Educators	--	--	--	2	--	--	2
Other	1	1	3	2	1	1	1
Total	19	10	12	8	7	10	14

Source: Compiled by the authors.

tee chairman and vice chairman, and a number of individuals who had held or were holding prominent positions in the states' political structures. Less than 10 percent of the leadership could not be identified by an important official position. Thus, what on paper appeared to be a very fluid leadership structure, in actuality was quite stable and redounded most frequently to the advantage of those individuals who had distinguished themselves in some way prior to the convention deliberation.

This aggregate analysis of leadership is necessarily general and hides the fact that the leadership structure that emerged was not monolithic. The range and scope in leadership within a convention was important in determining the output that emerged from the convention. We cannot examine fully the internal leadership structure of each of the conventions, but the following section describes the important relationship we found to exist between leadership perception and voting behavior in two of the conventions.

LEADERSHIP PERCEPTION AND VOTING BEHAVIOR

An interesting question posed by the data is the relationship between leadership perception and voting behavior. Specifically, was there a positive relationship between voting and the cue-giving and cue-taking process that occurred in the conventions? It is not possible to develop this relationship fully for all of the conventions, but we have selected one representative of the structured conventions (New Yori) and one from the unstructured types (Maryland) to illustrate the relationship.

The data for New York prove rather conclusively that a strong relationship between leadership perception and voting occurred. The impact of party within the New York convention can be measured by analyzing the scope and distribution of intra- and interparty leadership perception patterns that occurred both before and during the convention. Table 4.12 computes the percentage of maximum possible leadership perceptions among the delegates by party. On both interview schedules, Republicans and Democrats tended to perceive influence in members of their own party in far greater proportions than they did with opposition party delegates. For example, Democrats in the convention "looked to" other members of their party for leadership at a rate of 7.8 percent of the maximum possible perceptions before the convention began and 10.5 percent after the convention had completed its work. They looked to Re-

TABLE 4.12

Leadership Perception Among New York Convention Delegates,
by Party
(perception of maximum possible mentions)
(percent)

| | Democrats | | Republicans | |
Leadership	Pre-convention	Post-convention	Pre-convention	Post-convention
Democrats look to	7.8	10.5	3.7	4.0
Republicans look to	1.2	2.8	7.3	10.9

Source: Compiled by the authors.

publicans for leadership at rates of only 3.7 percent prior
to the convention and 4 percent following the deliberations.
When considered in conjunction with the attitude and voting
patterns discussed in earlier chapters, these data seem to
reinforce the notion that organized party activity was the
pivotal consideration in shaping the informal behavior pattern in New York as well.

In the unstructured context of the Maryland convention,
the process of identifying the relationship between leadership perception and voting behavior is more difficult. Table 4.13A plots the distribution of leadership nominations
within and among the four Maryland voting blocs. The voting
blocs are arranged on a continuum ranging from the most "reformist" at one extreme to the most "status quo" at the other. Cell scores represent a percentage distribution of leadership nominations directed by the members of each voting
bloc to their own group and to the other three voting clusters. Percentages are computed by dividing the actual number of leadership nominations directed by one group to itself or another group by the total possible nominations that
could have occurred if every member of the sending group had
nominated every member of the receiving group--for example,
if every "reform" delegate had nominated every other "reform" delegate as a leader, the percentage would have been
100 percent. Note that the actual number of mentions of
"reformers" by "reformers" consisted of 22.6 percent of

TABLE 4.13

Distribution of Leadership Nominations, by Voting Bloc
and by Four Group Variables
(in percents)

A. Distribution by Voting Bloc

	Sending Blocs*			
	I	II	III	IV
			Moder-	
		Moder-	ate	
		ate	Status	Status
Receiving Blocs	Reform	Reform	Quo	Quo
Bloc I. Reform	22.5	13.8	3.9	4.6
Bloc II. Moderate reform	16.8	26.9	11.4	9.0
Bloc III. Moderate status quo	16.8	25.1	28.0	18.1
Bloc IV. Status quo	2.5	2.0	2.1	13.3

B. Distribution by Four Group Variables

Variable	Within Variable	Without Variable	Solidarity Difference
1. Voting bloc	21.8	9.5	12.3
2. Committee membership	15.3	11.9	3.4
3. Region represented	14.8	12.1	2.7
4. Party	12.3	10.7	1.6

*This portion of the table should be read downward.
The nominating blocs are across the top of the table; the
nominated groups are along the side. For example, reformers nominated status-quo delegates at a rate of 2.5 percent; status-quo delegates nominated reformers at a rate
of 4.6 percent.

Source: Compiled by the authors.

the maximum possible nominations; "reformers" nominated "moderate reformers" at a rate of 16.8 percent of the total possible nominations, and so on.

The data confirm that a positive relationship existed between voting behavior and leadership perception. With the exception of the "status-quo" bloc, delegates nominated members of their own voting cluster more than they did other delegates. It is also significant that the percentages decline consistently the further the voting groups become separated on the reform/status-quo continuum.

To illustrate the predominance of voting blocs as a determinant of leadership selection, we also computed leadership distribution rates for party, regional, and committee subgroups within the convention. That data, together with a condensed version of voting bloc data, are summarized in Table 4.13B. The percentages are computed in the same way as 4.13A except that the scores appear only from a "within-group" and a "without-group" basis. The difference between the within and without scores we call the "solidarity difference." This figure is a measure of the extent to which a subgroup affiliation (party, region, committee, or voting bloc) was associated with broader scopes of leadership nominations among members of a specific subgroup as opposed to nonmembers of that category. The larger the solidarity difference, the more significant are within-group leadership nominations as opposed to without-group nominations.

Solidarity differences were positive on each of the four subgroup dimensions--that is, members nominated leaders from their own subgroups more than they did delegates from outside their groups. The range of solidarity differences, however, demonstrates that of the four group measurements, voting bloc affiliation, with a solidarity difference of 12.3 percent, was by far the most significant variable in structuring leadership perception. In a legislative setting remarkably free of preexisting party and factional groupings, leadership perceptions of the delegates generally paralleled the relationship that existed between voting behavior and shared attitudes on broad policy issues.

The major objective of the last two chapters has been to uncover the patterns of delegate behavior that characterized the internal politics of the seven constitutional conventions. To accomplish this task, a wide range of data was used to measure delegate attitudes and actual behavior patterns. The intent was to show how the transition from attitude response to actual decision-making choices was made. The hypothesis that underlay this endeavor was that there is an important relationship between attitudes and behavior that helps to explain the nature and direction of the policy output generated by the convention. The final link in this cycle is the actual product to emerge from the conventions. The next chapter will examine the revised constitutions produced by the seven conventions.

NOTES

1. See Samuel Patterson, "Patterns of Interpersonal Relations in a State Legislative Group," Public Opinion Quarterly 23 (Spring 1959): 101-09; Garland Routt, "Interpersonal Relationships and Legislative Process," Annals of the American Academy of Political and Social Science, 195 (January 1938): 129-36; Wayne L. Francis, "Influence and Interaction in a State Legislative Body," American Political Science Review 56 (December 1962): 953-60; and Cleo H. Cherryholmes and Michael J. Shapiro, Representatives and Roll Calls (New York: Bobbs Merrill, 1969).

2. Duncan Macrae, Jr., Issues and Parties on Legislative Voting: Methods of Statistical Analyses (New York: Harper & Row, 1970), pp. 4-5.

3. Wayne Francis, "The Role Concept in Legislatures," Journal of Politics 27 (August 1965): 568.

4. Richard D. Marvel, "The Nonpartisan Nebraska Unicameral," Midwest Legislative Politics, ed. by Samuel C. Patterson (Iowa City: University of Iowa Institute of Public Affairs, 1967), pp. 89-120.

5. A Lawrence Lowell, "The Influence of Party upon Legislation in England and America," Annual Report of the American Historical Association for 1901 I (Washington, D.C., 1902), pp. 321-544; Stuart A. Rice, Quantitative Methods in Politics (New York: Alfred A. Knopf, 1928); Julius Turner, Party and Constituency: Pressures on Congress (Baltimore: Johns Hopkins Press, 1951). More recent studies are David B. Truman, The Congressional Party: A Case Study (New York: John Wiley and Sons, 1959); and David Mayhew, Party Loyalty Among Congressmen (Cambridge, Mass.: Harvard University Press, 1966).

6. Samuel Patterson, "Dimensions of Voting Behavior in a One Party State 'Legislative,'" Public Opinion Quarterly 26 (1962): 185-200.

7. John G. Grumm, "A Factor Analysis of Legislative Behavior," Midwest Journal of Political Science 7 (November 1963): 336-56.

8. Bruce M. Russett, "Discovering Voting Groups in the United Nations," American Political Science Review 60 (June 1966): 327-39.

9. The factor analysis used for this study was adapted from MESA I, programmed by Clarence Bradford at the University of Chicago and described in Lee F. Anderson et al., Legislative Roll Call Analysis (Evanston, Ill.: Northwestern University Press, 1966), pp. 123-74, 196. The program performs a "Q" type analysis; in other words, it isolates clusters of delegates who vote together as opposed to the "R" analysis, which groups issues that evoke a common response. The program computes a principle-components solution and a varimax orthogonal rotation. It utilizes a product-moment correlation coefficient and under our adaptation can handle up to 200 variables. For a more complete account of the nature of the differences between "Q" and "R" type factor analysis see Grumm, op. cit., pp. 338-39. Two applications of the "R" type analysis can be found in Chester V. Harriss, "A Factor Analysis of Selected Senate Roll Calls, 80th Congress," Educational and Psychological Measurement 8 (Winter 1948): 583-91; and Gerald Marwell, "Party, Region, and the Dimensions of Conflict in the House of Representatives, 1949-1954," American Political Science Review 61 (June 1967): 380-99.

10. Elmer E. Cornwell, Jr., Jay S. Goodman, and Wayne R. Swanson, Constitutional Reform by Convention (New York: National Municipal League, 1973), Chapter 4.

5

THE CONSTITUTIONS

The ultimate concern of the student of state government and of constitutional revision is, of course, the
substantive product a convention turns out. The draft
documents in the seven states considered in this study
will therefore be the central consideration in the present
chapter. Any broad comparative or "macro'-analysis of the
links between the composition and operation of the conventions and their products is made difficult by the complexity of the relationships involved. To the extent that this
can be done, however, we will attempt it in this chapter.

The primary sources of difficulty are in the different
political cultures of the states and the sharply variant
documents with which each convention began its work, from
the point of view of archaic or modern qualities. Joseph
Schlesinger in a study of the power of the governorship in
the then 48 states found that when four dimensions of that
power were scored and an index figure was computed, the
range was from a "perfect" 19 points (enjoyed only by the
New York chief executive) to a low of 8 (in four states:
Mississippi, South Carolina, Texas, and North Dakota).[1]
Virtually every interval on the scale in between found
several governors functioning at that level.

Thus, a defender of the status quo in the Empire State
or one of the others whose governing arrangements had been
"modernized" over recent decades would find himself re-
sisting the "reform" of a system that to delegates in another state already represented the essence of revolutionary
radicalism. In other words, constitutional arrangements
and their revision efforts will vary from state to state.
They will vary as existing state constitutions compare
with the aspirations of local reformers for change in each

state. They also vary with local tradition and with what the culture of the state defines as acceptable.

From the point of view of documentary change, therefore, a convention may take a constitution that by any objective national standard is a museum piece, make fundamental and relatively quite radical changes in it, and still produce a result that in other jurisdictions would look old-fashioned and inadequate. The concepts of status-quo and reform orientation are, accordingly, themselves primarily relative notions. Therefore the only kinds of statements that can be made with assurance in comparing revised constitutions are statements (of the sort we will come to later in this chapter) that relate these to their predecessor charters, on the one hand, and to the National Municipal League's Model State Constitution[2] as a national standard, on the other.

Why conventions produce the results they do depends upon a number of complicated variables operating in a long time sequence. It depends on the mix of delegates, but that in turn depends on the cultural milieu from which they were chosen and the ways in which they were or were not representative of that milieu. It depends on the existing constitution and where it falls on a continuum running from the totally archaic to the ideally modern. This in turn depends on the history, traditions, cultural values (or prejudices), and sense of urgency that characterize the context in which the convention operates.

In this chapter, we will begin with the presentation and analysis of interview data relating to what the delegates to the various conventions saw as the key issues that would confront the bodies to which they had been elected. It is reasonable to assume that these perceptions were an important linkage between the public and the convention because they had to be formed in part at least by the delegates' interpretations of what was wanted or acceptable along with what they personally felt was needed. These perceptions are also important linkages between the convention and the final product, in that emphases existing in the delegates' minds would be expected to be goals that they would pursue in the operations of the body.

The question asked of the delegates was, "In your opinion, what would you say the five most important issues before the convention are?" They were then asked to rank these in order of importance. (This question was not asked in the single round of interviews used in the pilot Rhode Island study; hence data for Rhode Island do not appear in the tabulations in Tables 5.1, 5.3, and 5.4 or the accom-

panying discussion.) The data presented in the following
tables represent a tabulation of these replies. For immediate purposes the rankings were not taken into account,
and the five mentioned issues were treated as of equal
salience. (We decided not to use for this purpose the
point scoring system, which we had used elsewhere to rank
these replies. That had involved five points for first
choices down to one point for fifth choices. The risk
in such a system for the use being made of the data here
was that it would exaggerate differences that in many instances were not very great in the minds of the respon-
dents.) Table 5.1 summarizes the total pattern of replies
under the major headings that represent the topics dealt
with in state constitutions generally. All replies relating to each heading, whether general or specific (for example, whether citing the Bill of Rights without specification, or a particular "right," are tabulated under the one
heading). The figures are percentages computed to show the
proportion of the total number of individual replies given
that fell under the heading listed.

Several patterns emerge in the table. In each state
column, one finds, obviously, that the pattern is partly a
reflection of local concerns and the state of the existing
document but also a mirror of concerns that happened to be
uppermost nationally at the time. Generally, if one compares the states with one another by reading across the
rows on the table, we would expect that the greater the
variation in the percentages, the more likely it is that
the data reflect local patterns. On the other hand, where
the figures are more nearly similar from state to state,
one can presume that current national concerns were influential.

A comparison of the data relating to reform of the
executive branch with those for local government as an issue suggests the point. The figures on the executive range
from a 1.5 in Hawaii and 4.5 for New York to 25.5 in New
Mexico. Here is an area in which, as we have already noted
from the Schlesinger study, state variation is very high.
New York's constitution has long provided for a strong executive, as does the relatively new document in Hawaii.
Maryland, New Mexico, and Arkansas, on the other hand,
have provisions that are far from "modern" and leave much
room for "reform." In this policy area, therefore, convention attention seems to have varied in relation to existing
considerations in each state. The range of variation on
local government, however, is much narrower. If one takes
into account the fact that Hawaii has minimal provisions

131

TABLE 5.1

Delegate Perceptions of Five Most Important Issues: Summarized by Major
Constitutional Categories
(percentages of total replies in each state)

Constitutional Category	Maryland	New York	Hawaii	New Mexico	Arkansas	Illinois
Bill of Rights	8.0	11.0	3.0	3.5	1.0	8.0
Suffrage and elections	5.0	6.5	8.0	6.5	3.5	--
Legislative branch	13.5	23.0	39.5	5.5	10.0	12.0
Executive branch	21.5	4.5	1.5	25.5	18.0	8.0
Judicial branch	19.5	17.5	13.5	11.5	14.5	15.5
Local government	19.5	18.5	9.0	9.0	18.0	18.5
Shape of document, amending process	1.5	1.5	1.0	3.5	4.5	5.5
Substantive policy issues	10.0	17.0	23.5	34.0	26.5	30.5
Miscellaneous replies	0.5	--	1.5	1.5	3.5	1.5
Total	99.0	99.5	100.5	100.5	99.5	99.5

Source: Compiled by the authors.

for local government of any kind, then most of the remaining states reflect a relatively uniform level of concern, with "home rule" as the key issue.

Concern with the shape of the court system and the judicial branch is also shown to be widespread and relatively uniform, while the variations regarding the legislature are as great as any on the table. Judicial reform seems also to be a matter of nationwide concern, while legislative reform varies in interest both with the intensity of focus on reapportionment (as in Hawaii) and the desire for institutional reform or preservation of the institutional status quo. Among the most striking variations on the table are those relating to substantive policy issues. Note that, in four of the states, from a quarter to a third of all of the issue areas mentioned related not to structural considerations but to policy matters. This last finding serves to emphasize the differences in constitutional tradition and, ultimately, in political culture among the states.

Table 5.1 depicts the advance perceptions of the delegates about the central issues they faced. The next question is: What in fact did their respective conventions produce by way of revised documents? In the next section we shall summarize the draft constitutions and then relate them both to what the delegates anticipated and to the "ideal standard" for state charters represented by the model state constitution.

THE REVISED DOCUMENTS

Rhode Island

The 1842 constitution, which the delegates met in 1964 to change or replace, was (and is) a brief document, generally economical in its language and devoted for the most part to structural provisions and principles. It falls short of the ideal in several respects but not because of prolixity or inclusion of inappropriate legislative matter. By the same token, the prime issues that concerned the convention were ones relating to structure: the terms of executive and legislative officials, the composition of the General Assembly, the setup and personnel of the court system, and local government.

In discussing each of the revised documents, we will follow an outline starting with a bill of rights and suffrage, continuing through the legislative, executive, and judicial branches, local government, miscellaneous provisions, and constitutional change. The Rhode Island Bill of Rights was left largely untouched. Imprisonment for debt was dropped, a wiretapping ban was instituted, and federal due process and equal protection language were added. Regarding suffrage, a mass of detail in the original document and its amendments was superseded by a brief article that cut state residence to six months from one year, left local residence at six months, and gave the General Assembly broad powers to deal by statute with registration, absentee voting, shorter residence for presidential electors, and related matters. Most of these had been spelled out in the constitution before.

A concerted drive was mounted before the convention even met for a unicameral legislature. This failed, guaranteeing that the general structure of the legislative branch would remain more or less the same. Thus, the new document provided for a 40-member senate (slightly smaller than the last one elected pursuant to the provisions of the constitution of 1842 as amended), left the 100-member house unchanged in size, and stipulated that both should be elected strictly by population rather than by city and town, as previously. The Supreme Court would take over redistricting if the Assembly failed to do its duty after each census. The absurd $300 annual salary was eliminated in favor of a provision allowing the legislators to set their own pay. The veto power of the governor was strengthened a bit (though not via institution of a proposed item veto). Three-fifths in each house could still override, but the chief executive would now have 10 days (versus 6) to sign or veto and 30 days (as against 10) to deal with measures on his desk following adjournment.

As the last two sentences imply, there was no more disposition to make sweeping changes in the governorship than in the legislature. Proposals for strengthening the office in various ways, including a four-year term, did not make it into the revision. (The four-year term ultimately foundered on the insistence by the legislatively inclined delegates that the Assembly members should have whatever liberalized term was accorded the governor.) Therefore, the only changes to be found in the new executive article were essentially "housekeeping" ones. The right of the governor to appoint department heads with Senate approval was shifted from a statutory to a constitutional basis. The same was done with the existing legal mandate to submit operating and capital budgets.

Efforts to make currently elective officials like the
attorney general, secretary of state, and general treasurer
appointive, and to bracket the lieutenant governor with the
governor on the ballot, failed of acceptance, leaving the
status quo undisturbed. An elaborate provision to deal
with succession and disability among the "general officers,"
particularly the governor, and giving the Supreme Court
the role of final arbiter in case of dispute, was added.

A number of suggestions for revision of the court system and/or incorporation of more of it into the constitution (all courts now exist by statute save the Supreme
Court) were made, but most won only limited support. As
a result, the new judicial article added little beyond
rather elaborate retirement and disability provisions,
which had been largely lacking. By contrast, the convention did its most significant innovating in the local government area. This subject had only figured in the old
constitution in a home rule amendment. Now it was to become an article, based on the new principle that towns
and cities should, by constitutional mandate, be able to
legislate in any area not preempted by the constitution
or legislature. This reversed the Dillon rule presumption
that local governments could do nothing unless specifically
allowed.

In other ways the old document was tidied up. A lottery prohibition was removed. Provisions relating to
borrowing were updated. Amendment was made somewhat easier.
Now one General Assembly passage by absolute majority instead of two, followed by a referendum, was to be sufficient, and a simple voter majority could validate an
amendment instead of the former three-fifths. Finally,
the right of the General Assembly to call conventions was
written into the document, coupled with a requirement that
the question be put before the electorate at least every
10 years.

In general, the Rhode Island convention was a stand-
pat body bent on making relatively few changes in the status
quo. For the most part it did housekeeping chores while
leaving the overall document much in its original shape,
with structural prescriptions largely unchanged.

New York

Two features of the constitution of the State of New
York as it existed when the convention of 1967 met pro-
foundly affected that body's work. First, the Empire State

had, over the years, equipped itself with a charter that
in many ways was one of the most modern in the nation.
As the Schlesinger study indicated, no state in the union
had gone as far as New York in adopting the model of the
strong, unified executive under a powerful governor. Secondly, the state had developed a tradition of doing a good
deal of its substantive policy-making business via the
constitution. Often this was done through the amendment
procedure, but conventions of course lend themselves to
the same purpose on a broad scale. The Democrats, in control of the 1967 convention but often in a minority in the
legislature, put much of their effort into this kind of
substantive legislating.

A combination of these two factors shaped the kind
of changes that the convention made. For example, there
were a number of additions to the Bill of Rights. Federal
language on speech, press, assembly, petition, and the establishment of religion was added. Citizen lawsuits to
restrain unconstitutional acts or expenditures were provided for; stricter wiretapping and eavesdropping controls
were drafted; discrimination on the basis of sex, age, or
physical/mental handicap was proscribed; compensation
rights were broadened for public damage to private property; and governmental records were not to be open. Particularly illustrative of legislation by constitution were
provisions for the education and protection of consumers,
and a declaration of the policy of the state to foster
and promote economic security. In the suffrage area, literacy and property qualifications were ruled out, some adjustments were made in residence requirements, and the
legislature was given authority to lower the voting age
to a minimum of 18.

Relatively few revisions of consequence were made relating either to the legislative or executive branches--
areas that commanded major attention in states with less
modernized existing charters. Aside from slight adjustment
in the size of the Senate (it was increased from 57 to 60
members), the major new provisions related to reapportionment. Redistricting by statute was replaced with a five-
man commission and subsequent review by the Court of Appeals. A couple of minor procedural changes were made,
but overall the state's legislature was left very much as
it had been.

Even fewer changes were made in the executive branch.
As to the governor, the only addition was language on succession in case of vacancy. His powers to reorganize
state departments were somewhat broadened, the Public Ser-

vice Commission was increased from five to seven members
and the legislature was given a greater share in appointment. Controls on public authorities were tightened in a
couple of respects. A few relatively minor provisions
relating to the position and rights of public employees
were inserted.

New York has a complex court system, but the large
number of judges sitting as delegates helped to see to it
that little fundamental change was attempted. One provision was adopted that allowed the Court of Appeals to create
new judges subject to disapproval by concurrent legislative
resolution; another established a permanent court on the
judiciary to deal with removal and disciplinary cases;
and a third granted administrative authority over the court
system to the Court of Appeals. Others sought to accomplish a variety of relatively minor administrative and
jurisdictional changes in the detailed provisions in the
existing constitution. The most controversial proposal so
far as the general public was concerned mandated the state
to assume over a 10-year period the cost of operating the
whole state court system.

Regarding local government, the convention followed a
path pursued by several of the other states in our series,
namely, it inserted language to modify the Dillon rule regarding the powers of local units. Such bodies were to
enjoy all of the authority the legislature had the power
to confer subject to a Statute of Restrictions to be enacted.
Adjacent counties were allowed to create regional agencies
for specific purposes. Other provisions related to county
charter adoption by referendum, local redistricting, dual
officeholding by local officials, and one or two other matters of modest importance.

Most of the rest of the changes made by the convention
related in one way or another to substantive policy matters.
Under the heading of natural resources, a "forever wild"
provision was inserted relating to some forest lands in the
state. In the education sphere, a crucial decision was
made: to eliminate the so-called Blaine amendment, which
forbade public aid to denominational schools. Much of the
ratification campaign--and the election--revolved around
this action. Additionally, the legislature was required
to establish a system of higher education; the state and
city universities were granted constitutional recognition;
and discrimination in school admission on the basis of
race or religion was forbidden.

As to public finance, adjustments were made in the
methods of incurring bonded debt and in the ceilings im-

posed on the debt liabilities of the state and certain
public authorities and how these can be raised. Authorization was expanded for economic and community development
programs incorporating the present housing article, and
permission for state and local units to loan or grant money
to private persons or entities for public purposes was
broadened. Probably the most controversial provision required the legislature to authorize the assumption of local
welfare costs by the state over a 10-year period. A series
of adjustments were made in the complex provisions relating
to local debt limits and how these were to be changed.

A couple of minor changes were made in the amending
process and the requirement for periodic (20 years) votes
on convention calls. A miscellany of other matters were
dealt with, including a ban on gambling save for bingo,
parimutuel betting, and the state lottery. In general, as
noted earlier, the bulk of the changes sought by the convention pertained much less to governmental structure than
to the making of adjustments in or additions to the welter
of substantive policy matter in the existing constitution.

Maryland

If the Rhode Island and New York constitutional conventions were chary of making major changes, the Maryland
body was not similarly inhibited. Starting right off with
the Bill of Rights, often a low-priority area for wholesale
reform, the delegates did a major rewriting job, which cut
the number of articles from 45 to 18. (Though little if
anything substantial was lost, opponents claimed that the
rights of the citizen had been reduced.) Many of the
changes recast language and brought passages in line with
the wording of the federal constitution. Under this heading came updating of jury and court procedure provisions.
At the other extreme was an effort backed by strong lobbying to add a labor bill of rights. This failed following
protracted consideration. The delegates did add a new antidiscrimination provision and one on eavesdropping and
fair investigative procedure. Furthermore, they lowered
the voting age to 19 and cut residency to six months in
the state and three in the locality.

Maryland, like Rhode Island, found impassioned advocates of unicameralism among its convention delegates, but
tradition prevailed in spite of the generally reformist
thrust of the convention, which met at Annapolis. The
delegates did vote to reduce the maximum size of the legis-

lature (cutting the House from 142 to 120, for example);
they also liberalized considerably the allowable length of
sessions; and they tried to make it possible for the legislators to raise their own pay by removing the existing constitutional dollar limit. The convention also voted, in
one of its most bitterly fought decisions, to eliminate
multimember districts for the election of legislators and
institute a system of single-member districts. A redistricting commission was provided to force the legislators
to reapportion. Politically, these represented major reforms with far-reaching potential consequences.

The delegates also turned their attention to the
executive branch and made substantial changes there, primarily to strengthen the position of the governor. On
paper the Maryland chief executive is considerably weaker
than his political position allows him to be in practice.
Formal executive power is shared with an elected attorney
general and controller, plus a Board of Public Works and
a number of independent boards and commissions. The major
reforms written into the draft constitution that aimed at
solving these problems were a reconstruction of the Board
of Public Works, a substantial reduction of the authority
of the controller (a major effort to eliminate mention of
the controller as an elective office failed), a limitation
on the number of principal departments together with broadened gubernatorial appointive powers, and authority for
the governor to initiate executive reorganization.

The convention also created the office of lieutenant
governor (which the state had lacked for many years), revamped the language on succession and disability, and simplified the qualifications for the office of governor.
Adjustments were made in the veto power, broadening the
item veto, and eliminating the pocket veto. On balance,
these executive reforms added up to a quite significant
strengthening of the position of the state's chief executive.

Even more sweeping changes in the structure and functioning of the court system were contemplated in the revised
constitution. Maryland's system for administering justice
was at the time confused and chaotic in the extreme.
There were no less than 16 different types of courts. The
delegates approved a sweeping reform that would have replaced this with a four-tiered scheme headed administra-
tively by the chief judge of the state's highest court,
the Court of Appeals. All judges would be appointed by
the governor from lists prepared for him by nominating
committees. The existing system combined appointment and

election in a confusing array of provisions. At the same time, sheriffs and registers of wills were to have their offices eliminated from the constitution.

Reform of local government also came in for major attention by the convention. Maryland counties had had the option of home rule for years, but not many had taken advantage of it. The delegates thus wrote in mandatory home rule with a timetable and deadline for its adoption. At the same time, they adopted a "shared powers" concept for the allocation of power between the legislature and the local units, which had the same effect as Rhode Island's revamped home rule provision: to reverse the Dillon rule and grant communities all powers not specifically withheld. Language was put into the draft that, relatively speaking, limited the constitutional recognition of municipalities and made the county the primary unit of local government. This was not done without provoking sharp outcries from municipal officials and lobbyists. Finally, another con- troversial provision, to encourage the growth of regional governing units in the state, was written into the new constitution. All in all, though the reforms of local government may not have been revolutionary in any absolute sense, they were major changes in the eyes of many who would be affected.

Again, as in Rhode Island, there was a major and time- consuming debate over the lottery question, resulting in the retention of a modified ban. Archaic restrictions on state borrowing were liberalized. Modest changes were made in the referendum provisions in the existing consti- tution, generally having the effect of making the legisla- tive path somewhat harder to follow. Finally, the amend- ment process was left substantially as it had been.

All in all, the Maryland convention was a "gung-ho" reformist body compared with either Rhode Island's or New York's. In mandating major changes in the bill of rights, in the legislative, executive, and judicial branches, in local government, and elsewhere, it very substantially modernized and streamlined the state's basic law--but stirred up many a hornet's nest of opposition in the pro- cess. The Maryland convention comes closest of any covered in this study to the impartial "law-giver" model dear to the heart of the political reformer.

Hawaii

The island state's situation as of the meeting of her 1968 constitutional convention was substantially different

140

in one major respect from that of the other states being considered. Hawaii had written her first (and current) constitution in 1950 as a prelude to her subsequent admission to the union; hence, only 18 years had elapsed by 1968. Not surprisingly, the changes that the delegates found to make were scattered and relatively minor. The one area in which major change was necessary, and the problem that provoked the calling of the convention, was legislative apportionment.

Turning first, as we have done in the other states, to Bill of Rights changes, we find that the Hawaii delegates made a series of minor ones. An invasion-of-privacy section was added; existing practice on bail waiver was ratified in new language; a requirement for the supplying of counsel to indigents was put in, pursuant to recent federal Supreme Court decisions; "damaging" of private property for public purposes as well as actual "taking" was covered; and the language granting collective bargaining rights to public employees was strengthened.

The only issue that the citizens defeated at the polls was to be found in the area of voter rights: reduction of the voting age from 20 to 18. (The defeat of one out of 23 propositions was a quite remarkable record in light of the fact that in Rhode Island, New York, Maryland, New Mexico, and Arkansas, the whole convention effort went down to defeat.) Additionally, the Hawaiian conclave granted voting rights to felons who had served their time, and the literacy requirement was eliminated. Language urging the legislature to set up a presidential primary was added in spite of the fact that that body could so act without constitutional mandate.

Under the circumstances, it was not surprising that the legislative branch came in for major attention. The convention wrestled with the apportionment problem, made so difficult in Hawaii by the island makeup of the state and the great disparities of population. It also provided for the now familiar commission device to ensure future attention to reapportionment. The 1950 convention had set relatively high minimum ages for the legislature (30 in the Senate and 25 in the House), which the convention cut to the age of majority. The constitution had limited the legislature to a 60-day session every other year, with a 30-day budget session in the intervening years. This restrictive system was liberalized by sanctioning a regular session every year, lengthening this somewhat, and giving the legislature greater authority over its own sessions. A 24-hour waiting period was instituted between the dis-

tribution of a bill in its final form and action on it.
Legislative salaries were jumped from $2,500 to $12,000,
putting Hawaii for a time among the top six legislatures
in the nation. Finally, it is probably worth noting that
unicameralism also came up in Honolulu but was quickly
shelved.

Hawaii's first constitution had been written in the
heyday of the strong governor, integrated administration,
and short ballot. As a result the governor's powers were
considerable, and he shared them with no other elected officer (the lieutenant governor was the only other official
chosen by the whole electorate). Proposals were brought
to the convention to strengthen further the governorship
by making all department heads appointive and removable
by the chief executive without Senate concurrence in either
case. This change was not accepted, though the delegates
did grant the governor removal power without Senate agreement. A proposal to limit the number of terms an incumbent
could serve was debated but not adopted.

A protracted and well-organized effort was mounted to
replace selection of judges by gubernatorial appointment
with something like the Missouri plan for judicial selection, but the attempt failed and the status quo was retained. The terms of judges were lengthened to 10 years,
however, and a gubernatorially appointed commission device
provided to deal with questions of judicial removal for
cause. Otherwise, a generally simple and well-organized
court system was left as it had been set up under the 1950
document.

The remaining area to which the convention devoted
significant attention was local government. Probably none
of the 50 states has as highly centralized a governmental
system as Hawaii and, correspondingly, as weak and relatively functionless local units. Thus the requests by local
officials that the island state follow the same path as
Rhode Island and Maryland and abrogate the Dillon rule in
favor of leaving residual powers to their level of government bore little fruit. They were only able to gain modest
concessions in the direction of strengthened home rule.
These involved greater autonomy for the local citizenry in
choosing their form of government free of state control.

This assorted parcel of relatively noncontroversial
adjustments to the 1950 constitution represented the handiwork of the 1968 convention. As noted, all but one was
adopted. Their impact on the Hawaiian frame of government
was naturally marginal. But so recent a constitution,
whose 1950 framers had tried deliberately to write in much

of the current wisdom on what a state charter should contain, was hardly likely to need major change so soon.

New Mexico

The delegates to the New Mexico convention were in somewhat the same position as those in Arkansas in that both states had quite archaic constitutions and populations similarly skeptical of modernizing reform. Accordingly, efforts at compromise were necessary at many points, by virtue of which some measure of modernization was sought, but yet not on so thoroughgoing a basis as to alienate the electorate. (Actually, in both states, the voters turned down the work of their elected representatives in spite of the convention's concern to tread a middle and politically acceptable path.)

Some significant additions were made to the state's Bill of Rights, one of which seemed almost universally popular among the new documents we are considering. This entailed adding material on wiretapping and electronic eavesdropping to the provision about searches and seizures. Equal educational opportunity language was transferred from the educational article and inserted among the rights of the citizen. The right to bear arms was extended to include lawful hunting and recreation. Turning now to the elections article, the delegates reduced the voting age from 21 to 20. They also authorized the legislature to set special residence requirements for those voting for president and provided for absentee voting.

Changes of significance were made in relation to the legislative branch. The body could now determine the size of the respective houses within an overall maximum total of 112. Reapportionment, another perennial topic of concern in the aftermath of Baker vs. Carr and the subsequent decisions it fostered, prompted the New Mexico delegates to prescribe redistricting every 10 years. If the legislature were to fail to discharge its responsibility, a five-member commission appointed by the governor would do the job. Other provisions dealt with legislative salaries, the date of the legislative session (subject to change by the body itself), and a more flexible schedule for annual sessions than that prevailing.

The executive came in for considerable attention quite naturally, in light of its particularly archaic present structure. Three of the nine statewide elected officials were shifted to appointive status: treasurer, attorney general, and secretary of state. The term of office of those still to be chosen by the voters was extended from two to four years; however, the two-consecutive-term limit was retained, though with the right to run for another statewide office after serving the allotted eight years. The delegates voted to require the legislature to group administrative agencies and functions into no more than 20 principal departments under the supervision of the governor and gave the latter reorganization authority, thus mandating a major modernization of the executive branch structure.

There was significant innovation in the judicial area, specifically the establishment of an unified court system with supervisory and rule-making authority vested in the state supreme court. A series of essentially minor adjustments and revisions in other provisions relating to the court system were also mandated.

In the realm of local government, the New Mexico convention, like those in several of the other states, addressed itself to aspects of the question of local home rule. Actually it was less a matter of writing new provisions than of incorporating into the constitutional draft provisions already present in statute law. The courts were directed to construe the provisions of the local government article broadly so as to grant to local units powers they had by implication and that were not prohibited to them. Again, modification of the Dillon rule was thus undertaken.

Turning now to substantive policy areas, little was done to change provisions relating to taxation. The property tax millage and limitation on percent assessment were kept the same. Here too, existing practices and precedents were written into the draft. Provision was made for a college student loan program. In the area of education generally, an appointive board of education was instituted to replace the existing elective one, and budgetary power over school funds was transferred from a division of the Department of Finance to this new appointive board. The governor and the Senate were given authority to initiate removal proceedings against regents and members of the state board of education, with the Supreme Court retaining final authority in decisions on removal.

Finally, the amending process was altered to eliminate the present special voter majorities required to amend the education and elective franchise articles of the constitution. In sum, though the New Mexico delegates wrote many important revisions into their new document, they clearly felt they must pull their punches in key areas for political reasons and, overall, produced a draft that was at best modest by objective national reform standards. That it could still fail, in part no doubt because in terms of New Mexican attitudes it moved too far too fast, is again testimony to the relativity of standards and cultural preferences in the area of state government.

Arkansas

This largely rural southern state had the disadvantage, from the point of view of its convention delegates, of a more deeply entrenched governmental tradition than most of the other states in our sample. Resistance to change was bound to be high. On the other hand, as revision experience from elsewhere accumulated during the late 1960s, each successive conclave provided more precedents to serve as guides and warnings to Arkansas as it charted its own course. The delegates were painfully aware of the resounding failures in Maryland and New York and tried to profit by mistakes made there and in other states.

The convention that met at Little Rock tackled some of the same questions that had figured in the deliberations of other conventions whose work we have reviewed. It too added to the Bill of Rights a guarantee against invasions of the right to privacy. It clarified the right to counsel, and the protection against double jeopardy. Language was added to guarantee a preliminary hearing in felony cases, prohibit fees on the right to bear arms, broaden the ability of the citizen to file taxpayer's suits, and increase the protections against property seizure for debt.

In the elections area, though the convention declined itself to lower the voting age, it voted to allow the legislature to do so--down to 18. The residence requirement in the state was lowered from one year to four months, and the General Assembly was given authority to make provision for people to vote in presidential elections who did not meet that minimum.

The legislative branch was subject to several important changes--important both in a structural sense and in terms of the politics of ratification. The existing biennial session limitation was done away with, allowing the General Assembly to meet annually. Henceforth it would also have the power to call itself into special session. Much of the suspicion of state government endemic in the community seemed to focus on the legislature; thus, these changes were disturbing to many--as was the newly granted freedom of the legislators to set their own pay. Further changes included a shift to all single-member districts for legislative elections, some slight adjustments in the size of the houses to facilitate apportionment, and standardization at three-fifths of the special majorities required to vote tax measures. The General Assembly henceforth was to record all votes on substantive measures, and lost to the courts the right to make decisions on contested elections for its members.

Even more important changes were made in the executive branch. The governor and other state constitutional officers were to serve four-year terms, with a two-term limit for the chief executive. Changes were made in the roster of such officers--namely, the offices of lieutenant governor and secretary of state were combined in one, as were those of auditor and treasurer. The office of land commissioner was eliminated. The rest of the administrative branch in Arkansas was typical of the archaic system many states had had: some 180 separate executive departments and agencies. The convention mandated that these were to be grouped in 20 principal departments, which, however, would not include educational, quasi-judicial, or licensing and disciplining bodies, unless the legislature so required. The governor's veto was now to be overridden by a three-fifths vote of the legislature, rather than a simple majority. In general, these added up to a substantial modernization and streamlining of the executive branch.

Judicial reform was also viewed as overdue in Arkansas. The delegates tackled the problem forthrightly by setting up a unified court system with the Supreme Court at its head, equipped with supervisory powers over the lower courts. District courts were created to take over the functions of four existing separate courts, and county trial courts were created to consolidate five more lesser courts. Payment of court officials through fees collected was prohibited, and prosecuting attorneys (renamed district attorneys) were forbidden to carry on private practices. A judicial ethics commission was created, and other modifications in the system were made.

As to local government, the convention attempted major modernizations in structure, titles of officials, and the amount of autonomous power available to county and municipal authorities by reversing Dillon's rule. Generally that power was thus increased, and greater control was given the local citizenry over their form of government.

Intergovernmental cooperation was specifically encouraged. The existing constitution contained complex tax and borrowing provisions and limitations that the convention cautiously liberalized, mindful, however, of the political sensitivity of these limits and the protection they are felt to provide for the taxpayer.

One issue that caused much controversy was the "usury" provision that limits the rate of interest that may be charged by those who loan money. After long debate, the convention ended up retaining the (unrealistically low) 10 percent ceiling. A similarly explosive issue was "right to work," which the convention also retained in spite of strong labor union pressure for elimination of it. The existing method of constitutional amendment remained the same, but a new provision was added requiring a vote every 20 years on whether a convention should or should not be called.

In sum, the problem with the revised Arkansas document was not that it was radically innovative, though in comparison with the existing constitution it did represent a large number of major changes. Here, as in New Mexico, the issue as the voters apparently saw it was the relative extent of change, not its revolutionary nature. The traditions of the state simply would not admit of the degree of modernization the delegates attempted, however modest their changes might appear in a different context.

Illinois

The work of the Illinois constitutional convention of 1970, the last included in our series, was no less a compromise in many of its provisions than the others we have examined. The process of compromise was in some ways a different one, however, than in states like Arkansas or New Mexico. Since the representation at Springfield of the various major political interests in the state was more explicit and self-conscious, the delegates were more often involved in frank and relatively open bargaining and trading. One manifestation of these tendencies (and also a sign of the growing impact of referendum failures elsewhere on the thinking of the Illinois convention) was the decision to offer separate choices to the electorate in a few hotly disputed areas. In effect the delegates had fought issues like selection of judges and single-member versus multimember legislative districts to a draw and concluded that it was more prudent to leave them up to the

voters than force a narrow decision that might jeopardize
the whole document.

Unlike most conventions, Illinois' reworded the pre-
amble to update its description of the aims of modern
state government. To the Bill of Rights proper were added
some new provisions, including a guarantee against discrimination in housing and employment on the basis of race,
color, creed, national origin, sex, or mental or physical
handicap; protection against unreasonable invasions of
privacy; confirmation of the right to bear arms subject to
the police power; and equal protection of the laws for
both sexes. The question of the death penalty was put on
the ballot as a separate question for the voters, and they
chose to continue the use of that form of punishment.

On suffrage, the delegates took steps to reduce the
residence requirements parallel to actions of other conventions in the same area. The period of residence in the
state was cut from one year to six months and was eliminated for counties entirely, and the General Assembly was
permitted to impose a requirement at the election district
level of no more than 30 days. The legislature was also
allowed to prescribe special (shorter) requirements for
those wishing to vote in presidential elections. A State
Board of Elections with bipartisan membership was set up.
Again, on the issue of lowering the voting age to 18, the
matter was left to the voters, who concluded that 21 was
more appropriate.

As for the structure of the General Assembly, the
delegates decided to retain its present size, but they
were deeply divided on the question of single- versus multimember districts for House elections. (The latter was
the existing practice, with three chosen from each of 59
districts.) This question too was put up to the electorate, who opted for the status quo. Reapportionment every
10 years was stipulated, with alternative methods of doing
it if the General Assembly failed to redistrict itself.
Annual sessions of the legislature were provided for, a
very important change from the biennial session pattern
of the past. The minimum age for service as a legislator
was reduced to 21, and some other provisions relating to
the internal functioning of the lawmaking bodies were included.

Moves were made by the delegates to strengthen the
executive, particularly the power of the governor. The
item veto power that he had had was revamped so that from
now on he will be able to reduce appropriation items as
well as strike them out of bills sent to him. He is to

have authority to reorganize the executive agencies and reassign functions among them. One of the previously elective state officers, the superintendent of public instruction, was made appointive; the auditor was replaced by a comptroller, and the governor and lieutenant governor candidates were bracketed. Starting in 1978, elections for state officers will be held in even-numbered nonpresidential years instead of concurrently with contests for the White House.

The big issue in the judicial area was the selection of judges. There was a strong move in the convention to shift from Illinois' traditional electoral system to a scheme providing gubernatorial appointment from among nominees submitted to the governor by judicial nominating commissions. Ultimately, the electorate was asked to choose between these two systems and again opted for the status quo. The other changes were of a more limited nature and included the setting up of a Judicial Inquiry Board to receive or initiate and investigate complaints against judges, adjustments in the jurisdictions of the courts, provisions for filling vacancies on the bench, permission for two or more counties to join and choose a single states attorney, and alterations in the methods of selecting court clerks.

As in virtually every other state we have surveyed, home rule came in for considerable attention in Illinois. The existing constitution had not provided for it, but the new document granted it to all counties with elected chief executives and all municipalities with at least 25,000 population. Other units may by referendum choose to have home rule, and any home rule unit may by referendum give up that status. The powers of home rule governments were in effect enlarged by roughly the same kind of reversal of the Dillon rule that other conventions mandated for their states; and only by a three-fifths vote may the General Assembly limit strictly local powers to home rule units. The population of a local governmental unit has wide power over the structure of that government.

Finance and revenue claimed a good deal of the attention of the delegates. A new article was inserted in the document, which had no counterpart in the existing constitution, to improve financial mangement. It provided for an executive budget to be prepared by the governor and to cover all the financial affairs of the state. The General Assembly was to appoint an auditor general for a 10-year term and provide uniform systems of local government accounting.

The revenue article reflected not only the continuing concern that the citizens of many states feel to have limits in their basic charters protecting them against burdensome taxes but also the heightened anxiety of the time with high and rising levels of taxation. Provisions appear relating to the phasing out of the personal property tax; exempting certain things like food from sales tax; and requiring referendum approval of debts to be secured by the full faith and credit of the state (or a three-fifths Assembly vote). Other provisions relate to the debt and its repayment and to the property tax and its assessment. Two tax limitations were written in that had not been present in the old constitution: one prohibiting a graduated income tax for individuals and another limiting the amount by which corporate income tax rates might exceed the individual rates.

In part in response to recent court decisions, the delegates conferred primary responsibility for the funding of public education on the state, guaranteed free education to all through secondary school or higher if the General Assembly so provided, and set up a State Board of Education. The obligations of the state and the rights of individuals in the environmental area were spelled out for the first time. Finally, the process of amendment, which in the old document had been very difficult and cumbersome, was considerably streamlined. Lesser majorities both in the legislature and by the voters will now be required. A provision for changing the legislative article by initiative petition was introduced so that the voters could circumvent a balky General Assembly. And, lastly, a provision was added to ensure that a convention call be put on the ballot at least every 20 years.

Aside from Hawaii, only Illinois among the states covered in this study was successful in securing voter ratification for the work of its convention. This was the case in large measure because of the open and relatively comprehensive respresentation by the delegates of the major political groupings in the state and perhaps even more because of the careful segregation by the convention of the most controversial issues for separate voter decision. This tactic was the clear message of several of the earlier convention failures in other states, and the Illinois delegates had learned the lesson well.

THE CONSTITUTIONS: OVERVIEW

Table 5.2 is an effort to capsulize in a rough way
the relative degree of change accomplished by each convention in the draft they offered their fellow citizens, in
relation to the existing state constitution. Generally,
the notation in the table involves three codings designed
to signify (as their ordinary meaning would suggest) the
following: extensive and very basic changes, which are
labeled "major"; important but less extensive revisions,
labeled "significant"; and relatively unimportant, marginal alterations, labeled "minor." In most of the categories brief indication is also given of some of the specific changes made, which at least illustrate what was
done by the convention, and similarities from one state to
another.

Several patterns in Table 5.2 deserve comment. Reading down the columns one sees at a glance what could also
be discerned in the preceding summaries of convention action: The Maryland and Arkansas bodies produced substantially revised documents, with the New Mexico and Illinois
delegates not far behind. The New York and Hawaii conventions produced documents reflecting at best modest changes.

We are also in a position to examine such relationships as may exist not only among the draft documents but also
between the issue preceptions of the delegates when interviewed at the start of the respective conventions and the
work they later produced. To facilitate the understanding
of this comparison, we have included Table 5.3, which represents the same data presented in Table 5.1 but with more
detailed breakdowns under each of the major categories.

A cursory comparison of Tables 5.2 and 5.3 suggests,
as an initial impression, that, whereas there are some
similarities of pattern, there are other areas where comparability breaks down. To get at these relationships in
more detail, we might look at the individual constituional
issue categories. Based on the impressionistic judgments
recorded on Table 5.2, all six conventions made significant
changes or additions in the Bill of Rights area, and in
every single case there was included among these, language
on wiretapping and the right to privacy against eavesdropping. Yet, when one turns to Table 5.3, one finds that
the Bill of Rights area was of quite low saliency for the
delegates as the conventions began.

TABLE 5.2

Schematic Summary of Degree of Revision in Documents

Constitutional Category	Maryland	New York	Hawaii	New Mexico	Arkansas	Illinois
Bill of Rights	Major (wire tap)	Significant (wire tap) (discrimination)	Significant (wire tap)	Significant (wire tap) (discrimination)	Significant (wire tap)	Significant (wire tap) (discrimination)
Suffrage and elections	Significant (voting age) (residence)	Minor (voting age) (residence)	Major (voting age)	Significant (voting age) (residence)	Minor (voting age) (residence)	Minor (voting age) (residence)
Legislative branch	Significant (reapportionment) (sessions)	Minor (reapportionment)	Significant (sessions) (reapportionment)	Significant (sessions) (reapportionment)	Significant (sessions)	Significant (reapportionment) (sessions)
Executive branch	Major (departments) (short ballot)	Minor	Minor	Major (departments) (short ballot)	Major (departments) (short ballot)	Significant (reorganization) (short ballot)
Judicial branch	Major (total reorganization)	Minor	Minor	Significant (unified system)	Major (total reorganization)	Minor
Local government	Major (home rule)	Significant (home rule)	Minor	Significant (home rule)	Major (home rule)	Major (home rule)
Substantive policy	Significant (debt) (lottery)	Significant (finance) (Blaine)	Minor	Significant (finance) (education)	Significant (usury) (right to work)	Major (tax and revenue)
Amendment process	Minor	Minor	Minor	Significant	Minor	Major

Source: Compiled by the authors.

TABLE 5.3

Delegate Perceptions of Five Most Important Issues
(percentages of total replies in each state)

Constitutional Issues	Mary-land	New York	Ha-waii	New Mexico	Ar-kansas	Illi-nois
Bill of Rights	8.0	11.0	3.0	3.5	1.0	8.0
Suffrage and elections	1.5	6.5	a	0.5	3.5	a
Voting age	3.5	a	8.0	6.0	a	a
Legislative branch, general	7.0	10.0	10.0	a	6.5	7.5
Apportionment	1.5	13.0	21.5	0.5	0.5	3.5
Unicameralism	5.0	a	8.0	0.5	a	a
Miscellaneous reforms	a	a	a	4.5	3.0	1.0
Executive branch, general	14.5	4.0	1.5	2.5	9.5	6.0
Reorganization of	a	a	a	3.0	a	1.0
Short ballot	7.0	a	a	15.0	2.0	1.0
Four-year term (for governor)	a	a	a	5.0	1.0	a
Miscellaneous reforms	b	0.5	a	a	5.5	b
Judicial branch, general	19.5	17.5	a	7.0	10.5	14.5
Judicial selection	a	a	13.5	4.5	4.0	1.0
Local government and home rule	19.5	18.5	9.0	9.0	18.0	18.5
Education, general	3.5	b	6.0	5.0	1.0	6.0
Aid to parochial school and church-state relations	1.0	15.5	a	5.5	a	0.5
Finance, taxation, and revenue	5.5	a	15.5	17.5	11.0	21.0
Gambling, lottery	b	b	a	a	0.5	a
Social and welfare policies	a	b	a	0.5	a	1.5
Environmental, natural resources	a	1.5	0.5	3.5	a	1.0
Miscellaneous policy issues	a	a	1.5	2.0	14.0[c]	0.5
Shape of document, amending process	1.5	1.5	1.0	3.5	4.5	5.5
Miscellaneous replies	0.5	a	1.5	1.5	3.5	1.5
Total[d]	99.0	99.5	100.5	100.5	99.5	99.5
Number	530	783	373	326	445	517

[a]Signifies no replies in that cell of the table.

[b]Signifies replies amounting to less than 0.5 percent.

[c]6.5 percent of replies related to usury; 7.5 percent referred to "right to work."

[d]Because of rounding errors, totals do not equal exactly 100 percent.

Source: Compiled by the authors.

Very much the same points could be made about the area of suffrage and election reform. Here too, saliency was low at the outset, yet every one of the six states dealt in some way with the voting age question, and most dealt with residence requirements. How might one explain the difference between convention activity and initial lack of delegate interest? Probably the answer lies in a kind of issue "socialization process" that goes on in conventions, through which national currents of concern get reflected in the thinking of delegates and acquaint them with questions that their local milieu did not highlight in advance. Obviously, among the agents of that socialization are national groups (with, of course, local branches) like the American Civil Liberties Union and the League of Women Voters, plus the federal courts and the decisions they hand down, which state decision-makers must take into account, if at times belatedly and reluctantly.

It will perhaps be easier to evaluate patterns in relation to the three major branches of government if we construct a brief new table (Table 5.4) using the entries on Table 5.2 and, for simplicity, the total percentages from Table 5.1 discussed earlier. The disparities between initial assumptions of the delegates and what the conventions ended up doing are quite striking on this table. This is particularly true in the legislative area, where the states in which the highest levels of advance concern were registered turned out in one case to have made only minor changes and, in the other, "significant" but not "major" alterations. On the other hand, the two that scored lowest in delegate concern nevertheless did make rather substantial reforms in that branch of government. In short, there seems to have been little correlation between initial perceptions and convention activity in this area. Part of the explanation may be the fact that, as in Hawaii, reapportionment was a highly salient issue, which provoked the calling of the convention. This did not necessarily mean, however, that there was concern for major revamping of the legislative institution itself.

Turning next to the judicial area, the same general lack of congruence emerges. The two states in which the delegates were most persuaded in advance that reform of the court system was needed, Maryland and New York, emerged later with, respectively, major changes and relatively minor tinkering. Arkansas and Illinois, the next highest measured by delegate perception, paralleled Maryland and New York. It should be noted, however, regarding Illinois, that this finding is somewhat misleading. The convention

TABLE 5.4

Comparison of Issue Perception and Convention Action

	Mary-land	New York	Hawaii	New Mexico	Ar-kansas	Illi-nois
Legislative						
Perception	13.5	23.0	39.5	5.5	10.0	12.0
Action	Sig-nifi-cant	Minor	Sig-nifi-cant	Sig-nifi-cant	Sig-nifi-cant	Sig-nifi-cant
Executive						
Perception	21.5	4.5	1.5	25.5	18.0	8.0
Action	Major	Minor	Minor	Major	Major	Sig-nifi-cant
Judicial						
Perception	19.5	17.5	13.5	11.5	14.5	15.5
Action	Major	Minor	Minor	Sig-nifi-cant	Major	Minor

Source: Compiled by the authors.

did devote considerable attention to the issue of judicial
selection but ended up leaving the decision to the voters
--who opted for the status quo. Thus, the changes actually
made by the convention were minor.

In rather sharp contrast to convention performance
versus delegate anticipation in the legislative and judicial areas, the correlation is very high in the executive
issue category. The three highest preliminary scorers
rated "major" evaluations of the revisions actually made,
the two lowest rated "minor," and the remaining state,
Illinois, rated "significant" for its efforts. If one
were to offer an explanation for these issue area differences, it might be developed along lines of the interaction
between local or state traditions and trends in national
concern. Judicial reform, for example, was an "in" subject during the 1960s and hence, not surprisingly, was on
the minds of many delegates. Yet, once convention deliberation is under way, political forces both within and
outside the body could easily abort action. This clearly
happened in New York.

On the other hand, the far greater variations in perception in the legislative and executive areas probably
reflected local concerns and traditions and the way these
were represented in the delegate mix. Ultimately convention decisions would then depend on inputs into the convention deliberational process of theory, self-interest, and
pressure. Seemingly, perceptions in the executive area
were more readily translated into convention action than
in the legislative sphere--perhaps because legislators
generally have tended to have more clout in convention
decision-making than partisans of the executive.

COMPARING THE CONSTITUTIONS

There are no absolute standards about what provisions
should be included in the "ideal" state constitution. Yet
the National Municipal League's Model State Constitution
certainly comes closest to meeting the reformers' ideals
about what a constitution should contain. Thus, to compare
what happened in the seven states and also to indicate the
extent of reform success, we have constructed a reform
index. The index is constructed by awarding each of 29
selected constitution provisions, as listed in Table 5.5,
a specific number of points on the basis of their proximity
to the reform model construction. We scored two points
for a provision that met the reform standard listed in
Table 5.5; we gave one point to a semireform provision,
one that in part approximated the reform standard; and a
nonreform provision scored no points.

Table 5.6 presents the reform scores. A perfectly
reformed constitution, using the Model State Constitution
as the standard, would score 58 points. In contrast, in
Maryland, New Mexico, and Arkansas, the existing constitutions scored less than 10 points on the reform scale.
Hawaii, with its relatively new constitution, started out
at 34 points. All of the seven conventions moved their
constitutions further along the reform scale, most so in
states where the existing documents lagged in the beginning. For example, the average reform score for the seven
state constitutions before revision is 16-plus points; afterward, it is 34-plus points. Further, at the beginning
the range among them is 31 points; afterward it has been
reduced to 18 points. This movement in the direction of
reform and toward standardization across such a wide and
different spectrum of cases shows the national strength of
the reform movement.

156

TABLE 5.5

Model State Constitution as Reform Standard

Provision	Model State Constitution	Reform Points
Preamble	"Succinct statement of constitutional purpose"	2
Declaration of rights	"Sparse," modeled after federal constitution	2
Enumeration of powers	"Explicitly state that constitution is a grant not a limitation on State"	2
Suffrage and elections		
Voting age	18[a]	2
Residence requirements	Minimal, three months	2
Legislature		
Form	Unicameral[b]	2
Size	Set by statute	2
Term of office	Two years, lower house; six years, upper house	2
Type districts	Single-member	2
Compensation	Set by statute	2
Sessions (length)	Flexible	2
Procedure	Unspecified	2
Apportionment	Mandatory--every ten years	2
Postaudit	Specifically under legislative control	2
Executive		
Time of election	Odd-numbered years	2
Term	Four years, no limit	2
Elected state offices	None	2
Administrative organization	Consolidated	2
Succession	Explicitly provided for	2
Judiciary		
Organization	Unified	2
Selection	Missouri plan type	2
Administration	Centralized	2
Minor officials	Eliminated from constitution	2
Finance	Flexible	2
Local government	Broad local autonomy	2
Education	Specific grant	2
Intergovernmental relations	Free from obstacles to cooperation	2
Civil service	Specific grant	2
Constitutional change	Liberal, rather than cumbersome procedure	2
Total reform points		58

[a]No voting age is specified in the model; 18 years as a reform standard was set by the authors.
[b]Unicameral is optional in the model.

Source: Compiled by the authors.

157

TABLE 5.6

Reform Components of Old and New Constitutions
in Seven States

State	Reform Score of Old Constitution	Reform Score of New Constitution	New Reform Points	Reform Distance (percent)
Rhode Island	17	29	12	29
New York	30	36	6	21
Maryland	5	40	35	66
Hawaii	34	36	2	8
New Mexico	3	35	32	58
Arkansas	8	28	20	40
Illinois	18	36	18	45

Source: Compiled by the authors.

We also developed a measure called the reform distance, which illustrates the amount of "change" the constitutional convention accepted. The measure is a computation of the proportion of possible constitutional change actually enacted in moving toward the Model State Constitution standard, using the old constitution as the starting point. For example, in Rhode Island, there was a potential for 41 new reform points--58 in the Model minus the 17 in the old constitution. That the convention enacted 12 new reform points by the possible 49 points gives a reform distance score of 29 percent. Maryland achieved the most reform by this indicator, 66 percent, with New Mexico close behind at 58 percent. In both instances the starting point was a virtually completely unreformed document. The combination of an unreformed document and a reform-oriented and dominated convention could easily lead to very substantial change, as the reform distance score makes clear. In both states, the impact of the substantial change was reflected in press accounts and in the bitter ratification campaigns.

By contrast, in Hawaii, where the starting point was very reformed, the reform distance score was 8 percent. Overall, the seven states had a reform distance average of 38 percent, another indicator of the substantial success of the reform movements as measured by the documents themselves.

The subject matter of this chapter is, in many ways, least amenable to the kinds of behavioral analysis characteristic of this book. While it is possible to compare policy products such as state constitutions in the abstract, the comparison is complicated because these documents were produced by different bodies operating within somewhat different state political cultures and, most important, acting on the basis of very different starting points. What seems to us noteworthy, given the admitted primitive state of comparative policy studies that focus on outputs rather than on process, is that we were able to identify uniformities in some cases and also to indicate in what areas prior activist perceptions of what would be important were modified by the convention processes. The amount of such modification suggests that the conventions were more than mechanistic processors of perceived needs and demands as a simple systems model might suggest. As we have suggested throughout, they had important dynamic aspects as well as unique aspects in each state, and nowhere have we been able to illustrate both qualities as well as in the difficult data of this chapter. The great variety of the constitutional reforms made in the seven states is hard to quantify, but perhaps this effort has conveyed some of the richness of the specific changes that were made. For more detail, we have prepared separate behavioral monographs on each state. In the next chapter we turn to data more amenable to the quantitative techniques of our discipline and analyze the referenda on the revised constitutions.

NOTES

1. Joseph A. Schlesinger, "The Politics of the Executive," in Herbert Jacob and Kenneth N. Vines, Politics in the American States (Boston: Little, Brown, 1965), pp. 217-32.
2. New York: National Municipal League, 1968.

159

6

**CONSTITUTIONAL
REVISION: THE
PEOPLE DECIDE**

Constitutional conventions have to meet a requirement
that legislative bodies do not face. Everything a convention decides comes before the voters. Even in those states
that make the greatest use of referenda, only a limited
percentage of the total legislative effort goes before the
public. This link between citizenry and constitution-
makers is a final test of the representativeness of the
convention, of the public appeal of the product, of the
political skill of the delegates in achieving successful
ratification. Further, at least some of a convention's
work, it seems to us, has to be ratified if the institution is to be judged "successful," either in meeting the
problems that called it into being in the first place or
in justifying the effort and expense of its operation.
This chapter attempts to summarize the political events
that occur during the ratification campaign in each state
and to explain, using quantitative methods, the underlying
patterns of support of and opposition to revision.

THE POLITICS OF RATIFICATION

The bulk of this chapter, in the quantitative analysis, is an effort to discover which variables have the
greatest explanatory value in each state and to determine
the power of a basic contextual model. These techniques
alone cannot capture the flavor of the ratification campaigns, the personalities, the specific issues, and the
particularities of each state. As Table 6.1 shows, the raw
material of the quantitative analysis is seven state conventions, called by majorities of from 51 percent to 83

TABLE 6.1

Recent Referenda on State Constitutions

State	Convention Calls				Ratification Referenda			
	Date	Yes (per-cent)	No (per-cent)	Total Turnout	Date	Ap-prove (per-cent)	Disap-prove (per-cent)	Total Turnout
Rhode Island	11/3/64	69.0	31.0	228,708	4/15/68	20.2	79.8	86,404
New York	11/2/65	53.4	46.6	3,149,869	11/8/67	28.0	72.0	4,669,085
Maryland	9/13/66	83.5	16.5	191,960	5/14/68	43.5	56.4	651,134
Hawaii	11/8/66	65.7	34.3	181,217	11/5/68	65.3	34.7	220,137
New Mexico	11/5/68	69.0	31.0	116,239	12/9/69	48.5	51.5	123,072
Arkansas	11/5/68	51.4	48.6	441,924	11/3/70	42.6	57.4	524,529
Illinois	11/5/68	72.1	27.9	4,115,417	12/16/70	57.1	42.9	1,937,320

Source: Compiled by the authors.

percent and then receiving from a low of 20 percent to a
high of 65 percent support on the ratification referenda.
Further, ratification referenda came before voters in every
possible combination of on-year general election ballot,
off-year general election ballot, and special election
ballot. Turnout varied from very low to very high.

The best way to capture the flavor of ratification
politics in each state is through the full-chapter detailed
descriptions in the series of individual state monographs
now published or being published.[1] In this comparative
volume, the best descriptive treatment we can offer is a
brief state-by-state summary on how the new constitution
was presented on the ballot, what the major issues and
group alignments seemed to be, what campaign organizations
and techniques were used, and what the result was.

Rhode Island

In Rhode Island, the ratification campaign lasted
from September 11, 1967 until the referendum on April 16,
1968. After what everyone supposed was final convention
passage on September 11, a series of hearings was held
around the state, guided by the status-quo legislative
faction, which had dominated the convention product and
won four-year terms for both houses and freedom to set
legislative pay. The initial hearings revealed some public resistance, so the convention reconvened in October.
The convention modified its ban on wiretapping, provided a
safeguard for localities in merger procedures, and eliminated four-year terms for both the legislative and executive branch. This amended constitution was adopted by the
convention on December 4, and another round of hearings
was scheduled in eight localities.

The second round of hearings encountered less objection, and on March 25, 1968, the convention met again to
hear a final report and authorize spending $25,000 for a
public information campaign. Since the referendum was
only three weeks away, time was very short. The public
campaign lasted three weeks. Opposing the revised constitution were the popular incumbent Republican governor,
John Chafee, and the reform-oriented convention chairman,
Dennis J. Roberts, who jointly led a coalition of Republicans plus reformist Democrats under the rubric of the Committee for a First-Rate Constitution. The committee used
saturation radio commercials to attack the proposed document, hammering on the removal of the ban on lotteries,

the potential for legislative pay raises, and the changed
local government article. The commercials were simplified
and very specific and, in essence, urged voters who dis-
approved of one section of the constitution to vote "no"
and thus reject the entire document.

Proponents of the constitution had difficulty mount-
ing a strong campaign. A court suit forced the use of the
$25,000 only in the form of small-type comparisons of the
old versus the new document, article by article, without
argumentation. A Committee for the Adoption of the Proposed
Rhode Island Constitution was organized under the leadership of Professor Patrick Conley of Providence College,
a member of the convention research staff. Many prominent
citizens joined the committee, including Roman Catholic
Bishop Russell J. McVinney. The League of Women Voters,
which had seen many of their cherished reforms defeated,
felt on balance that the new constitution was an improvement and endorsed it. The Providence Journal, with statewide circulation, had been unenthusiastic about the convention and critical of the delegates' performance, particularly their attendance records. But in a somewhat equivocal editorial on March 24, the editors wrote, "The issue
is whether the document is better than the constitution we
have. We believe it is."[2] And again on the Sunday before
the referendum, an editorial "strongly" urged an approve
vote, on the grounds that "the long-range best interests
of Rhode Island will be served by adoption and implementa-
tion."[3]

In the end, however, the opponents were better organized and ran a much more sophisticated campaign than the
proponents. The opponents had the state's most popular
elected politician on the air campaigning against the document. Although the proponents had some blue-ribbon endorsements, their campaign relied upon printed ads prepared
in a dull format (as required by the court ruling). No
elected state official campaigned for the document (although several endorsed it mildly). Thus, the opponents
held the offensive in the ratification campaign. Nineteen
percent of the registered voters turned out, a moderately
high showing for a special election. The document was defeated 4 to 1. It lost in every community in the state,
although opposition was greater in the rural areas. A
less successful dénouement for a convention that had convened almost four years before could hardly be imagined.
For the moment at least, the move toward constitutional
change in Rhode Island appeared dead.

The five and a half months of deliberations of the
New York constitutional convention ended on September 27,
1967, when the full convention approved a new constitution.
The statewide referendum was scheduled for November 7, 1967,
allowing six weeks for a ratification campaign. The convention had not made enormous changes in the existing document, but it had taken a stand on several controversial
issues. Perhaps the most important modification was the
repeal of the so-called Blaine amendment to the existing
constitution, which prohibited in explicit language state
aid to parochial education. In place of the Blaine amendment, the convention substituted the language of the federal constitution guaranteeing freedom of speech, press,
assembly, petition, and forbidding the establishment of
religion. By removing Blaine, the convention opened the
way to state aid to parochial schools.

In addition, the convention lowered the voting age to
18 and provided stricter controls over wiretapping and
electronic eavesdropping and for state protection and preservation of natural resources. Perhaps the most important
decision the convention made was to present the document
to the voters in an all-or-nothing form. This decision
was made on the final day of the convention, after extensive lobbying by Convention President Anthony Travia. The
all-or-nothing plan passed by the exact minimum number
needed, and only with support from three Liberal Party
delegates against the opposition of all Republicans and
three defecting Democrats. The vote on ballot form reflected the organization and voting behavior of the convention along strict party lines, with the Democrats in a
narrow majority (although the Republicans were the majority
party by most political indexes in the state).

The political alignments during the ratification campaign were complicated. The convention Democrats were the
most active proconstitution campaigners within that party,
but endorsements came from other Democrats, including the
late Senator Robert F. Kennedy, who made television spots.
On the Republican side, although Governor Rockefeller gave
lukewarm support, Senator Earl Brydges and Assemblyman
Perry Duryea, the Republican leaders in the legislature,
campaigned actively against the constitution, as did most
other Republican delegates. Mayor John Lindsay, then a
Republican, did not support the document. The major GOP
opposition was based on the alleged cost of the new docu-
ment--an 80 percent increase in state taxes over 10 years

was a figure often used. The state's two smaller parties also were in opposition, the Liberals because of repeal of the Blaine amendment and the Conservatives on the basis of cost.

A great portion of the organized campaign was waged by interest groups. All the proponents of the constitution, with the exception of the state AFL-CIO and one other ad hoc group, based their support on the repeal of the Blaine amendment. The most active group was the Committee for Educational Freedom (CEF), which ran a sophisticated Madison Avenue print, radio, and television campaign reputed to have cost over $1 million. The main theme was that students attending parochial schools were discriminated against because of Blaine and that passage of the new document would end this situation. The pitch was very explicitly toward Catholics. On the other hand, of the 30 groups against the constitution, 18 based their position on opposition to repeal of the Blaine amendment. In this camp were major Jewish, Protestant, civil rights, civil liberties, taxpayers, and education organizations.

Almost every daily newspaper in the state opposed the new constitution editorially, including the New York Times, which stated:

> To our regret, the considerable improvements this document does make in the existing Constitution are insufficient in importance to offset a few features so highly objectionable that we can only recommend that the proposed Constitution be rejected at the polls in November.
> By far the most important weakness of the new Constitution is the absence of any ban on state aid to denominational schools.[4]

When the voters went to the polls on November 7, they defeated the new constitution by over 2 million votes, 72 percent against, 27 percent for. The margin was far greater than any observers had predicted, and the document lost in every county of the state. Even in more heavily Catholic New York City, no county mustered more than 38 percent in favor.

Maryland

The Maryland Constitutional Convention adjourned after voting a heavily reform constitution on January 10, 1968,

165

with the ratification referendum scheduled for May 14, 1968,
four months away. The convention, under the strong leadership of H. Vernon Eney, had been rigorously nonpartisan,
nonpolitical, and reform-oriented. Among the controversial
changes the convention made were lowering the voting age
to 19, elimination of constitutional status for a number
of state and local elected officials, imposition of single-
member legislative districts instead of the traditional
multimember system, and a provision making regional local
governments easy to form.

Proponents of the new constitution were overjoyed
when only three delegates voted not to support the revised
charter, which was to be put before the voters in the all-
or-nothing format. Convention President Eney predicted
that the voters would approve "so overwhelmingly that
there would be no question about it" because the constitution was "a Maryland document, made by Marylanders for
Maryland."[5] Yet even before the convention adjourned,
there were indications of potential opposition from those
status-quo-oriented political sectors that had been left
out of the convention and had lost perquisites in the final
document. Sheriffs and officials from the Maryland Court
Clerks Association had told delegates they would oppose
the new document if their constitutional status were
threatened.[6] Judge Philip Dorsey, from Maryland's Eastern
Shore, one of the three delegates to vote no, said that
"if ratified by the people, it [the constitution] will be
sowing the seeds for the destruction of democratic government in Maryland and will be a model for destruction of
democratic government in other states."[7]

The opposition seemed to operate at two levels. At
a local level, officials from county clerks and sheriffs
to big-city ward organizations (which stood to lose from
single-member legislative districts) worked against the
new document. Statewide, the main drive came from the
Save Our State Committee, led by the wife of a state court
of appeals judge. The SOS committee aimed its appeal
against specific aspects of the new document, in a radio,
television, and direct door-to-door campaign conducted at
a very emotional level. Arguments against the constitution
included the cost (helped on by an estimate of $153 million
from the state comptroller's office, which stood to have
its powers reduced substantially by the new document),
that the suburbs would be swallowed up by the central cities
under regional governments and, by implication, by blacks;
and that the new constitution was an effort by a national
reform movement, including the National Municipal League,

to impose standardization on state governments. The opposing groups appeared to benefit from the free time made available by local television stations. They spent around $15,000.[8]

The supporters of the constitution did not anticipate serious opposition and were slow to organize and grasp the challenge. By early March, a committee of 108 blue-ribbon leaders with Milton Eisenhower as titular cochairman was formed. "Pro-Con" was eventually to spend $60,000 on a high-level campaign that relied primarily upon radio advertising.[9] The basic strategy was to obtain extensive endorsements from the Maryland "establishment," including 30 college presidents and hundreds of businessmen. But the supporters had difficulty defending the entire constitution, whereas opponents could attack particular provisions. In addition, the rough and tumble of what ex-Governor Tawes (a supporter) called the "gutter-type" propaganda of opponents caught the reformers off-guard. Further, except in Montgomery and Prince George's counties, prime middle-class suburban territory, there was no grass-roots activity by Pro-Con. These two counties were the only ones where the document passed.

May 14, 1968 was a political and personal tragedy for those who had sought to make constitutional reform in Maryland a reality and a model. Voters rejected the constitution by 56 percent to 44 percent, and voted no in 21 out of 23 counties. Turnout was very high--43 percent. The Maryland product appeared to suffer from the nonpartisanship of the delegates and the convention. The Maryland reformers were not willing to compromise and appeared to be unaware of the importance, to those who were affected, of the proposed changes. Royce Hanson, president of the Washington Center for Metropolitan Studies and a Montgomery County convention delegate, observed that the constitution was defeated by the

> skillful use of a propaganda campaign that appealed to the anti-intellectual, anti-Negro, and anti-urban sentiments; and fear of unchecked power, change, and taxes. George Mahoney couldn't get elected governor, but his "little guy" let "the Establishment" know what it thought of its constitution.[10]

Hawaii

The Hawaii constitutional convention ended its working sessions on September 24, 1968, leaving six weeks un-

til the ratification referendum at the November 5, 1968
general election. The final document was signed, in a formal ceremony on October 21, by all of the delegates. The
Hawaii situation was unique in that the existing document
was a modern constitution written in 1950. The 1968 convention, working from this base and composed of a delegate
mix of officials and activists from both parties with a
"realistic" outlook, limited itself to incremental changes.

Nonetheless, there were some changes that might prove
controversial, including the elimination of the literacy
requirement for voting, lowering the voting age to 18,
granting collective bargaining rights to government employees, increasing legislators' salaries to $12,000 per year,
and reapportionment. Perhaps the most interesting and important decision the delegates made by way of ratification
strategy was the form of the ballot they chose. The delegates were conscious of the defeats of all-or-nothing new
constitutions in Rhode Island, New York, and Maryland. In
Hawaii, the Committee on Submission and Information devised
a unique yes/no/yes-but voting system.

This system provided for a three-part ballot. A
voter could cast a blanket "yes" vote for all the convention's revisions (Part A); or a blanket "no" vote (Part B);
or he could vote on any of the constitution's 23 sections
published individually as Part C, with the proviso that
those sections that did not receive an explicit "no" in
Part C voting would be counted as "yes" votes. In other
words, an automatic "yes" vote came under Part C for items
that the voter might be neutral on, and the system at the
same time allowed the public to vote against individual
provisions without rejecting the entire document. The convention's leaders hoped that this format would provide a
safety valve for focused one-issue opposition and also provide a sufficient number of "yes" votes (from Part A and
Part C) to meet the requirement of an affirmative vote of
a total of at least 35 percent of all those voting.

Support for the constitution came from organized labor
and the majority Democratic Party. The state central committee of the minority Republican Party assumed a neutral
posture but praised the work of Convention President Hebden
Porteus, a prominent Republican, who campaigned actively
for the new constitution. Republican State Chairman Edward
Johnson also personally strongly urged approval of all proposed amendments. The only opposition came from the Hawaii
Chamber of Commerce and the Business League for Sound Government, both of whom were against the raising of the ceiling on the state debt. No organizations emerged in opposition to the entire document.

The campaign for support of the document was managed largely by the Convention Committee on Submission and Information with the help of a public relations consultant and cost about $40,000.[11] Using the slogan "Know the issues . . . then vote on the amendments to Hawaii's constitution," the convention's campaign used all available media, including pamphlets, newspaper ads, and spot radio and television. Free time was provided on the local educational television station.

The convention had received a superbly favorable press throughout its deliberations, and both major newspapers praised the convention and endorsed all 23 amendments and urged a blanket "yes" vote (Part A). Norman Meller observed that

> reporters and commentators were so busy in the aid of "good government" that they either unconsciously ignored weaknesses of the convention, or deliberately avoided referring to them in order not to discredit the delegates and thereby run the risk of the voters becoming alienated.[12]

Thus with almost uniform political, business, labor, and civic support, the new document was tested at the polls on November 5. All but one of the 23 proposals were ratified by Hawaiian voters. Proposal 8, lowering the voting age to 18, failed by a small margin. Commentators generally attributed Proposal 8's defeat to backlash against student protest on the mainland and also in Hawaii, where a group of protestors had destroyed an ROTC building on the University of Hawaii campus shortly before the election.

The "yes-but" ballot procedure (Part C) turned out to be important in the revised document's success. Of the 23 amendments, none received blanket "yes" votes (Part A) equal to the required 35 percent of the 239,765 votes cast. The 22 successful amendments owed their ratification to the votes they received from Part C, the yes-by-implication count. Only four of the proposed amendments received more blanket "yes" than yes-by-implication votes.

New Mexico

The New Mexico Constitutional Convention adjourned on October 20, 1969, leaving only seven weeks until the December 9, 1969 ratification referendum. Sixty-five of the 70 delegates backed the new document. The main reforms were in the direction of executive efficiency and modernization. Some 300 autonomous boards were to be consolidated into a system of 20 cabinet departments under the governor, whose term was to be lengthened to four years. In addition, the elected offices of attorney general, secretary of state, and treasurer were to be made appointive by the governor. Finally, a major change was made to strengthen home-rule provisions for local government.

In the campaign, these major changes became the main issues. The supporters organized under the rubric of the "Vote Yes Committee of 1000." Among those endorsing the constitution were former governors Campbell and Mechem, the State Democratic chairman, the speaker of the State House of Representatives, the New Mexico Education Association, the League of Women Voters, the New Mexico Retail Association, the New Mexico AFL-CIO, and the powerful New Mexico Taxpayers' Association. Convention President Bruce King, a defeated candidate for the Democratic nomination for governor in 1966 and 1968 who finally won the nomination and the general election in 1970, stumped the state on behalf of the document. Proponents were disappointed that Republican Governor David R. Cargo gave only tacit support.

The opposition campaign was led by incumbent State Treasurer Jesse D. Kornegay under the organization Citizens for Better Government. The Citizens apparently drew heavily upon those officials and elected board members who stood to lose their positions, as well as the clienteles of these boards. For example, the New Mexico Sportman's Legislative Action Committee opposed the constitution because it would plunge the Fish and Game Department into "spoils politics." The main point of attack of the opponents hard-hitting campaign was the "Short Ballot." The point was hammered home again and again that elected officials were responsible to the people, whereas appointed officials were not. Unsigned fliers claimed that the new constitution would bring about a gubernatorial dictatorship.

The proponents campaigned on two levels. On one level was an endorsement-oriented campaign that also stressed high-level public education and the reform aspects of the new constitution. On another level was an effort to respond to intense charges of the opposition. Efforts were handicapped by the inability of the supporters to spend the $150,000 allotted to the secretary of state for running the ratification effort and publicizing the new document in any effective manner. By the provisions of the old

constitution, constitutional proposals had to be published
once a week for four consecutive weeks before the election,
and this was interpreted to be a set of binding and exclu-
sive instructions.

Press comment on the new constitution was almost uniformly favorable. Editorials praising the document appeared in the Alberquerque Tribune, the Alberquerque News,
the New Mexican, and the Farmington Daily Times. A television show that started eight weeks before the ratification date provided a weekly forum on the document. As in
Maryland, a heavily reform constitution appeared to have
virtually uniform "establishment" support. And again as
in Maryland, opposing individuals in relatively ad hoc campaigns managed to convert the contest into one between the
"little guy," whose representative institutions were going
to be taken away from him, and the "establishment." The
strong attack, the depth of whose appeal was not gauged
until much too late by the proponents, gained from the all-
or-nothing format of the ballot. The changes took things
away from specific individuals and groups, while the benefits of reorganization, efficiency, and home rule tended
to be diffuse and hard to recognize in advance.

The end result was a heartbreaking defeat for reform
proponents. With a record turnout in a snowstorm, the
constitution lost by less than 3,500 votes out of 123,072
cast, a margin of less than 3 percent. There was speculation that a more effective and well-financed professional
campaign on the part of proponents could have carried the
day.

Arkansas

The Arkansas constitutional convention adjourned on
February 10, 1970, leaving nearly nine months until the
ratification referendum on the November 3, 1970 general
election ballot. On the final convention vote, 98 of the
100 delegates backed the final document. The convention
product was a modest one in terms of reform, and the delegates were conscious of the need to be "realistic" and
write a document that could win voter approval. The form
of the proposed document was the all-or-nothing choice.

A number of changes turned out to be issues in the
campaign. Deleting the statement that the people of Arkansas were "grateful to Almighty God" drew criticism as
atheistic. What was intended to be a "state's rights"
section was later cited as giving dictatorial powers to

the state government. The new constitution provided for annual legislative sessions and allowed the General Assembly to set its own salaries and combined numerous agencies in executive reorganization. In addition, it reduced the autonomy of local judges and prosecutors and eliminated the jobs and fees of many local justices and county officials. Various provisions gave greater autonomy and tax powers to local governments through removing various limitations on fiscal operations. Eighteen-year-olds were given the vote. Existing provisions on interest rates and right to work were not changed, but liquor interests were angered because the new document jeopardized the fair-trade price-fixing systems.

Supporters of the constitution were brought together by Republican Governor Winthrop Rockefeller in a bipartisan committee, "Arkansans for the Constitution of 1970." Republican Lieutenant Governor Maurice Britt and former Democratic Governor Sid McMath were cochairmen, and Robert Meriweather, a political science professor, Study Commission member, and delegate to the convention, served as unpaid director. A leading public relations firm and a noted pollster were employed, and a strategy that relied primarily on endorsements from leading persons and groups became the main approach. One advertisement, for example, featured 31 leading political, civic, educational, religious, legal, and farm leaders.

Governor Winthrop Rockefeller endorsed the constitution, and so did the Republican Party in the first plank of its platform. The Democrats were somewhat cooler, although Rockefeller's opponent Dale Bumpers announced his support. In addition, 38 groups, including the Arkansas Farm Bureau, the League of Women Voters, the National Association for the Advancement of Colored People (NAACP), the Chamber of Commerce, and an Arkansas churchwomen's organization announced backing. The Farm Bureau supported the document strongly, to general surprise.

Using the endorsements approach on all media, the "Arkansans FOR" group also presented speeches around the state and radio and television panel presentations. Late in the campaign, some more issue-oriented and specific counter-attack ads were mounted against the anticampaign. All told, "FOR" spent about $130,000 in cash and an additional $20,000 in "in-kind" services on the campaign.[13]

The opposition did not run a unified campaign, nor did it have big names on its side. The largest of the anti-groups was the "Keep the Present Constitution Committee," organized in September with a former Supreme Court justice as its chairman. "KEEP" ran several newspaper advertisements, taped two television programs, and sponsored radio spots and literature, and its members made public appearances. Its major argument was that under the new document, taxes could and would be raised. Many judicial and county officials throughout the state apparently waged an intensive but low-visibility anti-campaign, especially in the rural areas. Covert financial support apparently came from liquor dealers and from real estate interests (who feared property tax increases). In addition, the American Independence Party opposed the document, and so did some gambling interests, which were allegedly disappointed that legalized gambling was not included in the new document. The anti-forces waged a specific emotional campaign, with taxes the major issue but with a variety of other points included also. It seems that about $20,000 was spent opposing the constitution, at least in open expenditures.

Press coverage in all media was adequate to extensive, and the convention printed hundreds of thousands of booklets and tabloid copies of the new document for distribution. Most of the leading newspapers backed the new constitution, but some small county papers and one northwest chain opposed it, and another chain stayed neutral. Although the path to ratification appeared smooth on the surface until near the very end, as the election approached, the depth of the opposition began to become obvious. In addition, ratification became entwined and to some degree submerged in the other aspects of the general election: a hotly contested gubernatorial campaign, a "taxpayer's revolt," and other referenda. In the end, the blue-ribbon delegates saw their carefully crafted document soundly defeated. The vote was 301,195 against to 223,334 for, a 57 percent to 43 percent defeat.

Illinois

On September 3, 1970 the Illinois delegates signed the proposed constitution. The referendum was scheduled for December 15, 1970, a little over three months away. The aim was to have the vote as soon as possible after concluding the writing, but not to blend the constitutional questions with the personalities and other referenda on the November 3 general election ballot. Very early in its deliberations, the convention had decided that the new constitution would not be submitted to the voters in a single package. With the Maryland experience well-known to the delegates, the instructions to committees had been to submit proposals that could be voted upon separately.

Throughout the convention, there was an awareness of the problems of ratification and the need to be realistic, which meant producing a document that could win support from the two major regions of the state and from both political parties. As the convention began, it was anticipated that state and local revenue and finance, along with the form of the judicial system, the method of electing legislators, and legislative apportionment would be the main issues. And indeed these questions occupied the main efforts of the delegates.

In the realm of finance, the convention removed existing debt limits on state and local governments, agreed to allow Cook County to keep its real estate tax classification system, to allow a nongraduated income tax, and to abolish the corporate ad-valorem personal property tax by 1979, along with other features. A compromise home rule provision provided for licensing for revenue and taxes upon income, earnings, and occupations by localities as allowed by the General Assembly, and set the cutoff point for home-rule communities at those above a population of 25,000.

On other questions, the convention removed the prohibition on lotteries and compromised on gun control and wire-tapping with equivocal language. On a series of thorny questions, the decision was made for separate submission to the voters. During the regular course of the convention, it was decided to put 18-year-old voting and capital punishment as separate propositions. Originally, decisions upon the method of selection of judges and on cumulative legislative voting were included in the "main package." But shortly before adjournment these two subjects, which raised almost irreconcilable differences, were shifted out of that main package. Instead, on each question voters were to be given a choice of two alternatives (either election or appointment of judges; either winner-take-all single-member districts or cumulative voting in multimember districts). These separations were felt virtually to guarantee passage of the basic document.

Support for the main package in the ratification campaign was very widespread, almost unanimous, coming from the governor, lieutenant governor, attorney general, treasurer, both U.S. senators, the Republican Party, the League of Women Voters, the State Chamber of Commerce, the Illinois Bar Association, the Illinois Congress of Parents and Teachers, the Illinois Agricultural Association, the Illinois Municipal League, the Illinois Association of Senior Citizens, the United Auto Workers, the Independent Democratic Coalition, the Chicago Better Government Association, the Welfare Council of Metropolitan Chicago, the Chicago Crime Commission, Operation Breadbasket, and the Urban League of Chicago. While the Democratic Party Platform was silent on the constitution, about half the party candidates for state legislature endorsed the document, and on November 30 Mayor Richard J. Daley of Chicago announced his support for the main package. Most newspapers across the state backed the main package also.

Supporters ran a generalized campaign, including a heavy dose of local-level workshops and courses organized by the League of Women Voters. Opponents remained relatively unorganized and specialized in their opposition to particular provisions. Among those opposing the main document were a few delegates to the convention, the Illinois Federation of Labor (AFL-CIO), the United Steelworkers of America, Joint Council 25 of the International Brotherhood of Teamsters, the Illinois Federation of Teachers, and such ad hoc groups as "Save Our State" and "Save Our Suburbs."

Positions on the separate proposals were more complicated. It was clear that voter disapproval of 18-year-old voting, abolition of capital punishment, appointment of judges, and cumulative voting was the prevailing downstate sentiment, where generalized opposition to the main package was also centered. In this context, the position of Mayor Daley's organization became the key. He backed election of judges and cumulative voting, in both of which the Chicago machine had a very tangible stake. On the other two separated questions the Chicago organization was silent, which meant in practical terms that the usual voter "caution" would prevail.

On December 15, the main package passed by a comfortable 56 percent to 44 percent margin. Cumulative voting passed with a narrow 51 percent majority, and the election of judges barely made it with slightly over 50 percent. Abolishing the death penalty was defeated and so was lowering the voting age to 18, receiving 34 percent and 43 percent support, respectively. Cook County voters, casting more than half the votes, provided the margin of victory for the main package, which was opposed downstate, and also carried the cumulative voting system. In Illinois, a combination of widescale support by powerful political parties and political leaders, a well-managed and realistic convention, and a shrewd system of presenting choices to voters led to successful ratification of a new constitution.

CONSTITUTIONAL REVISION: A
QUANTITATIVE ANALYSIS

Constitutional revision taps some complicated, and often negative, feelings in voters. Of 33 convention calls proposed since 1950, 21 have been approved, a rate of 63 percent. Once called, conventions do even worse. Of the nine ratification referenda since 1966, only three have passed. This success rate of 33 percent on convention or commission efforts compares with a rate of 71 percent approval that constitutional amendments win when submitted separately to voters after being written by a legislature, by initiative, or by limited conventions or commissions.[14]

There are obvious limitations to a comparative quantitative analysis of the ratification campaigns, and we have tried to overcome these inherent problems by describing the important specific circumstances of each state in the beginning of this chapter. In addition, in the discussion of the problem of the "specific no" application of Arrow's paradox in Chapter 2, we tried to indicate a particular contextual electoral problem that revised constitutions faced. With these caveats aside, however, we do think a rigorous quantitative study can add to our understanding of the bases of support and opposition within the general public to revised constitutions, a matter made more crucial for the whole process by the unhappy fate of so many new basic documents in our set. Our technique, simple correlation analysis and stepwide multiple regression analysis, is the same as we applied to voting on convention calls in Chapter 2.

There are a number of propositions that operationalize the hypotheses of this book in relation to the ratification process. Drawing upon the ideas of William C. Havard and Norman G. Thomas, we have:

Proposition 1: On ratification referenda, support is strongest among higher socioeconomic groups.
Proposition 2: If this is not exclusively the case, then traditional partisan patterns will be detected in support and opposition.[15]

There is an implicit negative counterpart to Proposition 1, and that is that lower socioeconomic groups will oppose the revised constitution. From the voting data alone, if this does occur, there is no way to separate causal possibilities. Opposition may be stronger as socioeconomic status decreases because, as we indicated, reform is initiated and supported by higher-status people under a good-government rubric. Thus, opponents would perceive a head-on clash of life-style and also whatever practical and symbolic benefits may be redistributed by constitutional change.

There is a related proposition, one that has received support in the literature of studies of constitutional referenda in both Michigan and Maryland.[16] That is:

> Proposition 3: In constitutional ratification campaigns partisan divisions will become more important than they were in votes on the call.

A broader model of state and local politics, often found in spending and voting studies, uses a set of contextual variables to try to explain various dependent variables.[17] The model holds, in effect that the observed phenomena can be explained, in a statistical sense, in terms of the independent variables drawn from the known social and political structure of the state. This approach can also be applied to constitutional revision. Then the question is: How powerful are these standard contextual variables in explaining voting variance on ratification referenda?

If the standard contextual variables explain most of the total variance on the ratification vote, then we would conclude that constitution revision is a process explicable in terms of the basic existing social and political alignments in the states. If the variables do not explain much of the variance, then an explanation would logically turn to the unique configuration of issues and personalities surrounding each convention and controversy.

We assume that contextual factors are the more important, and thus we hypothesize:

> Proposition 4: Contextual variables explain at least 60 percent of the variance of approve votes on ratification referenda.

METHOD AND DATA

We collected data by counties, utilizing 11 independent variables with "yes" votes on the calls and "approve"
votes on the revised constitutions as the dependent variables. The five socioeconomic variables were median income,
median education, percent owner-occupied dwellings, percent urban, and percent population change. The political
variables were percent Democratic vote in the closest two
presidential and gubernatorial elections. Finally, we include county employees as a ratio of population and per
capita county governmental expenditures because press coverage in several states indicated that county employees
were playing important roles in opposition to ratification.
Using counties as units has some drawbacks, most not-
ably that this method distorts their real voting weight
in the calls and referenda. Our analysis treats them as
equal units while in fact their populations vary. The
county units allow us, however, to identify sources of
support for calls and revised constitutions and to account
for variation in the impact of socioeconomic, political,
and county-employee/expenditure variables. We analyzed
the data first by simple correlations then by stepwise
multiple regression, omitting in the latter operations
Hawaii and Rhode Island, where the number of counties was
too small. We did four stepwise runs for each state.
Stepwise multiple regression identifies the most powerful
individual variables, the cumulative impact of additional
variables, and also the total power of all the variables
in the analysis, R and R^2.[18]

THE RATIFICATION VOTES

In Table 6.2 we present the simple correlations on
the ratification referenda. In New Mexico only socioeconomic variables prove significant. In Illinois and New
York, both socioeconomic and political variables are significantly correlated with approve voting. In Maryland,
socioeconomic variables are most powerful, although the
1960 Democratic presidential vote and county employees
are also significant. In Arkansas, two socioeconomic
variables are significant, and two political variables are
significant with a negative direction. In Rhode Island,
support is associated with Democratic vote for governor
in 1962 and 1966. In Hawaii, the only significant relationship is a negative one, with owner-occupied dwellings.

TABLE 6.2

Simple Correlations Among Contextual Variables and Approve Votes on Revised State Constitutions

Variable	Rhode Island (N = 5)	New York (N = 62)	Maryland (N = 23)	Hawaii (N = 4)	New Mexico (N = 32)	Arkansas (N = 75)	Illinois (N = 101)
Median income	-0.52	-0.48[b]	0.71[b]	0.22	0.50[b]	0.17	0.44[b]
Median education	-0.50	0.01	0.78[b]	0.14	-0.36[a]	0.08	0.57[b]
Percent owner-occupied dwelling	-0.64	-0.67[b]	0.04	-0.91[a]	0.46[b]	-0.32[b]	-0.30[b]
Percent urban	-0.12	0.70[b]	0.51[b]	-0.07	-0.30	0.33	0.29[b]
Percent population change	-0.68	0.07	0.71[b]	0.38	-0.31	0.13	0.35[b]
Democratic presidential vote							
1960	0.40	0.76[b]	0.49[b]	-0.25	0.003	-0.34[b]	-0.35[b]
1964	0.51	0.44[b]	0.33	0.39	0.09	-0.03	-0.28[b]
Democratic gubernatorial vote							
1959	--	--	--	--	--	--	--
1960	--	--	--	--	--	--	-0.19[a]
1962	0.75[a]	0.69[b]	-0.33	-0.64	-0.03	-0.19	--
1963	--	--	--	--	--	--	--
1964	--	--	--	--	--	--	-0.29[b]
1966	0.95[b]	0.46[b]	-0.30	0.44	0.19	-0.60[b]	--
County employees	--	-0.04	0.48[a]	--	--	-0.05	0.12
County expenditures	--	-0.12	0.37	--	--	-0.05	-0.07

[a]significant at 0.05 level.
[b]significant at 0.01 level.

Source: Compiled by the authors.

Table 6.3 contains the four selections of the stepwise multiple regression analysis on the ratification campaign. For three states, socioeconomic variables are the most important: education in Illinois, education in Maryland, and income in New Mexico. Thus, in combination with the simple correlation data, we have substantiation for Proposition 1, that support on the ratification votes is strongest among higher socioeconomic groups, and also for Proposition 2, that where SES is not alone in importance, it is joined by partisan political variables.

On the other hand, in New York and Arkansas, the most important variables in the ratification fights were political, for the former the 1960 Democratic presidential vote and for the latter the 1966 Democratic vote for governor. In New York, the 1960 Democratic presidential vote pattern reemerges as important because Catholicism was a factor in both the 1960 presidential election, with John F. Kennedy's candidacy, and the ratification referendum. On the latter, the main issue was repeal of the "Blaine amendment." In Arkansas, the document was apparently perceived as an urban, Winthrop Rockefeller document because the most important prior pattern in explaining the 1970 opposition to the constitution was 1966 support for segregationist Democrat James Johnson.

There is, in Table 6.3, little support for Proposition 3, that partisan divisions will become more important in the ratification votes than on the vote to call the convention. Table 6.3 shows partisan divisions, at least traditional partisan divisions, to be less important on ratification (see Table 2.7) in Maryland, Illinois, and New Mexico. Only in Arkansas and New York do they become more important. These are, of course, relative evaluations. In absolute terms it is interesting how little the nonpartisan delegate selection systems in Arkansas and Maryland insulated the ratification efforts from past partisan patterns. On the cumulative power of the contextual model to explain variance in voting on the ratifications, the model is quite powerful in two states, Maryland (Selection D) and New York (Selection C). It is less powerful for the other states. The average R^2 is 54.5 percent, or less than the 60 percent criterion set in Proposition 4.

CORRELATION BETWEEN SUPPORT FOR THE CALL AND SUPPORT FOR RATIFICATION

Another way to test Propositions 1 and 2 is to compare patterns of support on both votes. A scanning of the

TABLE 6.3

Stepwise Multiple Regression Analysis of Approve Votes on Revised State Constitutions

State	Socio-Economic Variables	Political Variables	Socioeconomic and Political Variables	All Variables
New York				
R	0.80^b	0.80^b	0.84^b	
Percent of total variance accounted for	64.7	64.9	70.7	
Most important variables and percent variance of each				
Percent urban	49.3			
Percent own dwelling	9.9			
1960 presidential		57.9	57.9	
1964 presidential		6.4	6.4	
Maryland				
R	0.79^a	0.82^b	0.89^b	0.92^b
Percent of total variance accounted for	63.1	68.8	79.4	85.1
Most important variables and percent variance of each				
Education	60.5		61.1	61.1
Percent own dwelling	1.2			
Percent population change	1.2			
1966 gubernatorial		36.1		
1960 presidential		24.0	6.2	6.2
Arkansas				
R	0.42	0.66^b	0.69^b	0.70^b
Percent of total variance accounted for	17.6	44.3	49.0	49.7
Most important variables and percent variance of each				
Percent urban	11.0			
Percent own dwelling	4.9			
1962 gubernatorial		5.2	8.3	8.3
1966 gubernatorial		36.5	36.5	36.5
New Mexico				
R	0.55	0.31	0.57	0.59
Percent of total variance accounted for	30.6	10.2	33.3	34.9
Most important variables and percent variance of each				
Income	25.7		25.7	25.7
Percent own dwelling	1.6			
1966 gubernatorial	3.6		2.6	
1960 presidential	3.1			
1964 presidential				2.6
Illinois				
R	0.59^b	0.43^b	0.66^b	0.67^b
Percent of total variance accounted for	34.9	19.0	43.6	44.9
Most important variables and percent variance of each				
Education	33.1		33.1	33.1
Income			2.6	2.6
Percent own dwelling	1.3			
1960 gubernatorial		6.6		
1960 presidential		12.0		

[a]Significant at the 0.05 level.
[b]Significant at the 0.01 level.

Source: Compiled by the author.

simple correlation in Tables 2.1 and 6.2 shows no clear
pattern. In Arkansas, socioeconomic variables were more
powerful in the call and political variables were more
powerful in the ratification. In Maryland, support for
call and ratification was much more similar; socioeconomic
variables were most powerful in each case, and correlations are higher in the ratification referendum. For Illinois, the voting support patterns for call and ratification
are the same, high socioeconomic status (SES) and Republican backing, except, in this instance, the correlations
are higher on the call. In New York, the patterns are the
same, high-SES and Democratic support, but the correlations are higher on the ratification. In New Mexico, however, there is a complete reversal of support patterns between the call and the ratification; in the first election,
support came from Democrats and high-SES people; in the
ratification, there was opposition in high-SES groups and
no clear political pattern. For Rhode Island, the pattern
in both elections was virtually identical: low SES and
Democratic support. For Hawaii, no visible pattern emerges
for either election.

Table 6.4 uses the vote on the call as an independent
variable in an analysis of the ratifications. The simple
correlations, Column I, are significant at the 0.01 level
in five of the states. The direction is positive except
in Rhode Island and New Mexico, where counties offering
support for the call opposed ratification. Columns II
through V add the call as a 12th independent variable to
the contextual model. In Illinois, the vote on the call
becomes the most important single variable, but it does
not add a great deal, only 7.7 percent in total explanatory
power. Only in New Mexico does the vote on the call add
a large amount to the power of the analysis.

What we have is continuity in votes for calls and ratification, but also some shifting, seen largely in the power
of the contextual model. Continuity with some shifts in
bases and magnitudes of support and opposition between call
and ratification is not a surprising finding. After all,
the calls were approved in all seven states, but the revised constitutions were approved in only two.

THOUGHTS ON THE DEFEAT AND SUCCESS
OF REVISED CONSTITUTIONS

Many explanations of the defeat of particular constitutions maintain the timing of the election played some

TABLE 6.4

Relationships Between Support for Convention Calls and Support for Revised Constitutions

	I r	II R^b	III R^2 (percent)	IV Percent Variance of Ratification Accounted for by Call Vote	V Additional Variance with Call Vote (percent)
Rhode Island	-0.51				
New York	0.52[a]	0.860[a]	74.1	1.8	3.4
Maryland	0.66[a]	0.896	80.3	5.8	-4.8
Hawaii	0.22				
New Mexico	-0.49[a]	0.712	50.8	1.5	15.9
Arkansas	0.52[a]	0.752[a]	56.6	8.3	6.9
Illinois	0.66[a]	0.725[a]	52.6	43.4	7.7

[a]Significant at 0.01.
[b]Contextual model with vote on the call added as an independent variable.

Source: Compiled by the authors.

role. Table 6.5 shows both convention calls and ratification referenda were presented to voters in virtually every
possible combination of time of election and with wide
range in turnout. In Arkansas, the vote on the finished
document was higher in an off-year than a presidential-
year general election. In Maryland, the special election
on the convention mobilized over three times as many voters.
In Illinois, switching from a presidential general election to a December special election cut the turnout more
than in half. In New York, the ratification election mobilized an extra 1.5 million voters. In New Mexico, in
one of the sharpest illustrations of the mobilizing power
of issues in state politics, more people voted in a December special election on the constitution than had voted on
the call in the 1968 presidential election. In Rhode Island, the switch from the 1964 presidential election to
an April special election cut turnout by almost 60 percent.
In Hawaii, as one might expect, turnout in the presidential
general election produced an increase in the vote on the
ratification of the constitution over the vote on the call
two years prior.

A STATE-BY-STATE EXPLANATION

Putting together these turnout patterns with our voting data on support and opposition and the descriptive sections on each ratification campaign leads to some explanations of individual outcomes. In Arkansas, the impact of
political cleavages heightened from call to ratification.
Opponents to the latter mobilized a rural Democratic vote
against Republicans and the blue-ribbon nonpartisan reformers who had written the document. In essence, the ratification campaign mobilized people who either did not vote
or supported the call and turned them into opponents.
In Maryland, the voting patterns of support and opposition were similar on the call and the ratification.
Here too a hard-sell campaign was waged against the document, which was portrayed as an elitist, intellectual,
problack outcome. Conservative Democrats were mobilized
against it in greater numbers than they were on the call,
and mobilization rather than conversions sank the document.
In Rhode Island too, patterns of support and opposition
reversed. What defeated the constitution was that the low-
income Democrats who backed the call in a general presidential election did not turn out for a special April election,
while the Republicans, agitated by a hard-sell anticonsti-

TABLE 6.5

Calls and Ratification Referenda: Some Timing and Turnout Characteristics

State	Timing of Election		Ratification Turn-out Compared to Call Turnout	Outcome
	Call	Ratification		
Rhode Island	General	Special	-142,304	Failed
New York	Odd-year general	Odd-year general	+1,519,216	Failed
Maryland	Special	Special	+459,174	Failed
Hawaii	Off-year general	General	+37,920	Passed
New Mexico	General	Special	+7,833	Failed
Arkansas	General	Off-year general	+82,605	Failed
Illinois	General	Special	-2,178,097	Passed

Source: Compiled by the authors.

185

tution radio campaign sponsored by Republican Governor
John H. Chafee, did.

In New York, where the final document got only 28
percent of the vote, specific opposition came from almost
all Republicans, and what Democratic support there was was
lukewarm at best. Although the issues that were most discussed were the Blaine amendment and a possible rise in
taxes, the partisanship of the convention, its high ex-
penses (the delegates each received $15,000 for five
months part-time work), and bad image were also probable
factors. We counted 5 interest groups in favor and 30
against. The call had barely passed originally, and what
happened afterward was a sharper focusing of political
cleavages and increased turnout of opponents.

New Mexico is a very interesting case. The voting
data show a turnabout between call and ratification refer-
endudum, with the original supporters becoming opponents
of the final document. The contextual model also lost
much of its power between the first vote and the second,
suggesting that the convention's product and the ratification campaign tapped new dimensions of public response.
The ratification campaign was bitterly contested, and the
turnout, while not markedly greater than for the call,
represented an unusual turnout for a special election in
a winter blizzard. The "short ballot" was used by opponents in a hard anticonstitution fight that won by less
than 3,500 votes.

In Illinois and Hawaii the revisions were successful.
Our voting data in Illinois are more powerful in explaining the call than the ratification referendum. Indications
are from the data that while shrinking turnout in a special election reduced the plurality, the same fundamentally
higher-SES and Republican groups managed to hold on and
win. In Hawaii, neither the call nor the ratification
evoked an identifiable pattern of support or opposition
in the political cleavages of the state, and, indeed, the
convention made few changes and produced a document that
won bipartisan support.

SOME TENTATIVE CONCLUSIONS
FROM THE QUANTITATIVE DATA

Using county data from seven convention calls and
nine constitutional ratification referenda, we used quantitative methods to test seven propositions about public
response to constitutional change and explored factors in

success and failure of proposed new constitutions. To summarize the findings:

1. There is evidence, but with several exceptions, supporting hypotheses stating that increased backing on ratification referenda comes from higher socioeconomic groups alone, or from a combination of these and partisan support (Propositions 1 and 2). In four of seven states there is a significant positive correlation between support on the call and support for ratification.
2. There is little evidence for the hypothesis that partisan divisions become more important in ratification votes than on the calls (Proposition 3).
3. There is less evidence that a contextual model can explain the variance in voting on the ratification referenda than on the call (Proposition 4).

The last finding suggests to us that the conventions and the constitutions they produce act as intervening variables, probably through the mechanism of the ratification campaigns, in the public consciousness. Support for the calls is probably generalized support for reform or change or at least responsiveness to elite or party cues on such matters. But in the ratification campaigns the public discovers that constitutional change involves pluses and minuses, and choice. Opponents in all the states found it easy to portray the choice as between the known system and unknown--and thus vividly characterized--evils. Thus how conventions acted, what they produced, and, we think, how the public relations of the campaigns were conducted, mattered in the outcomes of the ratification votes, within the framework of the broad patterns of public response to calls and referenda that we have identified. Only when drafters separated the most controversial proposals, could they win approval for their work. In our concluding chapter, we will bring all these elements together into an overview of constitution-making.

NOTES

1. See Elmer E. Cornwell, Jr. and Jay S. Goodman, The Politics of the Rhode Island Constitutional Convention (New York: National Municipal League, 1969); Leon S. Cohen, Elmer E. Cornwell, Jr., Wayne R. Swanson, and Jay S. Goodman, The Politics of the New York Constitutional Convention (New York: National Municipal League, 1973);

Wayne R. Swanson, Elmer E. Cornwell, Jr., and Jay S. Goodman, Politics and Constitutional Reform: The Maryland Experience, 1967-1968 (Washington, D.C.: Washington Center for Metropolitan Studies, 1970); John P. Wheeler, Jr. and Melissa Kinsey, Magnificent Failure: The Maryland Constitutional Convention of 1967-1968 (New York: National Municipal League, 1970); Norman Meller, With an Understanding Heart: Constitution Making in Hawaii (New York: National Municipal League, 1971); Sean A Kelleher, "The Politics of the Hawaii Constitutional Convention," unpublished doctoral dissertation, Political Science Department, Brown University, Providence, R.I., 1973; Arthur English, "The Politics of the New Mexico Constitutional Convention," unpublished doctoral dissertation, Political Science Department, Brown University, Providence, R.I., 1973; Calvin Ledbetter, George Dyer, Robert Johnston, and Wayne R. Swanson, Walter H. Nunn, The Politics of the Arkansas Constitutional Convention (Little Rock: Academic Press of Arkansas, 1973); Walter H. Nunn, The Arkansas Constitutional Convention, 1970 (New York: National Municipal League, 1973); Charles Pastors, Jay S. Goodman, and Elmer E. Cornwell, Jr., "The Politics of the Illinois Constitutional Convention, 1970" (forthcoming).

2. Providence Sunday Journal, March 24, 1968.

3. Ibid., April 14, 1968.

4. New York Times, September 27, 1967.

5. Baltimore Sun, January 8, 1968.

6. See Wheeler and Kinsey, op. cit., p. 211.

7. Baltimore Sun, January 12, 1968.

8. See Wheeler and Kinsey, op. cit., p. 198.

9. Ibid., p. 193.

10. Royce Hanson, "Maryland Proved Wholesale Change Just Won't Sell," Washington Post, September 6, 1968.

11. See Kelleher, op. cit., Chapter 6.

12. See Meller, op. cit., pp. 145-46.

13. See Ledbetter, et al., op. cit., Chapter 8.

14. Albert L. Sturm, Thirty Years of State Constitution-Making, 1938-1968 (New York: National Municipal League, 1970), p. 91.

15. William C. Havard, "Notes on a Theory of State Constitutional Change: The Florida Experience," Journal of Politics 21 (February 1959): 80=104; and Norman C. Thomas, "The Electorate and State Constitutional Revision: An Analysis of Four Michigan Referenda," Midwest Journal of Political Science 12 (February 1968): 129; see also the analysis of the calls in Chapter 2 of this book.

16. See Thomas, op. cit.; and Robert D. Loevy, "Vote Analysis Made of Maryland Defeat," National Civic Review 57 (November 1968): 159-522.

17. See, for example, Thomas R. Dye, Politics, Economics, and the Public: Policy Outcomes in the American States (Chicago: Rand McNally, 1966); and also Harlan Hahn, "Correlates of Public Sentiment about War: Local Referenda on the Vietnam Issue," American Political Science Review 94, 4 (December 1970): 1186-98.

18. For an illustration of this technique in political science, see James W. Clarke, "Environment, Process and Policy: A Preconsideration," American Political Science Review 57, 4 (December 1969). For an explanation, see Hubert M. Blalock, Social Statistics (New York: McGraw-Hill, 1960), pp. 346-51.

7

THE POLITICS
OF CONSTITUTIONAL
REVISION

Much of the fascination and many of the characteristics of the process of constitutional revision by convention lie in the fact that it is an occasional process. Unlike any of the other political processes at the state level—the legislative, the executive/administrative, the judicial, or even the party/electoral--constitution-making or remaking only takes place at rare intervals. For the student this means that he can examine a convention as a whole entity, tracing genesis and final results with an assurance denied to anyone bent on the study of ongoing political processes. For the participant, however, constitutional revision is, in varying degrees, an unfamiliar game whose rules and stakes must be learned or relearned each time.

For all these discontinuities, which make each episode (each convention) unique to a degree, even within the same state, the process is not without overall form and contours. The systematic study of politics assumes that despite diversity of culture, institutional patterns, perceptions, and stakes, there are overarching uniformities. Many of these are rooted in human nature, in the fact that men have ambitions and goals, exalted and mundane, which they seek to serve through the political process. However much the ground rules and structures may differ, human motivations are fundamentally similar.

Comparability also comes from the fact that though state political cultures and constitutional traditions differ, all are part of an overall American political culture. The very phenomenon of the constitutional convention is an American invention both in its political theory and its operational details. The notion that persons can by deliberate act at a given point in time restructure their governing systems has nowhere flourished as it has in American soil. Here constitutional revision is as much a part of the total array of political subprocesses as any of the others to which scholars have devoted their attention.

Indeed, we view our work as a continuation and extension of two very solidly established traditions within political science. One is the tradition of research into the legislative process, especially at the state level. The seminal work in the genre is, of course, the Walhke et al. study, The Legislative System. There is a voluminous literature of state legislative studies, as well as many studies of the federal congress and city councils, which have been relevant to our analyses, on broad terms and for specific hypotheses about behavior. We have drawn upon this prior work throughout and have indicated in the notes our extensive debt to the work others have done. The second tradition, a newer one in some ways and also owing a great debt to The Legislative System, is the comparative study of state politics (and, for that matter, the comparative study of local charter and legislative politics as well). We endorse the basic viewpoint of such comparative research--namely, that comparison provides the basis for a general understanding of uniformities and differences across a broad spectrum of cases and circumstances and thus contributes to the building of theory about politics. Again there is a voluminous literature, and we have tried to indicate in our citations our debt to those who have previously dealt with questions as diverse as comparative state political cultures and comparative voting behavior.

Although we deal repeatedly with very concrete processes and may often appear to be using methods that focus upon the micro-aspects of constitution-making, we like to think that we have not lost sight of the larger questions brought forth by our data. What kind of process is constitution-making? How can it be studied? We have tried to answer the latter question by bringing to bear, in the preceding chapters, a battery of techniques, each designed to illuminate one aspect of what goes on in and around conventions. Collectively they sketch a portrait of a complex, varied, yet in many ways uniform process of great importance to the operation of our state governments. In this final chapter we will attempt to describe that process in summary terms.

The first point we stressed is that constitutional revision is a political process. As such it does tap the full range of motives and interests called into play by the other political subprocesses at the state level. And like these other forms of state politics, it varies from jurisdiction to jurisdiction in response to local differences in political culture and style.

Americans like to pretend that much that goes on in their governing systems is not really political despite clear evidence that all government is political. This ambivalence is nowhere more prevalent than with constitutional conventions. The citizenry apparently reasons that nothing as important as the writing of basic law could or should be tainted by politics. Hence the need to elaborate three models of the convention process, with the "statesman" variant reflecting these cultural norms. Hence, also, are derived some of the problems that beset the conduct of conventions and the presentation of their work to the electorate.

For analytical purposes it was also necessary to posit a second "political" model, and this we did. A third model, a variation of this second, we labeled the "partisan-legislative" model. The basic political model we hypothesized would come closest to corresponding with the facts of the convention process. The partisan-legislative variant was designed to take into account situations in which, in the absence of a clear alternative convention model, the partisan legislative system in the state was taken to serve as a surrogate. This of course happened most obviously in New York.

THE PRECONVENTION PHASE

The actual convention revision process falls naturally into three phases. First come the events and decisions that precede the actual plenary meetings of the body. Second, there is, of course, the convention in operation and the decision-making process in which it engages. Finally, there is the ratification, or perhaps, in view of the fate of so many of the documents discussed in this study, it is better labeled the referendum stage.

Save in states whose constitutions call for the automatic submission of the question of a convention call to the electorate periodically, something must trigger the whole process. The various ways in which that triggering took place in the seven states we deal with are chronicled in Chapter 1. As these brief summaries make obvious, some combination of a pressing issue (reapportionment, for instance) and organized reformer activity, is ordinarily necessary. There is, in other words, an inertia that must be overcome, before a convention call finds its way onto the ballot and is approved by the voters.

We hypothesize, regarding the vote on the call, that the reform groups who initiated the movement would find their most dependable support among those in the population most like themselves—that is, people of relatively high socioeconomic status, high educational attainment, and urban or suburban residence. For all of the states covered, we tested this assumption against a series of variables characteristic of the populations involved and found, in general, that our hypothesis tended to be confirmed.

This finding is actually of much broader importance for the whole study of constitutional revision by convention. People of high socioeconomic status are sympathetic initially to reform and tend to support revised documents later, because they are most likely to grasp and be moved by the essentially abstract (and even abstruse) issues reform efforts involve. They, too, are less likely to be suspicious of change, more likely to be sanguine about the beneficial impact of effective government on the community, and least inclined to be cynical or alienated.

The other side of this coin is of course the inference that people of lower socioeconomic status, with less urban and more rural residence, and with lower levels of educational attainment are the potential opposition to constitutional reform. They are, for the obverse of the reasons that induce their better-situated fellow citizens to be sympathetic. In this division lies the root of the basic cleavage that explains much about the kind of political process that constitutional revision entails. The line of demarcation, in a word, is between those who want change for its own sake or because they see it as a means to other policy ends and those who want to retain the status quo because they fear change of the existing arrangements or are suspicious of government generally and thus want as little of it as possible. To this basic dichotomy we will be returning subsequently.

Once the convention call is approved, attention focuses logically on the process by which the delegates will be selected. We hypothesized that there is a theoretical range of possible selection systems whose affects on the work of the convention through determining the mix of delegates in it can be considerable. In cases like New York,

where the constitution specifies the method of selection
of the convention delegate group, there are of course
few choices to be made ad hoc at this stage. In most
states, however, choices must be made and conflicting forces
determine how the decisions will go.

The central actor at this point in the process is almost invariably the state legislature. It must enact the
legislation for delegate apportionment and election. The
lawmakers do not, as a rule, come at this task with wholly
open minds. In many cases--and this was often true among
the states studied here--they will have little enthusiasm
for the holding of a convention at all or will view it as
a potentially dangerous exercise from the point of view of
their personal or institutional interests or the interests
of political associates in other branches or organized
groups outside with which they are sympathetic. They may
thus be pulled in the direction of an electoral scheme that
will maximize their control or the control of those wishing to protect the status quo generally.

On the other hand, the simple fact that all but two
of the conventions we studied were elected on the basis
of nonpartisan systems of choice suggests that the legislatures did not give free rein to their own prejudices.
Actually, the statesman model of the convention process is
a very pervasive one, affecting even veteran politicians
to a degree. Our data show the power of this model among
the delegates themselves, and since the various delegate
groups had much in common with the legislators, one can
assume some similarity in attitude. Furthermore, there
obviously was considerable pressure in many states from
outside reform groups for "nonpolitical" selection systems.

The upshot in five of the seven states was an electoral system especially devised, and diverging in at least
some major characteristics from that used for the most
nearly comparable normal elections, those for the legislature itself. What kinds of recruitment processes could
one then anticipate? What impacts on the delegate mix in
the various states? And ultimately what sort of document
would each convention be induced to write by the characteristics of its membership?

We approached these questions with the general assumption in mind that the basic cleavage in all conventions
was likely to be reform versus status quo save where parties were inordinately strong. And even in those cases,
we assumed that the urge to "move" versus the urge to
stand pat would lurk somewhere beneath the surface. In
assessing the pool from which delegates were to be chosen,

though we surmised that reform and protection of the status quo would be heavily represented among the motives, we assumed the picture would be more complex than that. We therefore hypothesized a rather elaborate set of candidate categories that blended these general motivations with the personal motivation of political activists or aspiring activists. Our assumption was that convention operation and output would be a function of a set of forces involving both self-serving and public or group-serving elements and that the strength of each of these would have been more or less determined by the impact of the electoral system on the overall delegate mix.

When demographic data for the various conventions were examined, it became clear that though there were variations from state to state in the degree of representation of groups like women, blacks, and the young, in general, delegate rosters displayed the normal elitist characteristics of all legislative bodies. Our primary effort then became to test the impact of partisan versus nonpartisan modes of election. We theorized that partisan election would produce more representative delegate mixes than nonpartisan, but this did not prove to be uniformly the case. It was evident, however, that fewer experienced politicians turned up when the system was nonpartisan. On the other hand, nonpartisan election did not, as expected, help the minority party significantly. Perhaps most important of all, our data confirmed our assumption that nonpartisan election would result in a significantly higher percentage of reformers and a lower proportion of those devoted to the status quo, than partisan election.

Thus we were able to confirm the significance of the electoral system in structuring conventions by the effect it would have on the mixture of delegates, particularly along the key reform/status-quo dimension. We also found that the members of the nonpartisan conventions were more prone to see their work as above politics and indeed persisted in this view through to the end of their deliberations. The delegates chosen to the partisan conventions, on the other hand, were less idealistic at the beginning and, as the crucial role of parties impressed itself on them during the sessions, were still less idealistic at the end. In like manner, the nonpartisan delegates were more inclined to see their role as representing the whole state rather than their district, while the partisan delegates were more district oriented. Finally, as might well be expected, the partisan delegates perceived a considerably more central role for party in convention work and voting than the nonpartisan.

In sum, the alternative statesman and partisan models for convention operation, and the uncertainty they represent concerning what a constitutional conclave is, remain major "choices" until the convention has finally adjourned. Just what a constitutional convention really is actually never gets fully resolved. Depending in part on the electoral system chosen, the emphasis can be pushed one way or the other. If the shove is in the partisan direction, the reformist thrust in the final output will tend to be modified. If it is in the statesman direction, by virtue of a genuinely nonpartisan electoral scheme, the extent of reform in the product will be increased--perhaps very substantially, as in the case of Maryland.

Or to put the point a bit differently, the underlying potential struggle between the forces of reform and those bent on protection of the status quo can be tilted one way or the other during the preconvention period, and the slant imparted will likely persist during deliberations. To attribute this effect to deliberate, self-conscious preplanning would be a mistake in most contexts. The fact that conventions are new or rarely played games in most states means that a great deal happens by accident, or at best as a result of rather blundering and partial design. Little of the precise political craftsmanship that is often found in normal legislative politics is available in the convention setting.

THE CONVENTION ITSELF

Once a convention has begun meeting, a series of more or less simultaneous processes commence within it among its members. In several ways these are different from and more complex than those that go on in a normal legislature. These differences and added complexities are in large measure the result of the "new-game" quality of the convention as a political system.

The freshman members of any legislative body must be "socialized" in the folkways of the institution they are joining. In a convention, save for the few instances when members have served in a previous body of the same sort, all delegates are freshmen. Even those who have had legislative experience, though they may come with a valuable stock of general parliamentary lore, have much to learn about the special characteristics of a constitutional conclave. On the other hand, the varying proportions of past or present legislators in conventions that our interviewing revealed clearly have an important impact on convention operation. Many if not most delegates have not had previous experience in a legislative setting; hence they are in the full sense novices.

In a broader sense, all delegates, regardless of past experience, pass through a process of socialization. This has several obvious dimensions. In the first place, there is the impact of cumulative experience on the "statesman" model with which most of the delegates come imbued. As we have seen, in some conventions "idealistic" attitudes partially gave way to more "realistic" ones, while in others, for reasons that seem to depend on the delegate mix, idealistic assumptions were reinforced. In other words, each convention gradually hammers out, and its members absorb, its own definition of what a constitution-making body is. These individualized definitions partake in varying degrees of the antithetical "statesman" and "partisan" models.

Another dimension of socialization had to do with the perceived role of the political parties and party alignments. Here too, the ambivalence of attitude with which delegates entered into their duties was reflected in the role they saw for party in the first round of interviews. During the life of the body these patterns of attitude changed, and again, in some cases, as partisanship became more overt and unmistakable, the delegates came to admit a larger party role than they had first anticipated. In other cases, the initial nonpartisan spirit and perceptions were reinforced. Thus here too each convention added further dimensions to its own individual picture of itself.

Finally, perceptions of representational role changed and evolved. The basic dichotomy between representation of district from which elected and representation of the whole state altered. As one would expect from other evolutionary patterns discussed, perceived responsibility to constituents changed in a differential fashion, with some tendency for the more political conventions to shift in the direction of greater concern with district, just as in these same conventions, party role became clearly perceived and overall partisan quality more frankly accepted. These patterns of socialization and convention self-definition tended fairly uniformly in the opposite direction in the more genuinely nonpartisan bodies.

A second area of convention operation that relates quite closely to socialization might be called the "educational" process, for want of a better term. Again the differences between a state legislature and a state constitutional convention are evident. Even the freshman legislator, if he has followed the course of legislative politics prior to his election, is likely to have a pretty good idea as to what the chief categories of issues are that come up regularly for consideration by the lawmakers. Certainly the veterans know these categories and their political characteristics well--all too well in some instances.

Convention delegates are in a substantially different position. They obviously are keenly aware from prior public discussion and their own campaigns for election of the few salient issues that prompted the calling of the convention in the first place. Beyond these, however, as the data presented in Chapter 5 suggest, delegates must fall back on their (often scanty) contact with the reform literature, their awareness of issues that have become noteworthy nationally--such as home rule--and their knowledge of the several major topics with which any constitutional document must deal.

Only as they get into the actual deliberational process itself, get to know the concerns of their fellow delegates, of interests and organized groups, sit through hearings, snese and measure outside pressures (all virtually were aware of and favorably disposed toward lobbying activity), and learn in detail of the problems posed by the existing document they were chosen to revise, do the real issue contours emerge. And, as we also saw in Chapter 5, the resulting draft may incorporate a quite different set of substantive emphases than the ones that the delegates assumed would preoccupy them when they embarked on their work.

One of the most intricate and yet elusive aspects of internal convention operation is leadership. One form this takes, broadly defined, is of course the committee structure and the role of the committee chairmen. To this area, we devoted little direct attention. Rather, we focused on the broader question of overall convention leadership. As numerous a body as a constitutional convention must do its work through some sort of leadership. In most obvious terms, there were substantial variations among the ones we studied in that New York's, for example, following the "partisan-legislative" model, replicated in detail the party floor leadership patterns of the state legislatures to supplement the roles played by the convention president and other officers. Conventions like Maryland's ostentatiously avoided any semblance of party leadership, and in

198

that case, virtually the whole burden was assumed by the president. Various individual patterns were evolved in the remaining conventions.

These state-to-state variations showed up clearly in the responses we received to questions asked of the delegates regarding their attitudes in this area of operation. In every convention, at least a majority concluded that leadership had been important; in some cases half or more said "very important." Party leadership, on the other hand, was held to be important only in the basically political conventions (in New York, two-thirds said very important, not surprisingly). In the nonpartisan conventions it was sharply downgraded. Delegates were also asked their appraisal of the degree of concentration of power in the conventions, with considerably varied results. There seemed little correlation between perception of the importance of leadership, partisan or otherwise, and appraisal of power concentration. This last finding doubtless suggests that though the conventions tended to add further to their self-portraits by their responses in the leadership area, general ambivalence still persisted in the form of doubts about the legitimacy of centralized control.

Conflicting attitudes were also evident in responses to our question about the determinants of influence in the conventions. On the one hand, there was a definite tendency for the delegates to link influence with ability to speak and persuade in debate. This finding confirms the statesman model, which sees conventions as genuine deliberative bodies wherein truth emerges in the clash of ideas. That legislatures generally do not operate this way, but rather through log-rolling, party loyalty, and leadership pressure, is well known. The delegates, on the other hand, could not ignore the importance of formal convention position (president or other official officeholder) in ascribing influence. This too ranked high on the cumulative list. Here they swung back in the direction of the legislative rather than the statesman model. Of course, as the data presented earlier showed, conventions differed one from another in the weights given the various influence factors.

The key roles played by the presidents of the various conventions emerged unmistakably. All that we know descriptively about convention behavior underscores the vital importance of the role of the presiding officer. In our sociometric data, too, the convention presidents were cited most often for their influence, followed closely by various other individuals who, more often than not, either held some other convention position of formal leadership, or were past or present occupants of important public offices outside the convention itself. Thus, again, though leadership was viewed by delegates with some skepticism when they wore their "statesmen" hats, in their more practical and realistic moods, they accepted leadership from many of the same kinds of people to whom politicians and legislators have always looked.

As one tries to envision a constitutional convention in full operation, one imagines, as we have been doing in the foregoing paragraphs, simultaneous processes whereby the delegates are learning their role as convention member, are working out the style and model that will characterize the body, and are coming to terms with the problem of internal leadership. Yet these are peripheral, in a way, to the main business at hand, which is to make the decisions necessary to actually write a revised state charter.

Any effort to characterize this process must deal both with questions of how and questions of what. How were decisions arrived at? And what was the final product like? In Chapter 4 we used several methods to tackle the how problem. First we asked the delegates which of a series of familiar possibilities seemed to them best to describe the overall operation of their convention. What, in other words, was the major plane of cleavage that most often affected the convention's decision-making processes? In five of the seven conventions, the findings bore out our initial hypothesis--namely that the key basis of division and conflict in constitutional revision is between reformers and the guardians of the status quo. In four states, between two-thirds and three-quarters of the delegates agreed. In Rhode Island, over 80 percent chose that alternative, or the legislator versus nonlegislator one, which amounted to much the same thing. In New York and Illinois, for fairly obvious reasons, the city versus rest-of-state cleavage was seen as of overriding importance, with the party division about as important in New York.

Thus the delegates too had concluded that this is what constitutional revision is all about. The issues are not often liberal-conservative ones in the normal sense, nor even party-partisan ones very often, but simply change versus standing pat. Yet ultimate proof of this proposition requires more than analysis of the perceptions of the delegates. Did the convention members actually behave in a manner consonant with this perceived pattern? To find out, we performed a careful factor analysis of convention roll calls.

In the presentation of the results of this study, it became appropriate to divide the conventions into three

200

categories: the "partisan" conventions (New York and Rhode Island), two that we called "semi-structured" conventions (Illinois and New Mexico), and two best labeled "unstructured" (Maryland and Arkansas). Looking at the first pair, the term partisan was not chosen to describe strictly "party" partisanship. Rather, we used it to designate the two conventions whose voting patterns were most clearly polarized into two major clusters of delegates. In New York, of course, these were also clearly party groups, but in Rhode Island this was much less the case.

Actually there were three questions that needed to be asked about the factor analysis results from each convention: what kind of patterning emerged, did it show evidence of a status-quo/reform alignment, and finally, how well did the resulting delegate clusters correlate with groupings that emerged from our typology? As noted, New York and Rhode Island both displayed a bipolar mode of voting. Thus they conformed most closely to the normal manner of operation in regular legislative bodies. In New York this was so much the case that the two-cluster, two-party division largely submerged all other factional tendencies. Even in the Empire State, however, there was some suggestion of the reform/status-quo division (Democrats supporting reform more often than Republicans), and also some support for the validity of our delegate categorizations. Rhode Island also came out bipolar, but with a very clear reform/status-quo pattern overall and considerable support for the typology groupings of delegates.

Generally speaking, all of the rest of the conventions displayed a more fragmented pattern of voting clusters. The two we have called "semistructured" each settled into a voting pattern characterized by three major clusters of delegates. In Illinois, the reform/status-quo cleavage was in evidence, but across it cut the urban/downstate division; the typology was to a considerable extent confirmed. New Mexico roughly paralleled Illinois in that the Spanish-speaking group and its demands tended to crosscut the expected reform/status-quo division, and the representatives of this group formed the basis of one of the clusters, as the Chicago delegates did in Illinois. In other words, what might have been a bipolarity in both these states became a three-way division because of the injection of a grouping (which also represented an "issue") that could not be encompassed within the basic two-group pattern.

The patterns in Maryland and Arkansas were highly fragmented. Neither party divisions nor any other overarching pattern derived from the politics or demography of the state was present to impose a simpler, more straightforward pattern. In both, however, underlying the apparent chaos, there was a clear tendency for the reform/status-quo cleavage to emerge, and for the group typology to correlate in predicted ways with delegate voting behavior. The fact that this was the case in the states most lacking in other cleavage dimensions suggests that it is indeed the most basic line of demarcation in convention behavior generally.

The overall conclusion that emerges from analysis of all six states is that conventions structure themselves in ways that are induced by a combination of their partisan or nonpartisan character (the extent to which the electoral system and emerging convention style differentiates them from the normal partisan model), on the one hand, and the extent to which deep-seated divisions (urban-rural, cultural, or the like) imprint themselves on convention behavior on the other. But, underlying all of this, though camouflaged by these patterns in varying degrees, is the fundamental division over change or no change.

Thus, conventions as decision-making bodies may come to resemble the workings of the normally partisan, dichotomized state legislature, or may look very much like the statesman model with combinations and alliances shifting and changing from roll call to roll call. This tendency for voting behavior to follow either the statesman or the partisan model (or some hybrid of the two) further confirms the argument in earlier paragraphs that conventions gradually build an overall identity along one or another of these general lines. The study of roll call voting, however, while confirming convention individuality, also convincingly substantiates the basic similarity of such bodies as arenas in which the struggle between the forces of reform and the defenders of the status quo is the principal contest.

Thus far in this section we have been marshaling our conclusions about the "how" of convention operation. We must now turn to the "what." This can be dealt with rather more briefly. The essential questions posed in Chapter 5 were, what kinds of documents did the conventions produce, and what correlations can be made between the documents and the nature and operation of the deliberative bodies themselves.

Nowhere would one expect the uniqueness of each state culture, tradition, and the type of convention it spawned to be more clearly manifested than in the documents produced. This expectation is, as we have seen, well borne out. On the other hand, one of the obvious uniformities in the process of constitutional revision from state to state is to be found in the tendency for certain kinds of issues, certain institutional "problems" pinpointed by the reformers, to generate concern in nearly every jurisdiction. There are, in other words, styles and fashions in the reform of state government just as there are in other walks of life.

The data in Chapter 5 reveal, for instance, that all of the conventions dealt with wire-tapping and related "right-to-privacy" issues. All of them dealt with voting age, and more or less of necessity, with reapportionment. Judicial reform was also a sufficiently hot topic to come in for varying attention in all of the states, and the same can be said for local government and home rule. Other issues cropped up somewhat less consistently but fairly often, such as public aid to parochial schools, legislative sessions (often replacing biennial with annual), protection against various kinds of discrimination, and so on.

Doubtless one could take a cluster of constitutional conventions in any era--the Jacksonian period, the years of reconstruction or postreconstruction, the turn-of-the-century progressive era--and find patterns of issue uniformity in each. In other words, there are broad areas of agreement in any one period as to what "modern," "effective," "democratic" state government consists of, but little such agreement over time. Conventions in one era meet to undo the careful reforms of an earlier generation. Current attention to short-ballot issues is the reversed mirror image of earlier-long ballot enthusiasm.

More systematic comparisons of the documents as a whole were undertaken in Chapter 5, using a point system of scoring based on the Model State Constitution. Generalizing from the results, one could argue that either too much or too little reform is likely to cause trouble in the ratification referendum. Hawaii, given its relatively new existing document, would naturally be an exception to any such rule of thumb. Part of the problem in Rhode Island and New York doubtless was the fact that so much time (in Little Rhody) and inordinate expense (New York) produced such marginal changes. At the other extreme, there were really major changes in Arkansas, New Mexico, and Maryland that, in light of the extremely "backward" documents with which those three conventions started, were bound to be viewed as revolutionary. This was above all true in Maryland--and contributed heavily to defeat in all three. Illinois, seemingly, struck some kind of happy compromise.

203

A close linking of convention make-up and operation with documentary output is difficult. Yet the fact that the most extensive reforms were adopted in the less partisan, most fragmented, and most unstructured conventions may be significant. This point is underscored by the companion observation that the two most partisan conventions with the tightest internal group structuring produced the least movement toward reform, and that Illinois, which occupied a rough midway point between the New York and Maryland poles, was also midway on the reform scale and saw its referendum succeed.

THE REFERENDUM

One of the most obvious but most easily overlooked differences between a normal legislature and a constitutional convention is the fact that the work of the former emerges as a mosaic of generally unrelated actions, few if any of which are ever passed upon directly by the public. The output of a convention is usually a single unit and must gain voter approval. This means that, during the deliberations of a convention, attention should be given not only to individual decisions but also to the cumulative effect they are having--the amount of "reform distance" that will ultimately be traversed.

The convention, while still in session, must also decide how the results of its work are to be presented to the electorate. In most of the states covered by this study, an all-or-nothing vote on the document as a whole was the choice--and in the five states in which this method was followed, the draft was defeated. In Hawaii, where a complete new constitution was not the object, the scattered changes proposed were offered separately (though a blanket "yes" vote was also possible). Illinois adopted what probably makes the most sense as a strategy and presented the whole document but with some especially controversial areas offered in terms of separate either-or alternatives. The theoretical advantages of this kind of procedure were discussed in Chapter 2 in connection with Arrow's theory of voting.

In our multiple regression analysis of a number of variables in relation to county-level voting behavior on the referendum, we tested the proposition, among others, that people of higher socioeconomic status would be more likely to support the revised constitutions than people of lower SES. This was generally borne out by the findings,

as was the corollary proposition that where SES alone did
not provide the explanation of the vote, that combined
with partisan factors usually did.

The partisan variable tends, naturally, to relate to
the special characteristics of each state. That is, in
some, the parties might align pro and con; in some, both
pro; in some, both might remain more or less aloof because
they felt that they had been by-passed in the process.
Thus we looked to the finding regarding the kinds of people who supported or voted against reform for the most useful generalizations, not to party labels. And, as we first
saw in the analysis of the votes on the convention calls,
the referenda also confirm a systematic alignment that is
basic to the politics of constitutional revision and in
general accord with our other major findings.

Just as the delegates and the political activists in
each state tended to break down, ultimately, into "reformers" and supporters of the "status quo," so the electorate
divides in a similar fashion. The reasons activating the
latter are similar to but different in degree from those
motivating the former. Reform activists and citizen supporters of new constitutions both apparently share a level
of sophistication in their understanding of government
and its role, and both are sanguine about that role and
its potential enhancement through institutional reform.
These attitudes stem from their relatively high levels of
educational attainment, their urban or suburban residence
and the cosmopolitan attitudes thus acquired, and their
relative affuence. Increasingly in the decade of the
1960s, students of political behavior noted a liberal trend
among people of upper-middle-class status and a tendency
for them to be more willing to accept "big government,"
higher taxes, and innovative policies than those with lower
incomes and blue-collar status.

This latter trend has presumably meant that upper-SES
urban-dwellers were not only more receptive to structural
reform, but also to the financial implications, direct
and indirect, of constitutional revision. That is, they
neither feared institutional innovation nor the prospect
(real or imaginary) that reformed state government might
result in higher costs and hence higher taxes.

Opponents of reform among delegates and officeholders,
though they may share the skeptical portion of the electorate's doubts and fears, often have more concrete bases
for opposition. They or their political friends and associates stand to lose positions or advantages that they
currently enjoy. Or they act as spokesmen for an institu-

tional vested interest or the concerns of an organized private group that has reason to oppose specific changes. Opponents in the general public will, often, act out of more generalized concerns--about the loss of rights, lessened control over the legislature or over local officials, an open door to new taxes or expensive programs, or other threats to their security as they see it.

In short, constitutional revision potentially polarizes state communities, or the attentive portions of them, along predictable lines. Change and reform must win acceptance against groups and points of view that are latent in every state and, experience has shown, are readily mobilized. Thus the politics of constitutional revision pose the central problem of achieving enough reform to satisfy those who favor and work for such efforts, but at the same time not so much as to frighten or alienate too many vested interests or too many of the potential opponents in the citizenry.

FUTURE RESEARCH IMPLICATIONS

The implications of the research findings presented in this study, and the shape of the constitution revision process that emerges, are obvious for those who work in state government or seek its improvement. At the same time, both our methods of study and our findings will also be of importance to political scientists interested in the study of state government and politics. Both students of constitutional and governmental reform in the narrower sense and those interested in broader aspects of state political systems should find the foregoing chapters of interest. Our findings confirm not only the proposition that constitutional conventions are political institutions and parts of a political subsystem but also that that subsystem is closely related in many ways to the rest of the politics of state government.

Our researches have dealt with state political cultures, with electoral systems and their impact, with various dimensions of behavior in legislative-like institutions ranging from member socialization to roll-call analysis, with aspects of voter behavior in relation to public policy decisions, and with a variety of other questions that impinge on or overlap with most of the major issues of concern to the student of state political systems.

Perhaps most timely of all for the 1970s is the light that our findings shed on the process of political change at the state level. To the extent that Richard Nixon's "New Federalism" succeeds in shifting greater policy responsibility to the states, research that sheds light on state government will be increasingly important. To the extent that trends continue that began during the 1960s involving heightened resistance to policies designed to solve social problems, we will need to sharpen our understanding of the dynamics of social and political change and how it can be affected. State constitutional revision lies very close to the heart of these emerging concerns.

There is a great deal of discussion in reform and governmental circles about how state governments will have to "modernize" if they are going to meet the challenges of revenue-sharing and further decentralization from Washington. There is no question but that demands will be made upon these state governments from the citizen level to rethink and reprogram efforts to solve social problems in the face of rising citizen resistance. But our work indicates that if modernization and meeting citizen needs are interpreted to be synonymous with structural reform, resistance is very likely to be strong. Everyone must realize that devising increasingly sophisticated programs and making them work has to be carried on in an environment where electorates are no longer willing to assume that change and innovation are automatically beneficial.

ELMER E. CORNWELL is currently professor of Political Science at Brown University. His specialty is American politics, and he has written extensively in political science journals and is the author of <u>Presidential Leadership of Public Opinion</u> and <u>The Presidency: The Vital Center</u> and has coauthored <u>The American Democracy</u> and <u>Constitutional Conventions</u>. He was research director of the Rhode Island Constitutional Convention and codirector of the comparative study of state constitutional conventions. He is a graduate of Williams College, received his Ph.D. from Harvard University, and taught at Princeton University before joining the Brown faculty.

JAY S. GOODMAN is Professor of Government and Chairman of the Government Department at Wheaton College, Norton, Massachusetts. He is the author of <u>Democrats and Labor in Rhode Island, 1952-1962</u>, coauthor of <u>The American Democracy</u>, editor of <u>Perspectives on Urban Politics,</u> and author of the forthcoming <u>The Dynamics of Urban Government and Politics</u>. He was codirector of the comparative study of state constitutional conventions. He did his undergraduate work at Beloit College, studied at Stanford University, and received his Ph.D. from Brown University.

WAYNE R. SWANSON is Associate Professor of Government and Dean of the Faculty at Connecticut College. He is the author of a number of articles on American politics as well as <u>Lawmaking in Connecticut: The General Assembly</u>. He graduated from the University of Rhode Island and received his Ph.D. from Brown University.

LEGISLATIVE POLITICS IN NEW YORK STATE: A Comparative
Analysis
                Alan G. Hevesi

POLITICAL CLUBS IN NEW YORK CITY: A Comparative and Operational Analysis
                Blanche Davis Blank and Norman M. Adler

STATE LEGISLATIVE INNOVATION: Case Studies of Washington,
Ohio, Florida, Illinois, Wisconsin, and California
                Edited by James A. Robinson

STATE LEGISLATURES: An Evaluation of Their Effectiveness:
                The Citizens Conference on State Leg-
                islatures

SUPERCITY/HOMETOWN, U.S.A.: Prospects for Two-Tiered
Government
                League of Women Voters Education Fund